Picturing God

THEMES IN RELIGIOUS STUDIES SERIES

Series Editors: Jean Holm, with John Bowker

Other titles

Worship
Making Moral Decisions
Myth and History
Attitudes to Nature
Human Nature and Destiny
Sacred Writings
Women in Religion
Rites of Passage
Sacred Place

Picturing God

Edited by

Jean Holm

with John Bowker

PINTER
PUBLISHERS
LONDON, NEW YORK

Distributed exclusively in the United States and Canada by St. Martin's Press

Pinter Publishers Ltd.
25 Floral Street, London WC2E 9DS, United Kingdom

First published in 1994

Distributed exclusively in the USA and Canada by St. Martin's Press, Inc., Room 400, 175 Fifth Avenue, New York, NY 10010, USA

British Library Cataloguing in Publication Data

A CIP catalogue record for this book is available from the British Library

ISBN 1 85567 100 X (hb)
ISBN 1 85567 101 8 (pb)

Library of Congress Cataloging in Publication Data

Picturing God / edited by Jean Holm, with John Bowker.
p. cm. – (Themes in religious studies series)
Includes bibliographical references and index.
ISBN 1-85567-100-X (hb). – ISBN 1-85567-101-8 (pb)
1. Image of God. 2. Religions. I. Holm, Jean, 1922– .
II. Bowker, John Westerdale. III. Series.
BL205.P53 1994
291.2'11–dc20 94–13746
CIP

Typeset by Mayhew Typesetting, Rhayader, Powys
Printed and bound in Great Britain by Biddles Ltd., Guildford and King's Lynn

Contents

Series Preface

The person who knows only one religion does not know any religion. This rather startling claim was made in 1873, by Friedrich Max Müller, in his book, *Introduction to the Science of Religion*. He was applying to religion a saying of the poet Goethe: 'He who knows one language, knows none.'

In many ways this series illustrates Max Müller's claim. The diversity among the religious traditions represented in each of the volumes shows how mistaken are those people who assume that the pattern of belief and practice in their own religion is reflected equally in other religions. It is, of course, possible to do a cross-cultural study of the ways in which religions tackle particular issues, such as those which form the titles of the ten books in this series, but it soon becomes obvious that something which is central in one religion may be much less important in another. To take just three examples: the contrast between Islam's and Sikhism's attitudes to pilgrimage, in *Sacred Place*; the whole spectrum of positions on the authority of scriptures illustrated in *Sacred Writings*; and the problem which the titles, *Picturing God* and *Worship*, created for the contributor on Buddhism.

The series offers an introduction to the ways in which the themes are approached within eight religious traditions. Some of the themes relate particularly to the faith and practice of individuals and religious communities (*Picturing God, Worship, Rites of Passage, Sacred Writings, Myth and History, Sacred Place*); others have much wider implications, for society in general as well as for the religious communities themselves (*Attitudes to Nature, Making Moral Decisions, Human Nature and Destiny, Women in Religion*). This distinction, however, is not clear-cut. For instance, the 'sacred places' of Ayodhya and Jerusalem have figured in situations of national and international conflict, and some countries have passed laws regulating, or even banning, religious worship.

Stereotypes of the beliefs and practices of religions are so widespread that a real effort, of both study and imagination, is needed in order to discover what a religion looks – and feels – like to its adherents. We have to bracket out, temporarily, our own beliefs and presuppositions, and 'listen in' to a religion's account of what *it* regards as significant. This is not a straightforward task, and readers of the books in this series will encounter a number of the issues that characterise the study of religions, and that have to be taken into account in any serious attempt to get behind a factual description of a religion to an understanding of the real meaning of the words and actions for its adherents.

First, the problem of language. Islam's insistence that the Arabic of the Qur'ān cannot be 'translated' reflects the impossibility of finding in another language an exact equivalent of many of the most important terms in a religion. The very word, Islam, means something much more positive to a Muslim than is suggested in English by 'submission'. Similarly, it can be misleading to use 'incarnation' for *avatāra* in Hinduism, or 'suffering' for *dukkha* in Buddhism, or 'law' for Torah in Judaism, or 'gods' for *kami* in Shinto, or 'heaven' for *T'ien* in Taoism, or 'name' for *Nām* in Sikhism.

Next, the problem of defining – drawing a line round – a religion. Religions do not exist in a vacuum; they are influenced by the social and cultural context in which they are set. This can affect what they strenuously reject as well as what they may absorb into their pattern of belief and practice. And such influence is continuous, from a religion's origins (even though we may have no records from that period), through significant historical developments (which sometimes lead to the rise of new movements or sects), to its contemporary situation, especially when a religion is transplanted into a different region. For example, anyone who has studied Hinduism in India will be quite unprepared for the form of Hinduism they will meet in the island of Bali.

Even speaking of a 'religion' may be problematic. The term, 'Hinduism', for example, was invented by western scholars, and would not be recognised or understood by most 'Hindus'. A different example is provided by the religious situation in Japan, and the consequent debate among scholars as to whether they should speak of Japanese 'religion' or Japanese 'religions'.

Finally, it can be misleading to encounter only one aspect of a religion's teaching. The themes in this series are part of a whole interrelated network of beliefs and practices within each religious tradition, and need to be seen in this wider context. The reading lists at the end of each chapter point readers to general studies of the religions as well as to books which are helpful for further reading on the themes themselves.

Jean Holm
November 1993

List of Contributors

Jean Holm (EDITOR) was formerly Principal Lecturer in Religious Studies at Homerton College, Cambridge, teaching mainly Judaism and Hinduism. Her interests include relationships between religions; the relationship of culture to religion; and the way in which children are nurtured within a different cultural context. Her publications include *Teaching Religion in School* (OUP, 1975), *The Study of Religions* (Sheldon, 1977), *Growing up in Judaism* (Longman, 1990), *Growing up in Christianity*, with Romie Ridley (Longman, 1990) and *A Keyguide to Sources of Information on World Religions* (Mansell, 1991). She has edited three previous series: *Issues in Religious Studies*, with Peter Baelz (Sheldon), *Anselm Books*, with Peter Baelz (Lutterworth) and *Growing up in a Religion* (Longman).

John Bowker (EDITOR) was Professor of Religious Studies in Lancaster University before returning to Cambridge to become Dean and Fellow of Trinity College. He is at present Professor of Divinity at Gresham College in London, and Adjunct Professor at the University of Pennsylvania and at the State University of North Carolina. He is particularly interested in anthropological and sociological approaches to the study of religions. He has done a number of programmes for the BBC, including the *Worlds of Faith* series, and series on Islam and Hinduism for the World Service. He is the author of many books in the field of Religious Studies, including *The Meanings of Death* (Cambridge University Press, 1991), which was awarded the biennial Harper Collins religious book prize in 1993, in the academic section.

Peter Harvey is Reader in Buddhist Studies at the University of

Sunderland. His research is in the fields of early Buddhist thought, and the ethical, devotional and meditational dimensions of Buddhism. He has published articles on consciousness and *nirvāṇa*, the between-lives state, the nature of the *tathāgata*, the *stūpa*, *paritta* chanting, the signless meditations, self-development and not-Self, and respect for persons. Dr Harvey is author of *An Introduction to Buddhism: Teachings, History and Practices* (Cambridge University Press, 1990) and is currently working on *The Selfless Mind; Selflessness and Consciousness in Early Buddhism* (for Curzon Press), and a work on *Themes in Buddhist Ethics* (for Cambridge University Press). He is a Theravāda Buddhist and a teacher of Samatha meditation. He was a member of the CNAA Working Party on Theology and Religious Studies.

Douglas Davies is Professor of Religious Studies in the Department of Theology at the University of Nottingham, where he specialises in teaching the social anthropology of religion. He trained both in theology and social anthropology and his research continues to relate to both disciplines. His interest in theoretical and historical aspects of religious studies is represented in a major study of the sociology of knowledge and religion, published as *Meaning and Salvation in Religious Studies* (Brill, 1984), and in a historical volume, *Frank Byron Jevons 1858–1936, An Evolutionary Realist* (Edwin Mellen Press, 1991). Professor Davies is also very much concerned with practical aspects of religious behaviour and is a leading British scholar of Mormonism and, in addition to various articles, is author of *Mormon Spirituality* (Nottingham and Utah University Press, 1987). He was joint Director of the Rural Church Project, involving one of the largest sociological studies of religion in Britain, published as *Church and Religion in Rural Britain* (with C. Watkins and M. Winter, T. & T. Clark, 1991). As Director of the Cremation Research Project he is conducting basic work on Cremation in Britain and Europe and has already produced some results in *Cremation Today and Tomorrow* (Grove Books, 1990).

Sharada Sugirtharajah lectures on Hinduism at Westhill College in Birmingham. She has led sessions on topics ranging from Hindu spirituality to women's issues for clergy, nurses, social workers, counsellors and multi-faith groups. She has co-authored the text for a photo learning pack on Hinduism (a resource for primary and secondary religious education) published by the Westhill RE Centre. She has also contributed articles to journals.

Clinton Bennett is a Lecturer in Study of Religions at Westminster College, Oxford, and a Baptist Minister. His research interests include Islamic theology and philosophy, historical and contemporary encounter between Muslims and non-Muslims, Islam and anthropology, and religious beliefs as agents of social transformation. Dr Bennett is the author of *Victorian Images of Islam* (1992), has travelled and worked in the Muslim world, and was a member of the World Council of Churches' (WCC) working party that produced *Issues in Christian-Muslim Relations: Ecumenical Considerations* (1991). He currently serves on the WCC's 'Consultation on the Church and the Jewish People'.

Norman Solomon is founder and Director of the Centre for the Study of Judaism and Jewish/Christian Relations at the Selly Oak College, Birmingham. He is Visiting Lecturer to the Oxford Centre for Postgraduate Hebrew Studies, adviser to the International Council of Christians and Jews, and Vice Chairman of the World Congress of Faiths. Among his many publications is *Judaism and World Religion* (Macmillan, 1991). Rabbi Dr Solomon has a particular interest in Christian–Jewish dialogue and has been a frequent participant in international dialogue events with the World Council of Churches, the Vatican and the Ecumenical Patriarchate. He is also involved in trilateral dialogues of Jews, Christians and Muslims.

Beryl Dhanjal is a Lecturer at Ealing Tertiary College. She works on the programme for teaching ESOL (English to Speakers of Other Languages) and has special responsibility for developing community links, working mainly with people from the new commonwealth and with refugees. She studied Panjābi at the School of Oriental and African Studies, University of London. She has lectured at St Mary's College, Strawberry Hill, and the West London Institute of Higher Education, and has worked in adult education. She has written and translated many books, and particularly enjoys writing books for children and young people – she has written bi-lingual English/ Panjābi books for children.

Xinzhong Yao is Lecturer in Chinese Religion and Ethics, University of Wales, Lampeter. His research interests include philosophy, ethics and religion; he is currently focusing on comparative philosophy and comparative religion. Dr Yao is author of *On Moral Activity* (People's University Press, Beijing, 1990), *Ethics and Social Problems* (City Economic Press, Beijing, 1989), co-author of *Comparative Studies on Human Nature* (Tienjin People's Press, Tienjin, 1988), co-editor of *Applying Ethics* (Jilin People's Press, Changchun, 1994), and main translator of Charles L. Stevenson's *Ethics and Language* (Social Sciences of China Press, Beijing, 1991). He is also Deputy Director of the Institute of Ethics, People's University of China, Beijing.

Wendy Dossett is currently completing PhD research in the areas of Japanese Buddhism and religious studies methodology; her main research interests lie in Japanese religion and culture, and the phenomenology of religion. She has worked in Tokyo for the International Buddhist Study Center, an institution dedicated to the translation of Buddhist scriptures. She has lectured on Buddhism in the Department of Religious Studies at the University of Wales, Lampeter, and is a tutor in Religious Studies on the International Students' Programme there. Her publications include contributions on Hinduism to the *Chambers Dictionary of Beliefs and Religions*, (ed. Frank Whaling, Edinburgh, 1992), and on Japanese religions to *Contemporary Religions: A World Guide* (ed. Ian Harris et al., Longman, London, 1992).

Introduction: Raising the Issues

Jean Holm

Does this book have the right title? Almost all the contributors have felt it necessary to explain that dealing with the topic is not straightforward in the religion they are writing about. The problem is particularly acute in Buddhism: Peter Harvey begins his chapter, 'The phrasing of the title of this book . . . is more suited to the monotheistic, God-focused religions than to Buddhism'. Judaism and Islam are certainly 'God-focused religions', but although Norman Solomon and Clinton Bennett have no difficulty accepting the concept of 'God', they feel it important to qualify the word 'picturing', beginning their chapters respectively with: 'Judaism allows no visual representation of God, no image, icon or symbol', and 'Muslims picture God conceptually, not artistically or visually'.

The Far Eastern religions also have problems with the title. Wendy Dossett begins, 'God, in the western sense, does not generally figure in Japanese religions', and Xinzhong Yao opens with, 'Whether or not there is "God" in Chinese religions was not clear to the earlier sinologists'. At the other end of the spectrum lie the two Indian-based religions, with their authors facing the problem of how to confine within one chapter what could be said about God. Sharada Sugirtharajah opens with, 'The Hindu tradition is replete with a wide variety of images of the divine', and Beryl Dhanjal begins with, 'The Sikh Gurūs amassed one thousand four hundred and thirty pages on the subject of *Akāl Purakh* (God) without exhausting the possibilities'.

The fact that the title of this book presented the authors with a different – and more acute – challenge than that presented by the other titles in the series is a useful reminder not only that one cannot make a straightforward transfer from one faith to any other, but also that the concept of God lies at the heart of almost every religion, and contributes in large measure to its distinctiveness. As Raimundo Panikkar says, '*Brahman* is certainly not the one true and living God of the Abrahamic tradition. Nor can it be said that *Shang Ti* or the *kami* are the same as *Brahman*. And yet they are not totally unrelated' ('Deity' in Mircea Eliade (ed.) *Encyclopedia of Religion*, New York, Macmillan, 1984, p. 266).

Two of the religions represented in this book – Shinto and Buddhism – stand out from the others in not having the concept of 'a God'. There is a multitude of Shinto deities (*kami*), which may be spirits, or human, or natural forces such as mountains, and which are, in the words of Wendy Dossett, 'morally ambivalent powers of the universe', with spiritual power and authority. Buddhism also accepts the idea of a multitude of gods, but, in contrast to the *kami*, they play no part in the lives of ordinary people; they have been born into the 'realm of the gods' as a result of their previous lives, but eventually they will have to be reborn into the human realm. In the Mahāyāna tradition, however, *buddha*s and *bodhisattva*s function much as gods do in other religions: their devotees offer worship to them and seek their help. This is seen in its most extreme form in the Pure Land form of Buddhism, where faith in the Buddha Amida (Japanese)/Amitabha (Chinese) is believed to be all that is necessary for rebirth in the Buddha's Western Paradise. Even Theravadins tend to ascribe the functions of a deity to Gotama; the chapter on Buddhism includes Richard Gombrich's comment that although cognitively the Buddha is beyond worldly contact, affectively he is a living source of benefit.

In spite of the many differences among the religions, perhaps one of the most important similarities is an awareness of the impossibility of finite creatures being able to describe adequately that which transcends human experience. This is particularly true where there is a supreme being, who is, by definition, beyond comparison; language can never 'capture' God, and may well be misleading. In Hinduism and Buddhism the phrase *Neti, neti* ('Not this, not this') is used to express the belief that all that can be said about the Absolute has to be a denial of whatever qualities might be suggested. Similarly, in Christianity, but also in Judaism and Islam, *via negativa* is a phrase that is employed to emphasise that God cannot be compared or identified with anything known to humans. In the Judaism chapter Norman Solomon asks, 'If whatever we say about God is somehow wrong, can we really talk about God at all?'

Philosophers in the western world also discuss the possibility of talking about God. But their questioning is very different from that of the religious traditions; they ask not only whether it is possible to talk about God, but whether there is a God at all. For the religions represented in this book (with the exception of Buddhism), the existence of God, or, in the case of Shinto, the gods, is taken for granted. God is a given, and the emphasis is on knowing God, worshipping God, doing God's will, and the questions are more likely to be: What is God's nature? How is God's will to be known? What are the least inadequate ways of 'picturing' God?

Ways of imaging the divine

Because of the impossibility of providing any adequate 'picture' of what is perceived as ultimate reality, symbolism has a major role in all religions. Symbols point beyond themselves, and indicate something of the nature of what they symbolise, without ever being identical with it.

One of the most frequently encountered religious symbols is light. Both the Buddha and Jesus are referred to as 'the light of the world', the Jewish mystics described God as light, and in Islam, *an-Nūr* (the Light) is one of the names for God. Light is used in worship in most religions, as, for example, in the Hindu ceremony of *ārati*, when the lamp is waved before the image of the deity, and then taken round so that the worshippers can share the light, or in the use of candles in many Christian traditions. Light plays a particularly important part in festivals, as, for example, in Judaism, where candles are lit by the woman of the house to mark the beginning of *Shabbat*, where there are candles on the *Seder* table at *Pesach*, and where the progressive lighting of the nine-branched candelabrum is part of the celebration of *Hanukkah*. In the Hindu festival of *Divālī* the myriad of *diva*s (lamps) that are placed round every house as darkness falls symbolise the conquest of evil by good. Christians call Christmas the Festival of Light, but in the Eastern Orthodox churches it is an even more appropriate name for Easter: the resurrection is symbolised by light, and in the darkened church on Easter Eve the light spreads from person to person as they light their candle from that of the person next to them.

Ritual actions are also symbolic, and many ritual actions express something of the worshippers' beliefs about, and attitudes to, God. In Islam, the position of prayer in which worshippers place their foreheads on the ground shows the Muslim's willingness to submit completely to Allāh. Similarly, when Sikhs enter the prayer hall in a gurdwara they kneel and place their forehead on the ground in front of the Gurū Granth Sāhib, the scripture which represents the word of God. Bowing, kneeling, genuflecting, placing the hands together in prayer, or holding them with palms upwards, all symbolise a worshipper's response to the object of worship.

Another way in which religions express their beliefs is the names they give to manifestations of the divine. Names are not mere labels; they reflect what are believed to be attributes of the deity. Muslims have ninety-nine 'beautiful names' for Allāh, of which the most common one is 'the Merciful', and the rosary of 99 beads (or three times thirty-three beads) encourages believers to become familiar with these names through *dhikr* – remembrance of the names. Names are also highly significant in Hinduism. The same deity will be known by several different names, reflecting his or her different roles in Hindu mythology (though occasionally different names may be regional variations). Some of the major deities, Viṣṇu, for example, are credited with having a thousand names. In the *bhakti* tradition within Hinduism the repetitive chanting of the name of a deity, especially Rām and Kṛṣṇa, is a characteristic devotional activity.

Names given to deities can also indicate developments within a religion. As Xinzhong Yao explains, in early Chinese history God was known as *Ti* (lord, sovereign); later he was called *Shang Ti* (*shang* = above, first); and later still, with the development of the idea of the supreme God as righteous and universal, he was known as *T'ien* (roughly translated as Heaven). Among the names for God in the earlier part of the biblical period were 'the Lord of Hosts', and 'God Almighty', but later the Jews also used such names as 'the Holy One', and 'Saviour', and 'Father', and a frequently used prayer in Judaism addresses God as 'King of the Universe'. It is significant that Jews have, for over two millennia, considered the personal name of God so sacred that it is never pronounced, and they often refer to God as 'the Name' (*Ha-Shem*). In Sikhism, too, God came to be known as *Nām* (Name). The power inherent in a name is illustrated by the Shinto belief that the name of a *kami* written on a piece of paper represents the power of the *kami*.

In many religions the divine is pictured, quite literally, through the visual arts. This is probably most obvious in Hinduism, which cannot be understood apart from its iconography; the gods – as well as demons, spirits, legendary heroes – are depicted in paintings and sculpture, and, as Sharada Sugirtharajah shows, their attributes and their role in the mythology are symbolised by the objects they hold, their dress, their posture and the position of their hands. Hinduism's religious art also includes aniconic images, especially the *liṅga* associated with Śiva and *śālagrāma* associated with Viṣṇu. Iconography also plays an important part in Buddhism. Peter Harvey points out that in early Buddhist art the Buddha was shown only by symbols; later he was shown in human form, though any representation of him eventually had the requirement that it must include what came to be accepted as the classical 'thirty-two signs'. Wendy Dossett comments on the richness of the iconography of Japanese Buddhism, and on the fact that Zen paintings are pictures of ultimate truth.

Islam has a strict prohibition against any visual representation of God, but art and architecture do make a contribution to its 'picture' of God. The symmetry and the geometric patterns on mosques reflect Muslim belief in the order of the universe and in Allāh's sovereign control of it, and the absence of any representation of sentient beings – human or animal – is a reminder of the conviction that God, and God alone, is to be worshipped.

Religious art has played an important part in Christianity's expression of its beliefs about God. In the Western churches this has often taken the form of the use of biblical material, or scenes depicting heaven (sometimes hell as well), with God represented either in human form or by a symbol such as a triangle or a down-stretched hand. In the Eastern churches the most significant form of religious art is the icon. Icons are described as 'windows into heaven', and, as Douglas Davies points out, in icons Christ stands as God and for God.

The human and the divine

The relationship between the human and the divine has provided religions with both possibilities and problems in picturing God. The distinction is at its sharpest in Islam, with the most serious sin being *shirk* – associating anything or anyone with God; its firm rejection of the use of 'Father' as one of the names of God reflects its determination to avoid the suggestion that God could be in any kind of physical relationship with human beings, and certainly could not have a son. The distinction between creation and creator is also marked in Judaism, although Judaism has made much more use of anthropomorphic imagery than Islam. In Christianity such Jewish forms of mediation between God and humans as God's Word or his Wisdom or his Spirit were 'enfleshed', with the incarnation becoming a central belief of Christian theology, and with the person of Jesus being seen as the most complete way of picturing God.

In Chinese religion *T'ien* was regarded as the supreme being, as creator, and as in complete control of the world, but, as Xinzhong Yao explains, at a popular level there developed a belief in the God, *Yu Huang*, who was seen as the incarnation of *tao*, and as the counterpart in heaven of the emperor on earth. In Japanese religion the Shinto *kami* were believed to be close to the human realm, both physically and in their personality.

It is in the religions of Indian origin that there is no sharp dividing line between the human and the divine (and between humans and the rest of the animal kingdom), although this features far less in Sikh thought than in either Hinduism or Buddhism. The belief in rebirth, or rebecoming, means that the kind of life individuals lead affects the situation into which they are born in their next life. In Mahāyāna Buddhism, those who have achieved enlightenment may, as *bodhisattva*s, remain in contact with the world instead of 'entering' *nirvāṇa*, because of their compassionate concern for the enlightenment of all people, and, as we saw above, their help will be sought by those further back on the Path. In Hinduism, the line between the human and the divine – and between both and the animal kingdom – is even more blurred. This is probably most obvious in the concept of *avatāra*, in which the God Viṣṇu 'descends', in times of great wickedness, to conquer evil and restore righteousness, incarnating himself in either animal or human form, or, as in the case of Narasiṃha ('man-lion') as half animal, half man. In addition, the Hindu pantheon includes Gaṇeśa, the elephant-headed god and Hanumān, the monkey god.

There is another aspect to the relationship between humans and God. In the chapter on Christianity, Douglas Davies comments that one of the ways in which the human imagination pictures God is through the lives of men, women and children; Christians believe that one can 'see' God in the lives of people. This does not apply only in Christianity. Clinton Bennett describes the Ṣūfī position in Islam: 'If you want to picture God, picture the perfect man, picture the individual whose life is so tuned into the will of God, whose life so reflects the qualities of God, that duality between creature and creator is annihilated'.

A feature of several religious traditions is the reconciliation of opposites in their picture of God. This most commonly relates to the tension between transcendence and immanence. This is a characteristic concern in Judaism, where God is creator and ruler of the world but also a God who acts, who is with his people; one resolution of this tension, as Norman Solomon shows, is the concept of *shekhinah* – God's hidden and yet manifest presence. Christianity's belief in the incarnation might appear to have resolved the question of transcendence and immanence, but it has led to endless theological discussion about how Jesus could be both divine and human. Islam faces a slightly different problem: how to reconcile Allāh's complete control of everything that happens with individuals having to account for the way they have lived their lives.

The reconciliation of 'opposites' is at its most obvious in Hinduism. Sharada Sugirtharajah emphasises that the qualities of the deities are not opposite but complementary. They include: with form and formless, immanent and transcendent, benign and terrible, male and female. Śiva is the god who perhaps more than any other holds apparent opposites in a 'harmonious unison'. In one of his forms he is even *Ardhanāri* – half male, half female. Complementarity is also expressed through the role of goddesses in Hinduism. The goddess is the god's *śakti*, his creative energy, without which he is not able to function.

In this introduction it has been possible to make only brief reference to individual religions, by way of illustration of the issues raised. This can be very misleading, partly because the illustrations have had to be taken out of their proper context, and partly because, in the main, they have been drawn from what anthropologists call the 'great tradition' of the religions: the teachings of the classical texts or of the principal expounders of the faith. The 'little tradition' refers to the way of understanding or practising the religion at a popular level, and this can vary considerably from the classical exposition – and is often the form of the religion of the majority of its adherents. This is more noticeable in the understanding of God than in most other aspects of a religion, because of the difficulty of 'picturing' the transcendent. In the chapters which follow, many of the authors include some discussion of the variations which developed in the popular forms of the religions, and the suggestions for further reading should help to extend the understanding of what is, in religious studies, a most important aspect of any religion – the little tradition.

1. Buddhism

Peter Harvey

The phrasing of the title of this book, 'Picturing God', is more suited to the monotheistic, God-focused religions than to Buddhism. However, Buddhism does accept a range of beings and levels of reality which go beyond our everyday world, and these will be the subject of this chapter. In the Buddhist world-view, ultimate reality is generally not personalised, as a God, much less as a single God. It is seen in more impersonal terms as a state to be attained or realised: *nirvāṇa*. The personal dimension comes in when one looks at those who experience this reality: for Theravāda Buddhism, *arahant*s ('saints') and earthly *buddha*s; for Mahāyāna Buddhism, Heavenly *buddha*s and advanced *bodhisattva*s, who are on the brink of buddhahood.

All schools of Buddhism also accept a range of gods: divine beings who have attained heavenly rebirths due to their good deeds, but who will sooner or later die and be reborn. *Buddha*s, *arahant*s and *bodhisattva*s are said to be 'teachers of humans and gods', and even gods are said to revere the 'three treasures': the Buddha, the *Dhamma* and *Saṅgha*. Here, the *Dhamma* is the *buddha*s' teaching, the timeless truths they point to, the path of practice, and the states realised on the path, culminating in *nirvāṇa* itself. The *Saṅgha*, as a 'treasure' or 'refuge', are those who have fully or partially realised *nirvāṇa*, who are conventionally symbolised by the monastic community, also known as the *saṅgha*. Buddhism thus lacks a simple contrast between the 'human' and the 'divine'. There are humans, limited gods, and, further, holy beings who have fully or partially experienced that which is truly transcendent, *nirvāṇa*.

The gods

The gods (*devas*) are said to live in twenty-six heavens of a progressively refined and calm nature (Harvey 1990: 34–7, 4–5; Conze 1959: 222–4). Those of the six lowest heavens gain their rebirth by generosity and moral virtue, and are not too distant from humans to be called on for help with such things as a good harvest, or to discipline troublesome nature spirits (Gombrich 1971: 191–213). The remaining heavens are all of a more subtle nature, and are only reachable by having attained a corresponding level of meditative calming. The life-span in the heavens is said to vary from 84,000 eons in the highest, down to nine million years in the lowest. Yet time passes more quickly for the gods: in the lowest heaven, fifty human years pass in one divine 'day'. While many gods tend to be somewhat complacent about the need for further spiritual effort, some are wise. These include the helpful Sakka (or Indra: ruler of the early Hindu pantheon), who is said to have had a first glimpse of *nirvāṇa*, so as to become a 'Stream-enterer'. Also, the gods of the 'pure abodes' (heavens 18–22) are 'Non-returners', who almost became *arahants* as humans, but who will attain *nirvāṇa* in their present state. In the fourth, Tuṣita heaven, is Metteyya (Sanskrit Maitreya), who is a *bodhisattva* who will be the next Buddha.

Among the higher gods are also the Great Brahmās, said to have attained their level by deep meditation on lovingkindness, compassion, sympathetic joy and equanimity. Such glorious beings, though, have the unfortunate tendency to think themselves eternal creator Gods. The reason for this is explained in Walshe (1987: 75–6, 213–15): periodically, the heaven of Great Brahmā, and lower realms, come to an end. After an eon, they re-appear, and a being is reborn, from a higher heaven, as a Great Brahmā again. In time, he becomes lonely and longs for the presence of others. Soon his wish is fulfilled, simply because other higher gods die and happen to be reborn, due to their *karma*, as his ministers and retinue. Not remembering his previous life, Great Brahmā therefore thinks, 'I am Brahmā, Great Brahmā . . . the Maker, the Creator . . . these other beings are my creation'. His godlings agree with this erroneous conclusion, and when some eventually die and are reborn as humans, they develop the power to remember their previous life, and consequently teach that Great Brahmā is the eternal creator of all beings! Buddhism sees no need for a creator of the world, as it postulates no ultimate beginning, and regards the world as sustained by natural laws. Moreover, if there were a creator, he would be seen as responsible for the world's sufferings. Yet a Great Brahmā's compassion is much valued, for such a being requests a *buddha* to teach after his enlightenment, when he wonders if anyone else could understand his profound discovery (Walshe 1987: 213–15).

Nirvāṇa in Theravāda Buddhism

Nirvāṇa fits within the Theravāda framework of belief as the third of the Four Holy Truths: *dukkha* (suffering/unsatisfactoriness), craving as its cause, *nirvāṇa* as its cessation, through the ceasing of craving, and the Holy Eightfold Path, of morality, calming meditation and wisdom, as the way to the end of *dukkha*. *Dukkha* is equated with the five 'groups' (*khandhas*) of processes making up a person: material form, feeling, cognition, constructing activities and (discriminative) consciousness. *Nirvāṇa* is both a state realised during life, by one who thus becomes an *arahant*, and a state entered when such a person dies, never to be reborn (Conze et al. 1954: 96–7). *Nirvāṇa* literally means 'extinction' or 'quenching', being the word used for the 'extinction' of a fire. *Nirvāṇa* is the extinction of the 'fires' of attachment, hatred and delusion – the causes of *dukkha* – and of the processes of 'birth, ageing and death' – *dukkha* itself. *Nirvāṇa* during life is defined as the destruction of attachment, hatred and delusion, the 'defilements'. When individuals who have destroyed these die, they are totally beyond the remaining 'fires' of birth, ageing and death.

Nirvāṇa is seen as truly profound and mysterious (Harvey 1990: 60–4; Conze 1962: 69–79; Brown and O'Brian 1989: 17–18, 62–4; Conze et al. 1954: 92–102; Conze 1959: 155–9). It is therefore not so much to be talked about as experienced, so more is said on how to attain it than the experience itself. Descriptions of *nirvāṇa* are not absent, but they tend to be negative, saying what *nirvāṇa* is *not*. This is to ensure it is not wrongly identified with any limited worldly phenomenon. One famous description is: 'Since, monks, there exists the unborn, unbecome, unmade, unconditioned (*asaṅkhata*), then there is apparent the leaving behind, here, of the born, become, made, conditioned' (Brown and O'Brian 1989: 63–4). This sees *nirvāṇa* as not subject to birth or, as said elsewhere, to dying; it is the Deathless which is beyond time and change. It is not the product of any process, is not constructed or conditioned by anything else: it can thus never fall apart or come to an end. Again:

> There exists, monks, that sphere where there is: i) neither solidity, nor cohesion, not heat, nor motion; ii) nor the sphere of infinite space, nor the sphere of infinite consciousness, nor the sphere of nothingness, nor the sphere of neither-perception-nor-non-perception; iii) neither this world, nor a world beyond, nor both; iv) nor sun-and-moon; v) there, monks, I say there is no coming or going, nor maintenance, nor falling away, nor arising; vi) that, surely, is without support (*patiṭṭhā*), it has no functioning, it has no object (*ārammaṇa*); vii) just this is the end of *dukkha*.
>
> (*Udāna* p. 80; numbers added. See Conze et al. 1954: 94–5)

That is, *nirvāṇa* is (i) totally beyond the four elements of matter, and (ii) beyond even the four 'formless' heavens, where only mental states occur. It is thus (iii) beyond *any* world, human, divine or whatever (for they all have their limitations). It is (iv) not any place in the cosmos, yet has its own intrinsic brilliance, outshining anything else. It is (v) beyond the processes involved in dying and being reborn. It is (vi) unsupported, as it exists without dependence on anything else; it is not something that 'functions', according to conditioning factors; and unlike all mental states, it does not have an object which it is aware of (and which would condition it). Finally (vii), it is the end of all *dukkha*: of all that is suffering, unsatisfactory, limited, imperfect. It is thus truly worthy of realisation.

Among 'negative' characteristics of *nirvāṇa* are three emphasised in the developed Theravāda meditative tradition (Conze 1962: 59–71). In this, a meditator is said to perceive *nirvāṇa* as either the 'signless', the 'undirected' or as 'emptiness' (*suññatā*). It is 'signless' in lacking any signs or indications that the mind can become attached to, being known in this way by those with strong insight into the ephemeral, limited nature of all conditioned processes. *Nirvāṇa* is 'undirected' in that it is attained by the total 'letting go' which comes when all conditioned processes are seen as *dukkha*. *Nirvāṇa* is 'emptiness' in being void of any grounds for the delusion of a permanent, substantial Self, and because it cannot be conceptualised in any view which links it to 'I' or 'mine' or 'Self'. It is known in this respect by one with deep insight into everything as not-Self (*anattā*), 'empty' of Self (Brown and O'Brian 1989: 42–3, 50–1, 54, 77; Conze et al. 1954: 91). Not only does Buddhism see ultimate reality as impersonal, then; even a human 'person' is seen as a collection of mutually conditioning mental and physical processes (*dhammas*) which are not a substantial Self, I or personal entity. As an overall collection, these changing states have no more than a relatively stable 'personality' or character-style.

Positive descriptions of *nirvāṇa* are generally of a poetic, suggestive nature. Thus it is said to be: the 'further shore' (beyond this 'shore' of life and its inherent suffering); the 'island amidst the flood' (a refuge from danger and suffering); the '(cool) cave of shelter' (a powerful image of peace and rest in the hot Indian climate); the marvellous. Certain positive descriptions give a less poetic indication of its nature. Thus it is 'the real, beyond the realm of reason, stable . . . the sorrowless, stainless state . . . the calming down of constructing activities, bliss' (Brown and O'Brian 1989: 64). It is peace, truth, and purity, (Woodward 1927: 261–4). Some early canonical passages hint that it may be a radically transformed state of consciousness (*viññāṇa*). Such passages talk of *nirvāṇa* as a consciousness 'in which nothing can be made manifest' (Walshe 1987: 179–80), and of *nirvāṇa* being realised when consciousness, through non-attachment, is without any object (*ārammaṇa*) to act as its support (*patiṭṭhā*) (Woodward 1925: 45–6): which accords with item vi) from *Udāna* 80, above. Nevertheless, the developed Theravāda tradition does not take up this hint. While *nirvāṇa* is itself seen as objectless, an enlightened person's consciousness has it as its object. For the commentator Buddhaghosa's discussion of *nirvāṇa*, seeking to avoid an over-negative or over-positive view, see Conze et al. (1954: 100–2).

As *nirvāṇa* is beyond space and time, no place or time is 'nearer' or 'more distant' from it; but it exists as an ever-present possibility to be realised. Indeed, it is said that it is 'in' – i.e., to be realised in – the body (Brown and O'Brian 1989: 53–4). It is often thought that *nirvāṇa* during life is an ever-present state of the *arahant*, but it would seem that this cannot be so. As *nirvāṇa* is synonymous with the cessation of all *dukkha*, and *nirvāṇa* during life is not seen as inferior to *nirvāṇa* beyond death in any respect, it cannot be ever-present; for the *arahant* will sometimes have physical pain, and his normal mental processes are all changing and impermanent, hence *dukkha* (Conze et al. 1954: 66–7). *Nirvāṇa* during life must thus be a specific experience, in which the defilements are destroyed for ever, and in which there is a temporary stopping of all conditioned states. During life or beyond death, *nirvāṇa* is the unconditioned cessation of all unsatisfactory, conditioned phenomena. During life, it is where these phenomena stop, followed by their recurrence in the arising of normal experiences of the world; once attained, this stopping can be returned to. Beyond death (not 'after' it: *nirvāṇa* is beyond time), it is where they stop for good. Yet *nirvāṇa* is seen as existing whether or not anyone attains it. So one could perhaps say that the *arahant*'s experience of *nirvāṇa* during life is one of 'participating in' that unborn, unconditioned blissful reality.

As a proximate goal, *nirvāṇa* is the focus for a minority of Theravāda Buddhists. It has never been seen as *easy* to attain, and it is orthodox belief to say that people's true understanding and practice of the *Dhamma* has declined over the centuries since the Buddha's time. Most laypeople and many monks aim for a better rebirth next time, as a god or wealthy human, and aspire that, over many lives, they will become spiritually mature enough to make the effort to attain *nirvāṇa*. A common aspiration is that, in a future life, they will be in the presence of the next Buddha, Metteyya, and attain *nirvāṇa* under his guidance. A minority of middle-class laypeople now aspire for *nirvāṇa* within a few lifetimes. The minority of monks who are ascetic 'forest-dwellers' specialising in meditation, also seek to attain arahantship or stream-entry (a first glimpse of *nirvāṇa*) in this life or soon after. For discussions of contemporary attitudes to the attainment of *nirvāṇa*, for Myanmar (Burma) see Spiro (1971: 76–84); and for Sri Lanka see Gombrich (1971: 16–7, 214–24, 290–2). Whether or not a person has *nirvāṇa* as a proximate goal, the 'contemplation of peace' – of the qualities of *nirvāṇa* – is recommended as a meditation leading to the arising of bliss, peace and self-confidence.

The Buddha and *arahants* in Theravāda Buddhism

The person known to history as 'the Buddha' is generally known to Theravadins as Gotama Buddha. As a '*buddha*' he is one of the 'Awakened Ones' who arise over the ages. It is held that a 'hundred thousand eons ago', in a past life, he met and was inspired by a previous *buddha*, Dīpaṅkara (Conze et al. 1954: 82–4; 1959: 20–4). He therefore resolved to strive for buddhahood, by becoming a *bodhisattva*. He knew that, while he could become an *arahant* under Dīpaṅkara, the path he had chosen would take many more lives to complete. It would, however, culminate in his becoming a perfect *buddha*, one who would bring benefit to countless beings by rediscovering and teaching the timeless truths of *Dhamma* in a period when they had been lost to human society. He then spent many lives as a human, animal and god, building up the moral and spiritual perfections necessary for buddhahood. Over the ages, he meets and is taught by a number of past *buddha*s. All these are said to go through a series of parallel events in their lives, for they are seen as fulfilling an eternal pattern of *Dhamma* that is of cosmic importance (Walshe 1987: 199–221). In descriptions of his life and character, Gotama is portrayed as a humane, tranquil, compassionate figure, who used his sharp, analytic intelligence and acute observation to guide those who sought the Beyond in which lies true happiness and an end to *dukkha* (Harvey 1990: 14–31). His charismatic presence inspired many, and is even said to have drawn to him many divine beings. While modern Theravadins sometimes say that he was 'just a human', this is usually meant as an implicit contrast to Jesus, seen as the 'Son of God', or to the more divinised Mahāyāna view of the Buddha. It may also be due to a modern demythologising. In the Theravāda Canon, Gotama was seen as *born* a human, though one with extra-ordinary abilities due to the perfections built up as a *bodhisattva*. Once he had attained enlightenment, though, he had gone beyond the deep-rooted unconscious traits that would make him a god or human, so he was neither of these, but a *buddha* (Conze et al. 1954: 104–5). In perfecting his human-ness, he had transcended it.

The Buddha is seen as having a mysterious nature closely linked to the *Dhamma*: 'Who, Vakkali, sees *Dhamma*, he sees me; who sees me, sees *Dhamma*' (Conze et al. 1954: 103). He is one who 'has *Dhamma* as body' and who is '*Dhamma*-become' (Conze et al. 1954: 112–13). That is, he has fully exemplified the *Dhamma*-as-Path, in his personality or 'body', and has fully realised *nirvāṇa*, the supreme *Dhamma* (Brown and O'Brian 1989: 63). The *arahant* is no different in these respects, for he is described as 'become the supreme' (*brahma-bhūta*) (Conze et al. 1954: 42), a term equivalent to '*Dhamma*-become'. While Christians see Jesus as God-become-man, then, Buddhists see the Buddha (and *arahants*) as man-become-*Dhamma*. A *buddha* or *arahant* is 'deep, immeasurable, hard-to-fathom as is the great ocean' (Conze et al. 1954: 106). Having 'become *Dhamma*', their enlightened nature can only really be fathomed by one who has 'seen' *Dhamma*, as *nirvāṇa*, with the '*Dhamma*-eye' of stream-entry.

The *arahant* is one who has been radically transformed by the complete destruction of attachment, hatred and delusion (Katz 1982; Brown and O'Brian 1989: 81; Conze et al. 1954: 42–5). His or her actions are pure and spontaneous: 'Calm is his mind, calm is his speech, calm is his behaviour who, rightly knowing, is wholly freed, perfectly peaceful and equipoised'. He 'keeps his cool' under all circumstances. While he may experience physical pain (as a result of past *karma*), no mental anguish at this can arise, for it is not identified with as 'mine' (Conze 1959: 159–62). Even the threat of death does not ruffle him, for he has transcended the idea of 'I', and so has nothing to feel threatened. The *arahant* has a strong mind, 'like a thunderbolt', in which flashes of insight arise, and he has fully developed the 'seven factors of enlightenment': mindful alertness, investigation of *Dhamma*, vigour, joy, tranquillity, concentration and equanimity. While he is one who has seen through the delusion of a permanent Self or I, lacking the 'I am' conceit, he nevertheless has an empirical self, or character, which is very well developed: he is 'one of developed self' (*bhāvit-atta*), not a 'small' person.

The Buddha is himself called an *arahant* – one who has fully experienced *nirvāṇa* – but he had a more extensive knowledge than other *arahants*. For example, he could remember as far back into previous lives as he wanted, while other *arahants* had limitations on such a power, or may not even have developed it. A *buddha* is seen as one who can come to know anything he pleases about the past and present, and can make many valid predictions about the future, such as how a person will be reborn. From his vast knowledge (Woodward 1930: 370), he selects what is spiritually useful. Having rediscovered the Path, he skilfully makes it known to others, thus enabling them to become *arahants* (Brown and O'Brian 1989: 82). Like him, they then become a *tathāgata*, a 'Truth-attained One'.

The Buddha was often asked about the destiny of a *tathāgata* after death: could it be said that he 'is', that he 'is not' (being annihilated), that he 'both is and is not', or that he 'neither is nor is not'? The

Buddha set aside these questions without answering them: they were 'undetermined' (Harvey 1990: 65–8; Woodward 1927: 265–83). One reason for this was that he saw speculating on them as a time-wasting side-track from spiritual practice. Demanding answers to them was like a man, shot with a poisoned arrow, refusing to let a doctor cure him until he knew everything about who shot the arrow, and what the arrow was made of: such a man would soon die. The important thing was to get on with the task of overcoming *dukkha*. Moreover, the Buddha also saw that his questioners were really asking about what they conceived of as the fate of an (enlightened) substantial *Self* after death; as no such thing could be found during life, it was meaningless to discuss its state after death (Woodward 1927: 278–9).

Besides the above, what might the Buddha's silence on this issue mean? It is clearly unacceptable to say that a *tathāgata* is annihilated after death, for this is the view of the second undetermined question, which is seen as particularly pernicious: for only *dukkha* (the conditioned personality factors) ends at death (Woodward 1925: 93–6). Having destroyed all causes of rebirth, though, it cannot be said that a *tathāgata* 'is' after death, in a rebirth; nor that a *part* of him is reborn ('both is and is not'); nor that he is reborn in the very attenuated 'sphere of neither-perception-nor-non-perception ('neither is nor is not'). Asking the four questions on a *tathāgata* is said to be like asking the meaningless question of which direction a quenched fire had gone in: east, west, south or north (Conze et al. 1954: 106). Having said this, the Buddha stressed that a *tathāgata* (even in life) is 'deep, immeasurable, hard-to-fathom as is the great ocean'. While to a western-educated person, an extinct fire goes nowhere because it does not exist, the Buddha's audience in ancient India would generally have thought of it as going back into a non-manifested state as latent heat. The simile of the extinct fire thus suggests that the state of an enlightened person beyond death is one which is beyond normal comprehension, not that it is a state of nothingness: 'There exists no measuring of one who has gone out (like a flame). That by which he could be referred to no longer exists for him. When all phenomena are removed, then all ways of describing have also been removed' (Conze 1962: 77–9, cf. 113–14). Silence again. The only whisper in the silence is a hint that, beyond death, an enlightened person's consciousness may remain, in a radically transformed, 'unsupported' form (Conze et al. 1954: 43);

it would thus be objectless, unlimited, unconditioned, timeless: *nirvāṇa*.

The Theravāda tradition emphasises that the Buddha, since his death, is beyond contact with the world and cannot respond to prayer or worship. There is, though, a widely held belief in a kind of compassionate '*buddha*-force' which will remain in the world for as long as Buddhism is practised. This power-for-good can be drawn on through the Buddha's teaching (*Dhamma*) and even through the bodily relics which remained after his cremation. The chanting of certain texts known as *paritta*s is also seen as drawing down a protective power, both by releasing a truth-power inherent in the words of the Buddha, and by pleasing those gods who are Buddhist (Harvey 1990: 180–2). At the popular level, Buddhists can also behave as if the Buddha is a being who actively responds to prayer. Richard Gombrich has described this situation by saying that while, *cognitively*, the Buddha is acknowledged as beyond worldly contact, *affectively*, at the level of feelings, he is often looked on as a living source of benefit (Gombrich 1971: 81–2, 122, 139–42).

The Mahāyāna perspective on *arahant*s and the Buddha

In the Mahāyāna, the final goal is not arahantship, but full, perfect buddhahood, a state of omniscience and compassion, which facilitates the liberation of countless beings. The teaching directed at the attainment of arahantship, the Four Holy Truths, is seen as simply a provisional teaching given by the Buddha to those not yet ready to understand the full teaching (Conze et al. 1954: 124–7). The *arahant* is seen as still having a subtle pride, and as lacking in compassion in his hope of escaping the round of rebirths, thus leaving unenlightened beings to fend for themselves. For the Mahāyāna, true *nirvāṇa* is only attained at buddhahood, and the way to this high goal is the path of the *bodhisattva*, which takes many, many lives of selfless striving. In the ten-stage path to buddhahood, *bodhisattva*s, at stage six, reach a level akin to that of the *arahant*s and could leave the round of rebirths if they wished. However, from compassion, they continue in the round of rebirths until they have sufficient spiritual perfections to attain full buddhahood (see further, pp. 23–4, 27–8).

According to the standards of arahantship preserved by the

Theravāda, the charge that the *arahant* is proud and selfish is absurd. By definition, he or she is one who has finally destroyed the 'I am' conceit, the root of all egoism and selfishness. He is also described as imbued with lovingkindness and as compassionately teaching others. The Theravāda still acknowledges that the long path to buddhahood, over many many lives, is the loftiest practice, as it aims at the salvation of countless beings. Nevertheless, while this *bodhisattva*-path has been and is practised by a few Theravadins (often laypeople), it is seen as a way for the heroic few only. Most have gratefully made use of Gotama Buddha's teachings so as to move towards arahantship.

In the Mahāyāna perspective, Gotama is referred to as Śākyamuni (Sage of the Śākyas) Buddha. Unlike in the Theravāda, he is not seen to have attained Buddhahood in his life in the fifth century BCE. In the *Lotus Sūtra*, the Buddha explains that he became enlightened an unimaginable number of eons ago (Conze et al. 1954: 140–3; Williams, 1989: 167–84). Since that time, over the ages, he has already appeared on earth in the form of past *buddha*s such as Dīpaṅkara (Brown and O'Brian 1989: 220–1). All such earthly *buddha*s teach those of lesser understanding that *buddha*s pass into final *nirvāṇa*, beyond contact with living beings, when they die. This is only a skilful means, however, to ensure that people do not become overly dependent on *buddha*s, but actually use the spiritual medicine that *buddha*s give. In fact, the heavenly Buddha (also known as Śākyamuni), who appeared in the form of earthly *buddha*s, will live on for twice the time that has passed since he became enlightened; only then will he pass into final *nirvāṇa*.

The historical Buddha is thus seen as a manifestation skilfully projected into earthly life by a long-enlightened transcendent being, who is still available to teach through visionary experiences (Conze et al. 1954: 139–40). At the popular level, the omniscient Śākyamuni Buddha is seen as an omnipresent, eternal being, watching over the world and supremely worthy of worship. While he is seen as enlightened for a hugely long length of time, however, the idea is still expressed that he became a *buddha* by practising the *bodhisattva*-path, starting out as an ordinary being. He is, then, neither a recently enlightened human who has passed into final *nirvāṇa*, nor an eternal monotheistic God-type figure. As a *buddha*, he does not exist forever, and is only 'eternal' in that he knows, and has become identical with, that which lies *beyond* time.

The Mahāyāna on *nirvāṇa*

The Mahāyāna perspective not only sees the Buddha in a different way, but also reassesses the relationship between *nirvāṇa* and the world (Eliade 1987: X, 448–56). For early Buddhism and the Theravāda school, *nirvāṇa*, as the blissful unconditioned, is a clear contrast to the conditioned world in which we live: *saṃsāra*, the realm of rebirth and of constant change and suffering. Yet for the Mahāyāna, *nirvāṇa* and *saṃsāra*, when properly understood with insight and wisdom by the advanced *bodhisattva*, are seen as not different at all! The earliest expression of this perspective is found in the *Perfection of Wisdom* (*Prajñā-pāramitā*) *Sūtra*s (first century BCE and following) and in the philosophical school related to them, the Madhyamaka (founder Nagarjuna, *c.* 150–250 CE) (Harvey 1990: 95–104; Williams, 1989: 37–76).

In the earlier literature known as the *Abhidharma*, personality had been analysed down into sets of interacting mental or physical processes known as *dharma*s (Pāli: *dhamma*s). All of these were said to be 'empty' (*śūnya*) of a permanent, substantial Self. In the *Perfection of Wisdom* texts and the Madhyamaka school, the *dharma*s were said to be 'empty' in a further sense. As they could only be understood as part of an interacting web of *dharma*-processes, no *dharma* could exist or be anything on its own. All that a *dharma* 'is', is derivable from the other *dharma*s which condition it; but the same applies to them also. So a *dharma* has no 'nature' of its own, nothing 'belonging' to it apart from its relationship to other *dharma*s. *Dharma*s are thus said to be 'empty' of 'own-nature' (*svabhāva*), to lack any inherent nature of their own. They are thus said to share the mysterious quality of 'emptiness' (*śūnyatā*). This term points to the radical inter-relationship of *dharma*s, and thus to their relativity: they only exist in relationship to each other. More than this, the term points to the indescribable nature of reality. Language splits the world up into separate bits, and then tries to fit these back together to some extent by talking of various kinds of relationship between them. But on the *Perfection of Wisdom*/ Madhyamaka analysis, there really *are* no truly *separate* bits in the first place, so language will always distort to some extent. The term 'emptiness', though, can be used as a pointer to the fact that, in its true thusness or suchness (*tathatā*) – its as-it-is-ness or whatness – reality is not capable of being grasped in concepts. Yet this is precisely how *nirvāṇa* had always been seen: as an 'emptiness' that was beyond being grasped in positive concepts. Thus the unconditioned *nirvāṇa* cannot be differentiated from, is not different from, *saṃsāra*. As expressed in the brief text known as the *'Heart' Perfection of Wisdom Sūtra*, none of the five aspects of personality can be differentiated from nirvanic emptiness, for example: 'material form is emptiness, and the very emptiness is material form; emptiness does not differ from material form, material form does not differ from emptiness' (Conze et al. 1954: 152–3; Brown and O'Brian 1989: 200–2). In the inconceivable interacting field of emptiness, moreover, nothing stands out as a separate entity, so the *Heart Sūtra* continues by saying that 'in emptiness' there are none of the five aspects of personality, or even any of the Four Holy Truths, including *nirvāṇa*. All such provisional, limited concepts are transcended when the mind can truly let go, from insight into emptiness. And yet in doing so, true *nirvāṇa* is attained. As expressed in the *Diamond-cutter* (*Vajracchedikā*) *Perfection of Wisdom Sūtra*, to attain *nirvāṇa*:

> the *Bodhisattva*, the great being, should produce an unsupported (*apratiṣṭhita*) thought, i.e., a thought which is nowhere supported, a thought unsupported by sights, sounds, smells, tastes, touchables, or mind-objects.

Such a *nirvāṇa* is seen as experienced by advanced *bodhisattva*s, of stage seven onwards, who remain in (the heavenly levels of) *saṃsāra* while knowing it is no different from *nirvāṇa*. The *nirvāṇa* they will reach at buddhahood is only superior to this in involving omniscience. The *nirvāṇa* experienced by advanced *bodhisattva*s is known as *apratiṣṭhita-nirvāṇa*: 'unsupported *nirvāṇa*', also translated as '*nirvāṇa* without standstill'. It is seen as a state in which the *bodhisattva*s are not resting content in *saṃsāra*, but nor have they abandoned it to rest content in *nirvāṇa*. Their minds can fluidly move between both. How these ideas might relate to earlier hints on *nirvāṇa* as a consciousness which is 'unsupported' (*apatiṭṭhita*: Pāli equivalent of Sanskrit *apratiṣṭhita*) is yet to be determined.

While the Madhyamaka was one of the major philosophical schools of Indian Mahāyāna, the other was the Yogācāra (Harvey 1990: 104–13; Williams 1989: 77–95). This school produced a slightly different perspective on *nirvāṇa*. In its analysis, the world as we experience it is something which is purely mental. *If* there is anything beyond consciousness and mental states, we have no way of knowing: for these are all we ever experience. The content of a person's experience is said to be projected out of his or her deep unconsciousness, the *ālaya-vijñāna*, or 'storehouse consciousness' (Brown and O'Brian 1989: 106–7). This stores the traces left by one's previous *karma*/actions, which later mature to produce details of a world of apparent 'sights' and 'sounds' etc. The aim of Yogācāra meditations is to stop being taken in by these apparently 'external' objects, and to recognise them as mental projections. Further than that, the meditator should come to realise that the very idea of an inner 'subject' is itself linked to the contrasting idea of 'external' objects. When 'external' objects are transcended, so must a supposed 'inner' subject or Self be transcended. There is simply thought-only, with no 'inside' or 'outside' (Conze et al. 1954: 209–11; Brown and O'Brian 1989: 205–6). When this is fully realised, there is said to be 'reversal of the basis' (*āśraya-parāvṛtti*): that is, a revolution in the storehouse consciousness which is the 'basis' (*āśraya*) of the world as we know it. This 'reversal' or 'turning back' disrupts the normal flow of apparent objects, and lets the interpreting mind, the *manas*, turn round to know its basis. As is stated in a Yogācāra-related text, the *Laṅkāvatāra Sūtra*, *nirvāṇa* is, then, 'the storehouse consciousness which is realized inwardly, after a reversal has taken place' (Conze et al. 1954: 207; Brown and O'Brian 1989: 203–4). Yet as *nirvāṇa* is beyond time, this cannot be an actual change, just a cessation of delusions, so, as in the Madhyamaka, 'there is no difference between *saṃsāra* and *nirvāṇa*' (Conze et al. 1954: 207).

The *Laṅkāvatāra Sūtra* also contains elements of a strand of thought which became very influential in China and other parts of East Asia. This relates to the idea of the *tathāgata-garbha*, the 'embryo of the *tathāgata*', also known as the *buddha*-nature (Harvey 1990: 113–18; Williams 1989: 96–115; Brown and O'Brian 1989: 105–6; Conze et al. 1954: 181–4, 216–17). In the *Laṅkāvatāra Sūtra* (pp. 190–3) this is equated with the storehouse consciousness. The *tathāgata-garbha* is seen as an inner radiant purity which is the seed of enlightenment, though it is obscured by spiritual ignorance and other defilements. Indeed, without these obscurations, it is itself enlightenment: while being empty of all defilements, it is replete with the qualities of buddhahood. These, then, do not so much need to be developed, as uncovered, known and shown in one's actions. This approach is that favoured by the Ch'an (Chinese; Japanese, Zen) school. Like most schools of Chinese and Japanese Buddhism, this talks little of *nirvāṇa*, with its Indian associations of escape-from-rebirth, and links with the 'discredited' *arahant* ideal. Rather, it focuses on 'awakening' (Chinese *wu*) or buddhahood. In the dominant, 'southern' strand of Ch'an/Zen, it is emphasised that one does not need to work at gradually purifying the mind of defilements, for these are empty, not ultimately real (Brown and O'Brian 1989: 210). Rather, one should seek insight into one's pure, innate *buddha*-nature, and seek to express this in all one's actions. Thus Dōgen (1200–53), who introduced the Soto form of Zen into Japan, emphasised that sitting in meditation is not something done so as to become a *buddha*; one is already a *buddha*, and meditation is simply the best way to manifest this (Brown and O'Brian 1989: 265–7). Besides meditation, Ch'an/Zen has also seen enlightenment expressed in actions that are done with great awareness and compassion, and which combine the disciplined restraint of personal desires and spontaneous creativity, seen as an outpouring of the *buddha*-nature. The masters embodying these ideals have varied from fierce, unconventional, iconoclastic characters, to clowning 'fools', to saintly ascetic figures. All have emphasised: look within and find the *buddha*-nature.

Also influential in East Asian Buddhism, particularly in the Hua-yen school, is the outlook of the *Avataṃsaka Sūtra* (Harvey 1990: 118–20; Williams 1989: 116–38; Brown and O'Brian 1989: 207–8). This sees enlightenment as the omniscient vision of reality as the *Dharma*-realm: a vast, harmonious and wonderful array of phenomena which exist as an interpenetrating network of processes. In this, each particular reflects and is related to everything else in the cosmos, and the whole mystery of reality is present even in a grain of dust.

The Mahāyāna view of *bodhisattva*s and *buddha*s

The Mahāyāna is focused on the *bodhisattva*, whose task is to help beings compassionately while maturing his or her own wisdom (*prajñā*) (Harvey 1990: 121–4; Williams 1989: 185–214; Conze et al. 1954: 127–35). From this, he knows that the beings helped are not ultimately different from himself, for 'self' and 'other' are equally empty of separate reality (Brown and O'Brian 1989: 158–60). He or she can also rub shoulders with wrong-doers, in an effort to 'reach' them, knowing that their bad characteristics are not inherent realities. Any potential pride at the good done is tempered by the reflection that his or her goodness-power is also 'empty'. A person may even do a deed leading to hell, if this is a necessary part of helping someone else and giving them a more wholesome outlook on life.

*Bodhisattva*s begin as ordinary human beings who have been stirred by the sufferings of all sentient beings to seek to become *buddha*s. With compassion as the driving force, they begin to practise the six 'perfections' of a *bodhisattva*; generosity, moral virtue, patience, vigour, meditation, and intuitive wisdom (Brown and O'Brian 1989: 168–86; Conze et al. 1954: 135–9). When insight reaches a deep level, they attain a first glimpse of emptiness, at the 'Path of Seeing'. This is the entry to the path of the Holy (*Ārya*) *Bodhisattva*. They then develop the perfections through the first six stages of the Holy *Bodhisattva* Path. On the sixth, they attain the true perfection of wisdom, and from the seventh to tenth stage, they are 'Great Beings': heavenly saviour-beings who aid beings in a variety of ways. They send manifestations into many worlds, so as to teach and help beings in appropriate ways; they also transfer karmic goodness-power ('merit') from their vast store, so that beings who pray to them receive it as a free spiritual uplift of grace. Beyond the tenth stage, they finally attain buddhahood, in a heavenly realm of existence.

Buddhahood is understood according to the *Tri-kāya* or 'Three body' doctrine (Harvey 1990: 125–8; Williams 1989: 167–84). This sees it as having three aspects: i) the *nirmāṇa-kāya*, or 'Transformation-body', ii) the *sambhoga-kāya*, or 'Enjoyment-body', and iii) the *dharma-kāya*, or '*Dharma*-body'. The 'Transformation-body' refers to earthly *buddha*s, seen as teaching devices projected into the world to show people the path to buddhahood. The 'Enjoyment-body' is seen as a refulgent subtle body which is the product of the goodness-power of a *Bodhisattva*'s training. It is adopted by a *buddha* for the 'enjoyment' of Holy *Bodhisattva*s: in this form, the *buddha* teaches them through visionary experiences or, for the heavenly Great Beings, by a direct presence. The heavenly Buddha Śākyamuni is of the Enjoyment-body type, but there are many others, 'as numerous as there are grains of sand on the banks of the river Ganges', dwelling in various regions of the universe. Their form and wondrous powers vary slightly according to their past *bodhisattva*-vows and goodness-power. Each Enjoyment-body *buddha* is seen as presiding over his own 'Buddha Land' (*Buddha-kṣetra*), the world-system where he finally attained buddhahood in its Akaniṣṭha heaven. Many such Lands are said to be 'Pure Lands', mystical universes created by the appropriate *buddha* using his immeasurable store of goodness-power. While these are described in paradisaical terms, they are primarily realms whose conditions are very conducive to attaining enlightenment. Pure Lands are outside the normal system of rebirth according to personal *karma*. To be reborn in one requires a transfer of some of the huge stock of goodness-power of a Land's presiding *buddha*, stimulated by devout prayer. Once faith has led to rebirth in a Pure Land, individuals can develop their wisdom and so become either an *arahant* or a Great Being *bodhisattva*. Besides the 'Pure' Buddha Lands, there are also 'impure' ones, normal world-systems like our own, Śākyamuni's realm.

The '*Dharma*-body' has two aspects, the first being the 'Knowledge-body' (*jñāna-kāya*), the inner nature shared by all *buddhas*: the omniscient knowledge, perfect wisdom, and spiritual qualities through which a *bodhisattva* becomes a *buddha*. It is regarded as having a very subtle, shining, limitless form from which speech can come, due to the autonomous working of the *bodhisattva* vows. In this respect, the *Dharma*-body is given a semi-personalised aspect, making it somewhat akin to the concept of God in other religions. The *Dharma*-body is thus sometimes personified as the Buddha Vairocana, the 'Resplendent One' (Eliade 1987: XV, 126–8; Brown and O'Brian 1989: 240). In the tenth century, the process of personification was carried further, in the concept of the *Ādi*, or 'Primordial', ever-enlightened Buddha. The second aspect of the *Dharma*-body is the 'Self-existent-body (*svabhāvika-kāya*)'. This is the ultimate nature of reality, thusness, emptiness: the non-nature which is the very nature of *dharmas*, their *dharma*-ness. It is what is known and realised on attaining buddhahood, it is *nirvāṇa*. Only for convenience of explanation are the Knowledge and Self-existent bodies described as different. In emptiness, there can be no differentiation between a *buddha*'s thusness and the thusness of all *dharmas*: *buddha*-ness is *dharma*-ness (Conze 1973: 193, 291).

On the ultimate level, only the *Dharma*-body exists; the other *buddha*-bodies are just provisional ways of talking about and apprehending it. They, Pure Lands, and Great Beings, then, are not truly real, any more than the book you are now reading or the eyes with which you read it! (Brown and O'Brian 1989: 258). In emptiness, nothing stands out with separate reality. At the conventional level of truth, however, such *buddhas* etc., are just as real as anything else. Indeed, in popular Mahāyāna practice, the Enjoyment-body *buddhas* and Great Beings are treated as wholly real, and rebirth in their Pure Lands is ardently sought through faith. From the conventional perspective, such beings are those who have heroically striven to be close to, or attained to, buddhahood. From the ultimate perspective, they are the symbolic forms in which the 'minds' of empty 'beings' perceive the *Dharma*-body (Brown and O'Brian 1989: 283–4). *Buddhas* can know it directly, Holy *Bodhisattvas* experience it as Enjoyment-bodies, while ordinary beings only know it when it appears as a Transformation-body. Those with great insight, though, can glimpse it in the thusness of any worldly object. To non-Buddhists such as Hindus, the *Dharma*-body appears in the form of the gods of their religion (Suzuki 1932: 165–6). Thus in Japan, the major *kami*, or deities of the indigenous Shinto religion, became identified with particular heavenly *buddhas* or Great Beings.

The Mahāyāna pantheon

Of the 'countless' heavenly *buddhas* and *bodhisattvas*, some of the named ones became focuses of devotion (Harvey 1990: 129–33, 182–9; Williams 1989: 224–76). Besides Śākyamuni, important heavenly *buddhas* include Bhaiṣajya-guru, the 'Master of Healing', who offers cures for physical and spiritual ailments (Eliade 1987: II, 128–30), and Amitābha, 'Infinite Radiance' (Eliade 1987: I, 235–7; Brown and O'Brian 1989: 219). The latter became of central importance in the Pure Land schools of East Asian Buddhism. The Larger *Sukhāvatī-vyūya*, or 'Array of the Happy Land', *Sūtra* tells how, as a *bodhisattva*, he had vowed that he would only become a *buddha* when his goodness-power was sufficient to produce the most excellent Pure Land possible. Its inhabitants would have the highest 'perfections', memory of previous lives, and the ability to see myriads of other Buddha Lands. They would immediately hear whatever teaching they wished, would have no idea of property, even with regard to their own bodies, and would have the same happiness of those in deep meditative trance. This Happy Land (Sukhāvatī) would be a paradise full of 'jewel-trees', which stimulate calm and contemplative states of mind, where everything would be as beings wished, in a realm free from temptation and defilement (Conze et al. 1954: 202–6; Conze 1959: 232–6). Most importantly, he vowed that he would appear before any dying being who aspired for enlightenment and devoutly called him to mind, so as to conduct him or her to his Pure Land (Brown and O'Brian 1989: 251–2). Entry to this is said to come from deep faith in Amitābha and the power of his gracious vows.

The notion of gaining rebirth in the Happy Land has long provided a hope to people struggling with existence, living less than perfect lives. If currently unable to behave like true *bodhisattva*s, the environment of the Happy Land will enable them to do so, and the immeasurably long life-span there will encompass the hugely long *bodhisattva*-path. Yet other perspectives on the Happy Land are also found. One idea which developed in the Japanese Jodo school is that the Happy Land is everywhere: seeing it just needs an attitude transformed by faith. In the Japanese Jodo-shin school, even one's faith is seen as coming from Amitābha; one must simply be open to his wondrous power: humans are seen as too sinful to attain salvation by their own power (Brown and O'Brian 1989: 254, 257). This school sees Amitābha as the embodiment of the *Dharma*-body, and even sees the Happy Land as the same as *nirvāṇa* (Brown and O'Brian 1989: 258).

Maitreya, 'The Kindly One', is said to be a heavenly *bodhisattva* who, after attaining buddhahood, will send a Transformation-body to be the next *buddha* on earth (Eliade 1987: IX, 136–41). In China, he is often portrayed in the form of one of his recognised manifestations, the tenth-century Pu-tai. This Ch'an monk was a jolly, pot-bellied, wandering teacher who carried presents for children in his cloth bag (*pu-tai*). In the West, images of him are often known as 'Laughing Buddhas'. Another important Great Being is Mañjuśrī, 'Sweet Glory', a helper of the heavenly Buddha Śākyamuni (Eliade 1987: IX, 174–5). He is seen as the greatest embodiment of wisdom and has the special task of awakening spiritual knowledge. Accordingly, he is shown holding a copy of a *Perfection of Wisdom Sūtra*, and wielding a flaming sword, symbolic of the wisdom with which he cuts away delusion. He is seen as the patron of scholars and a protector of *Dharma*-preachers. Those who devoutly recite his name, and meditate on his teachings and images, are said to be protected by him, to have many good rebirths, and to see him in dreams and meditative visions, in which he inspires and teaches them.

By far the most popular of the Great Beings is Avalokiteśvara, who is said to aid Amitābha in his compassionate concern for the world. He is in fact seen as the very embodiment of compassion, the driving force of all *bodhisattva*s (Eliade 1987: II, 11–14; Blofeld 1977). His vows are such that he will not become a *buddha* till all beings are saved. As a *buddha*, he would have a limited, though huge, life-span, but as a *bodhisattva* he can remain in closer contact with suffering beings, helping them till the end of time. The name Avalokiteśvara means 'The Lord Who Looks Down (with compassion)'; in China he is called Kuan Yin, 'Cry Regarder', or Kuan Shih Yin, 'Regarder of the Cries of the World'. In all Mahāyāna lands, he is the focus of devout worship, contemplation, and prayers for help (Brown and O'Brian 1989: 287; Conze et al. 1954: 194–6). He is seen to manifest himself as various compassionate beings: these may mysteriously disappear after they have appeared to help someone, or may live out a full life, or even a series of them, as in the case of the Dalai Lamas of Tibet. He even manifests himself in hells or as an animal. In one Chinese painting, he is shown appearing in the form of a bull, in order to convert a butcher from his wrong livelihood.

Like most other Great Beings, Avalokiteśvara is portrayed crowned and with royal garments, rather than the monastic robes of a *buddha* (Figure 1). This is to show that *bodhisattva*s are more in contact with the world than *buddha*s, and more actively engaged in helping beings. Avalokiteśvara holds a lotus bud, which symbolises the pure beauty of his compassion, or the worldly minds of beings which he encourages in their efforts to 'bloom' into enlightenment. He is often shown with his hands cupped together around a 'wish granting jewel', an emblem of his willingness to grant righteous wishes. Its clarity also symbolises the natural purity, hidden by coverings of spiritual defilements, in the minds of beings. These defilements are suggested by the cupping hands, also said to be like a lotus bud. One of the many types of images of Avalokiteśvara shows him with one thousand arms, each with an eye on its palm; this suggests his being ever on the look out for beings in distress, and his reaching out to help them.

Great Beings also include female forms, such as Prajñā-pāramitā, 'Perfection of Wisdom', symbolically seen as the 'mother of all *Buddhas*', for buddhahood comes from wisdom (Conze et al. 1954: 47–9). In Tibet, the Green Tārā, or 'Saviouress' became the ever-popular patron-deity of the country (Figure 1). She is seen as graceful, attractive and approachable, and as ever-ready to care tenderly for those in distress (Eliade 1987: XIV, 337–9; Conze et al. 1954: 196–202). Her compassionate nature, in responding to those who call on her, is reflected in the story that she and the White Tārā were born from two tears of Avalokiteśvara when he saw the horrors of hell. In the Tantric form of Buddhism in Tibet and Mongolia, male and female holy beings are often paired, as consorts. In such pairs, the female is known as the *Prajñā*, or 'Wisdom' of her partner, and represents the wise, passive power which makes possible the active and energetic compassionate skilful means of the male. The pair is often represented, as *Yab*, 'Father', and *Yum*, 'Mother', in discreet sexual union. This form symbolises the idea that, just as sexual union leads to great pleasure, so the union of skilful means and wisdom leads to the bliss of enlightenment (Eliade 1987: II, 472–82).

The Buddhism of Tibet and Mongolia, and the Korean Milgyo and Japanese Shingon schools, are all Tantric, or Mantra-yāna forms, making use of *mantras* (Eliade 1987: IX, 176–7; Blofeld 1978). These sacred words of power are mostly meaningless syllables or strings of syllables. When pronounced in the right way, with the right attitude of mind, the sound-arrangement of a *mantra* is seen as 'tuning in' the meditator-devotee's mind to a holy being he or she wishes to visualise. This may perhaps be compared to the way in which certain musical chords naturally tend to evoke reactions of sadness or joy in people. In the Yogacarin 'thought-only' perspective, the visualised being is seen as not 'external' to the devotee, but as a psychic force or level of consciousness latent within the person's own mind. A *mantra* is seen as acting like a psychic key which enables a person to visualise and communicate with a being/force whose *mantra* it is. Each holy being has its own *mantra*, which is seen to express its essence. For example, that of Tārā is *oṃ tāre, tuttāre ture svāha!* Each holy being also has a short 'seed' *mantra*: *trāṃ* in the case of the Buddha Ratnasambhava. The most famous *mantra* is that

Figure 1 A Tibetan painting showing some of the main holy beings and symbols of Tibetan Buddhism, from Samye-Ling Tibetan Buddhist Centre, Scotland

of Avalokiteśvara: *oṃ maṇi padme hūṃ*. *Oṃ* and *hūṃ* are sacred sounds from the Hindu Veda, the first being seen as the basic sound of the universe. *Maṇi padme* literally means 'O jewelled-lotus lady'. In later exegesis, *maṇi* is seen as referring to the jewel that this *bodhisattva* holds, while *padme* refers to his symbol, the lotus. A complex set of symbolic explanations is also given to this *mantra*. For example, its six syllables are associated with the six perfections, or the six realms of rebirth. Figure 1 shows Avalokiteśvara with the syllables of his *mantra* emerging from him. Above him is Amitābha Buddha, his inspiration; to his left Tārā, to his right Padmasambhava, the founder of Tibetan Buddhism. Below are two symbols: a *stūpa* and a *dharma*-wheel.

In Tantric Buddhism, the pantheon came to include beings portrayed in 'wrathful', as well as the more normal 'peaceful' forms

(Harvey 1990: 261–4; Blofeld 1970: 110–17). Male and female wrathful beings may be focused on by strong, unconventional people who are disgusted with the impermanent world and its dreary round of rebirths. The anger which the being shows is not that of a vengeful god, but, hate-free, it aims to open up the practitioner's heart by devastating his hesitations, doubts, confusions and ignorance. One such being is Yamāntaka, 'Conqueror of Death', the wrathful form of the Bodhisattva Mañjuśrī. He is depicted as free and unbridled, trampling on corpses, representing the 'I-am' conceit and its limiting, deadening influence. His head is that of a raging bull, on which is a crown of skulls, representing human faults.

These strongly symbolic forms are used as part of a system of meditative training in which a person's Guru (Tibetan: *bLama*) selects a 'chosen deity' (Tib. *yi-dam*) appropriate for the pupil to work with (Blofeld 1970: 174–82). A *yi-dam* is a particular holy being which is in harmony with the pupil's nature. By visualising and meditatively identifying with it, a practitioner identifies with his own basic nature purged of faults. The *yi-dam* reveals aspects of his character which he persists in overlooking, for it visually represents them. Acting as a guide for his practice, the *yi-dam* enables the practitioner magically to transmute the energy of his characteristic fault into a parallel kind of wisdom, embodied by the *yi-dam*. The *yi-dams* may be 'peaceful' or 'wrathful', and are grouped into five 'families', each associated with a particular fault and with one of the main Mantrayāna *buddhas*. The first of these is the 'central' Buddha, seen as a personification of the *Dharma*-body: the ever-enlightened *Ādi* Buddha. As *Dharma*-body, he is seen as unifying and manifesting the other *buddhas*.

Buddha-images and symbols

In early Buddhist art, Gotama, even before his enlightenment, was only shown by symbols. This must have been due to the feeling that the profound nature of one nearing or attained to buddhahood could not be adequately represented by a human form. In Figure 2, he is portrayed by a throne surmounted by a *dhamma*-wheel, symbolising the *Dhamma* that the Buddha embodied. In ancient India, the wheel had associations with the eye (cf. the Buddha's wisdom 'eye') and the sun (cf. the Buddha as the 'light' of the

Figure 2 An aniconic representation of the Buddha, from a carved relief from Nāgārjunakonda, third-century CE

world). A celestial wheel is said to have moved through the air when a compassionate Universal Emperor (*Cakkavatti*) peacefully spread his influence through the world. In parallel to this, the Buddha's inauguration of his influence in the world, the first sermon, is called 'The Setting in Motion of the *Dhamma*-wheel'. Just as the spokes of a wheel diverge from and are firmly rooted in the hub, so the various aspects of the *Dhamma*-as-teaching come from the Buddha. And just as the spokes converge on the hub, so the aspects of *Dhamma*-as-Path converge on *nirvāṇa*.

In time, the absence of the long-dead Buddha was keenly felt, and there arose a need for a representation of him in human form to act as a more personalised focus of devotion (Snellgrove 1978). The development of Buddha-images, in the second century CE, was probably preceded by the practice of visualising the Buddha's form. The period was also one in which a change in mood was affecting all Indian religions, leading to the portrayal of the founder of Jainism, and of major Hindu gods, as foci of *bhakti*, or warm 'loving devotion'. In Buddhism, this change had also contributed to the origin of the Mahāyāna. The craftsmen who made Buddha-images drew on the tradition that Gotama had been born with the 'thirty-two characteristics of a Great Man', which indicated that he would become either a *buddha* or a Universal Emperor. These bodily features are described as karmic results of specific spiritual perfections built up in past lives (Walshe 1987: 441–60). The most obvious one shown on images is Gotama's 'turbanned-head', meaning that he had a head shaped like a royal turban, or that one with spiritual vision could see a royal turban on his head. In art, it came to be shown as a protuberance on the top of the head. The early texts see it as a result of previous moral and spiritual prominence; later texts see it as a kind of 'wisdom bump' to accommodate a *buddha*'s supreme wisdom. A feature of Buddha-images not among the 'characteristics' is the elongated ear-lobes. These signify Gotama's royal upbringing, when he wore heavy gold ear-rings, and thus his renunciation of the option of political greatness. They may also be seen as a common symbol for nobility of character, or indicative of the Buddha's 'divine ear', a meditation-based psychic ability. Such features were used in the portrayal of all *buddha*s: the earthly Gotama, past earthly *buddha*s, and heavenly Mahāyāna *buddha*s.

A good image, as in Figure 3, has life, vigour and grace, and its features suggest joy, compassion, wisdom, serenity and meditative concentration. Images remind a Buddhist of both the actions and the spiritual qualities of a holy being. Contemplation of an image helps to inspire, and also to stimulate the arising of similar qualities. In Mahāyāna Buddhism, except perhaps in Ch'an/Zen, images also function in other ways. Especially in Tantric schools, they are seen as infused with the spirit and power of the being they represent. Moreover, as image and being 'meet' in both being ultimately 'thought-only' or emptiness, the image comes to be seen as an actual form of the being. For this, it must have the traditional form and symbolism and be consecrated. This is done by chanting prayers and *mantra*s over it; by placing in it scriptures or relics, and even internal organs of clay, and by completing and wetting the eyes. This

Figure 3 A nineteenth-century Burmese image of Gotama Buddha. His lowered hand, touching the earth, recollects his 'conquest of Māra', just prior to his enlightenment, when the earth is said to have shaken in response to his request for affirmation of his many lives of spiritual cultivation. It is a symbol of Gotama's conquest of the evil Māra, who is said to have then given up his attempt to prevent his attaining enlightenment. Other image forms show, for example, the Buddha with his hands together in his lap, in meditation, or at his chest, as if turning the 'wheel' of *Dhamma*, when teaching

associates it with holy sounds and objects, giving it a power-for-good, and animates it, the wet eyes suggesting the response of a living gaze. Even in Theravāda Buddhism, a temple image seems to act as more than a reminder; for it is generally thought that it must be consecrated before it can function as a focus for devotion. Consecration involves the placing of relics in the image, and a monk reciting some Pāli verses over it. In Sri Lanka, these verses are the ones said to have been spoken by the Buddha immediately after his enlightenment. This harmonises with the fact that the eyes are often completed at around 5am, the time at which Gotama became fully enlightened. These two aspects seem to suggest that the consecrated image is seen as a representative of, rather than just a representation of, the Buddha. Other aspects of consecration reinforce this idea. In Sri Lanka, the lay craftsmen completing the eyes act as if this were connecting the image to a source of power which, like electricity, is dangerous if handled carelessly. They ritually prepare themselves for hours, and then only look at the eyes in a mirror while painting them in; till completed, their direct gaze is considered harmful (Gombrich 1971: 138–40). Some westernised monks deny that there is any need to consecrate images. In fact, the '*buddha*-force' which many Therevadins believe in is particularly associated with images, especially ones which have been used in devotion for centuries, suggesting that these are seen as having been thus 'charged up' with the Buddha's power-for-good. Less educated Theravāda Buddhists sometimes even see the Buddha as still alive as an individual, and as somehow present in consecrated images.

A key Buddhist symbolic monument, found at many temples, is the *stūpa* or pagoda. This is essentially a relic-container, but it also symbolises the Buddha and his *nirvāṇa*-at-death. Relics placed in *stūpa*s are said to have been those of Gotama, *arahant*s, and even of past *buddha*s. Having been part of the body of an enlightened being, they were considered to have been infused with something of the power-for-goodness of an enlightened mind, and to bring blessings to those who expressed devotion in their vicinity. Where funerary relics cannot be found, hair or possessions of holy beings, copies of bodily relics or possessions, or Buddhist texts have come to be used in their place.

A famous early *stūpa*, dating from the first century CE in its present form, is at Sāñcī in central India (see Figure 4). The four gateways, or *toraṇa*s, place the *stūpa* symbolically at a cross-roads,

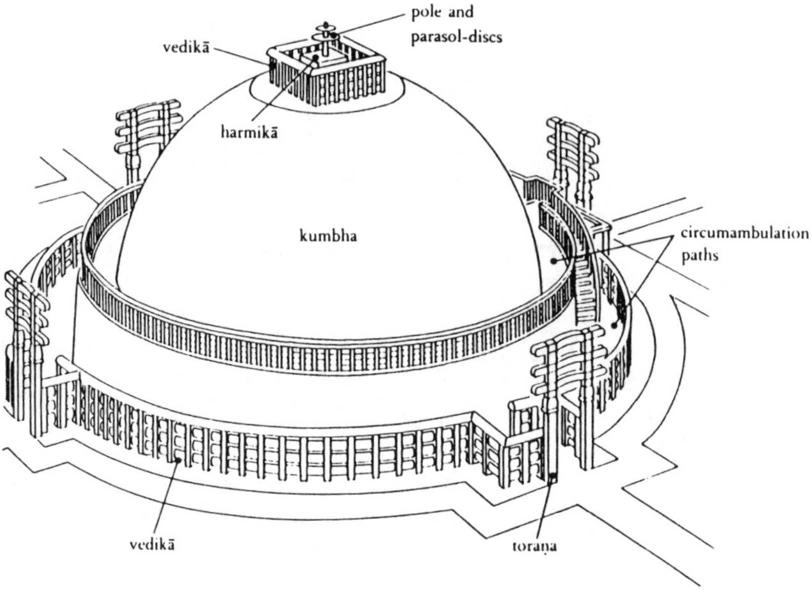

Figure 4 The Great *Stūpa* at Sāñcī

as the Buddha had specified, perhaps to indicate the openness and universality of the *Dhamma*. The circular *vedikā*, or railing, marks off the site dedicated to the *stūpa*, and encloses the first of two paths for respectful circumambulation. The *stūpa* dome, referred to in early texts as the *kumbha*, or 'pot', is the outermost container of the relics. It is associated with an Indian symbol known as the 'vase of plenty', and symbolically acts as a reminder of an enlightened being as 'full' of uplifting *Dhamma*. On top of the Sāñcī *stūpa* is a pole and three discs, which represent ceremonial parasols. As parasols were used as insignia of royalty in India, their inclusion on *stūpa*s can be seen as a way of symbolising the spiritual sovereignty of the Buddha. The kingly connection probably derives from the ancient custom of rulers sitting under a sacred tree at the centre of a community to administer justice, with mobile parasols later replacing such shading trees. The parasol-structure on *stūpa*s also seems to have symbolised the Buddhist sacred tree, the *bodhi*-tree, under which the Buddha attained enlightenment. In later *stūpa*s, the top

Figure 5 A simplified *maṇḍala*, showing the five main *Buddhas* in symbolic form, from C. Trungpa (1976) *The Myth of Freedom*, Boston, Shambhala Publications, p. 146

part fused into a spire, and several platforms were often added under the dome to elevate it in an honorific way. It then became possible to see each layer of the structure as symbolising a particular set of spiritual qualities, such as the 'four foundations of mindfulness', with the spire symbolising the powers and knowledge of a *buddha*.

In Tantric Buddhism, an important symbol is the *maṇḍala* or '(sacred) circle' (Eliade 1987: IX, 155–8; Blofeld 1970: 102–9; Conze et al. 1954: 246–52) (see Figure 5). A *maṇḍala* may be temporarily constructed, for a particular rite, out of coloured sands or dough and fragrant powders, using a raised horizontal platform as a base. In a more permanent form, it may be painted on a hanging scroll. The *maṇḍala* symbolises a related set of holy beings, represented by metal statues, painted images, symbols or seed-*mantras*. The pattern of a *maṇḍala* is based on that of a circular *stūpa* with a square base. It can, in fact, be seen as a two-dimensional *stūpa*-temple, which contains the actual manifestations of the deities represented within it. The bands encircling the *maṇḍala* mark off its pure, sacred area from the profane area beyond, and also suggest the unfolding of spiritual vision gained by practitioners when they visualise themselves entering the *maṇḍala*. Having crossed the threshold, they then enter the central citadel, representing the temple of their own heart. Depending on the rite, the beings in the citadel will vary, though the five main *buddhas* are most common. By being introduced to their *yi-dam*'s *maṇḍala*, practitioners can familiarise themselves with the deity's luminous Pure Land, with associated holy beings arrayed around the *yi-dam*. By vivid visualisation of all this, meditators may master and integrate the psychic forces it represents, and achieve a wholeness in their life.

In contrast to this stylised form, Zen Buddhism often dispenses with either images or symbols, and seeks to hint at the Beyond by trying to capture the living thusness of a natural scene or event. It has thus inspired arts as various as landscape painting and the seventeen-syllable *haiku* poem form. A good example of the latter is:

> Under the water,
> On the rock resting,
> The fallen leaves.

A NOTE ON LANGUAGE

This article uses both Pāli and Sanskrit terms. Pāli is the textual and liturgical language of Theravāda Buddhism, while a form of Sanskrit was the original language of most classical Mahāyāna texts, which now exist mostly in Chinese and Tibetan. Some of the terms are the same in both languages (*bodhi*, Buddha/*buddha*, *deva*, *kumbha*, *saṃsāra*, *tathāgata*, *toraṇa*, *vedikā*). In sections discussing Mahāyāna Buddhism, Sanskrit terms are generally used. In sections on Theravāda Buddhism (and on the gods), Pāli terms are generally used. The exceptions are certain terms which have become well known in their Sanskrit form: *nirvāṇa* (Pāli *nibbāna*), *bodhisattva* (Pāli *bodhisatta*), *stūpa* (Pāli *thūpa*); the Pāli term *arahant* (Sanskrit *arhat*) is also used throughout. The form of the term *Dhamma/dhamma* (Pāli), *Dharma/dharma* (Sanskrit) is used as is appropriate to the context. The terms *Saṅgha* and *Cakkavatti* are Pāli, and *bhakti* is Sanskrit.

A pronunciation guide for Pāli and Sanskrit words is found in Harvey (1990: xxi). As an initial guide, note that a, i and u are pronounced short unless they have a bar over them (ā, ī, ū), in which case they are pronounced long (as are e and o). C is pronounced ch, th as an aspirated t, ph as an aspirated p, ṣ and ś as sh and ñ as ny.

FURTHER READING

Blofeld, J. (1970) *The Tantric Mysticism of Tibet*, New York, Dutton.

—— (1977) *Compassion Yoga: Mystical Cult of Kuan Yin*, London, Unwin.

—— (1978) *Mantras: Sacred Words of Power*, London, Unwin.

Brown, K. and O'Brian, J. (eds) (1989) *The Essential Teachings of Buddhism*, London, Rider (translation extracts plus comments, all schools).

Conze, E., Horner, I.B., Snellgrove, D. and Waley A. (eds) (1954) *Buddhist Texts Through the Ages*, New York, Harper and Row (translations from all schools).

Conze, E. (1959) *Buddhist Scriptures*, Harmondsworth, Penguin (translations from all schools).

—— (1962) *Buddhist Thought in India*, London, Allen & Unwin.

—— (1973) *The Perfection of Wisdom in Eight Thousand Lines*, Bolinas, Four Seasons (translations).

Eliade, M. (ed.) (1987) *The Encyclopedia of Religion* (16 vols), New York, Macmillan.

Gombrich, R. (1971) *Precept and Practice: Traditional Buddhism in the Rural Highlands of Ceylon*, Oxford, Clarendon.

Harvey, P. (1990) *An Introduction to Buddhism: Teachings, History and Practices*, Cambridge, Cambridge University Press.

Katz, N. (1982) *Buddhist Images of Human Perfection*, Delhi, Motilal Banarsidass.

Snellgrove, D.L. (ed.) (1978) *The Image of the Buddha*, London, Serindia.

Spiro, M.E. (1971) *Buddhism and Society*, London, Allen & Unwin.

Suzuki, D.T. (1932) *The Lankavatara Sutra*, London, Routledge & Kegan Paul.

Walshe, M. (1987) *Thus Have I Heard*, London, Wisdom (translation of the Dīgha Nikāya).
Williams, P. (1989) *Mahāyāna Buddhism: The Doctrinal Foundations*, London, Routledge & Kegan Paul.
Woodward, F.L. (1925, 1927, 1930) *Kindred Sayings*, vols II, IV, V, London, Pali Text Society (translations from the *Saṃyutta Nikāya*).

2. Christianity

Douglas Davies

For many people the phrase, 'picturing God', will trigger the idea of paintings, stained glass windows and statues. But the human imagination also has other ways of picturing God through architecture and ritual, and through the lives of men, women and children. All these help express the sense of God at the heart of Christian faith.

In this chapter we think about picturing God both in the literal sense and in other ways which provide people with working ideas of what God is like, and enable them to worship and talk about God as understood by Christianity.

Many pictures

At the most literal level, books and sacred texts give verbal descriptions of God as pictures to the mind's eye, through the verbal descriptions of poetry, sermons or talks. Sometimes these accounts speak in a logical way and try to give a systematic account of what God is like, as in the case of formal systematic theology. But other types of account are more suggestive and poetic, hinting at the nature of God by analogy with human relationships, especially through ideas of love.

Music evokes another realm of sensing what God is like. Not only in hymns and chanting, where words also play a significant part, but also in music on its own; many moods can be formed and a sense of God fostered. The great majority of religious traditions of the world make use of music in worship. And this also applies to Christianity which has, with a few exceptions, taken music as a serious medium for expressing religious faith.

Words and music often benefit from a particular setting and this has certainly been the case in Christianity where cathedrals, churches and chapels regularly serve as the context for worship. Not only can God be 'pictured' through the very architecture of buildings, but the sheer availability of quiet places where people may think, meditate and worship, gives opportunity for God to be pictured within the personal experience of individuals.

A final way of picturing God comes through the example of saintly lives, as humble and self-sacrificing people give themselves in a life of love for others. This is true not only as Christians look out at other people, but also as they gain their own experience of living in a Christian way.

In this chapter we consider all these avenues as ways of picturing God, for each one can enable the imagination to catch a glimpse of what God is like. In practice, these media work together to build up a knowledge of God within individuals, drawing as they do from the tradition of their church, from their own experience of worship, and from the facts of daily life and service.

Are pictures valid?

At the heart of Christianity lies the question which is posed several times in the Jewish scriptures, and which the spirituality of Israel has always taken as its own guide: 'To whom then will you liken God, or what likeness compare with him?' (Isa. 40: 18). The answer of *Tanakh* (Jewish Scripture, referred to by Christians as the Old Testament) is resoundingly clear: there are no comparisons whatsoever that can be made, so that it is wrong even to begin to think of entering God into any set of comparisons. And, to press the logic of this argument further, models, statues, or pictures of God were forbidden.

Some scholars have assumed that this Jewish attitude passed on into Christianity to produce opposition to artistic representation of God which has, in some churches, been a very strong feeling at particular moments in their history. Some other scholars have taken a different line, believing that early Christians used art in a creative way to express their belief in Christ as the saviour of the world, incorporating into their work stories from Old Testament texts along with episodes drawn from the classical mythology of that pagan world in which many early Christians lived (Murray 1981: 13ff).

Idolatry

The Jewish prophets tended to ridicule the idea of any images of God. To choose special, long-lasting wood, and to cover it in gold, to set it up and worship it, was nothing but folly. Isaiah 40 explores this theme, and simply points to the heavens as well as to the creation of the earth to show that the one who made all that is beyond comparison.

In fact, as the Psalmist also makes disparagingly clear:

> Our God is in the heavens;
> he does whatever he pleases.
> Their idols are silver and gold,
> the works of men's hands.
>
> (Ps. 115: 3–4)

The description of idols presents the ridiculous spectacle of idols that have mouths through which they cannot speak, ears that cannot hear, feet that cannot walk, etc. Idolatry is obviously ruled out of court as dealing with inferior products rather than with the creator of all. In fact, this is the critical point. It is precisely because God is the creator of all that it is wrong to represent deity in or through any one created thing. A created thing cannot represent the Creator; it is by definition a lesser object, an inferior and unworthy focus for worship.

The Ten Commandments, which lie at the heart of the Jewish Law and which have entered so fundamentally into Christian belief, stress the primacy of God with an immediate command not to make any graven image of anything in heaven or earth (Exod. 20: 1ff.). God is transcendent, and beyond any such futile art-work of humanity. God is not to be pictured.

The divine name

Even when God is addressed or referred to in words, the divine name itself must not be taken in vain, as another of the Ten Commandments puts it. The ancient Jews developed the practice of substituting the Hebrew word *Adonai*, or Lord, for the tetragrammaton, or four letters (JHVH), which stood in their scriptures as the word for the deity. In the Hebrew scriptures special vowel-points are placed around the basic consonants to give the pronunciation of words. Unusually in this case, the vowel pointing for 'Adonai' was placed around the consonants JHVH, leading to the compound word 'Jehovah', which has come to be common in some Christian use. What this shows is that even in words where, in one sense, God is depicted or identified, respect had to be shown. It is an interesting fact that in Great Britain the letters GOD have never been issued for use on car licence plates, presumably out of some similar respect both for the deity and also for believers who might be offended by such a number plate.

Divine encounters

There are several incidents in the Hebrew Bible dealing with the early mythical history of Israel, which hint at a physical encounter with God, as when Abraham encounters certain visitors (Gen. 18: 1ff), when Jacob wrestles with someone until the break of day (Gen. 32: 30), or when God speaks with Moses, 'face to face, as a man speaks to his friend' (Exod. 33: 11). But these are all profoundly exceptional moments in the encounter between God and Israel in the formative period of their mutual covenant relationship. For the greater part of *Tanakh*, encounter with God is expressed in worship (as through the Psalms) or else as inspired utterance by the prophets.

Reflecting God

The divine will, nature, and intention, are all expounded in detail through the prophets and priests of the Jewish religion. The picture that emerges focuses on moral issues rather than on any physical aspect of the divine. God is mirrored in the moral life of Israel. The priestly writers and the stream of the biblical tradition also depict God through rules for the ritual life of Jews.

This led the anthropologist Mary Douglas to propose that the Holiness Codes, as represented, for example, in Leviticus, gave laws for social life that tried to make the chosen people a model of the moral nature of God (Deut. 14; Lev. 11). God was, in a sense, to be mirrored or reflected in the dynamic social and moral life of the Jewish people rather than in any static picture. Even the food laws expressed an ordered world in which animals that conformed to a clear type could be eaten and those that seemed to straddle different groups could not be touched. In *Purity and Danger* (Routledge and Kegan Paul, 1966) Mary Douglas says the dietary laws were:

> like signs which at every turn inspired meditation on the oneness, purity, and completeness of God. By rules of avoidance holiness was given a physical expression in every encounter with the animal kingdom and at every meal.
>
> (Douglas 1966: 57)

These practical rules for life were contained in scriptures that were of vital practical consequence for Jews. Given the history of Israel, it is no accident that God is approached through the words of scripture both in the synagogue and in private prayer. The scrolls of the law were and are treated with respect and honour and they replaced any other representation of God. The symbolic focus of all this lies in the tables on which the Ten Commandments were believed to be written, tables that were, according to tradition, kept in the Ark of the Covenant (Deut. 10: 1–5).

Background

It is important to recognise that the scriptural religion of Jews emerged and continued in a world of many cultures where gods, heroes, and mythical figures played an important part in the apparatus of worship, as did altars, standing stones, wooden posts symbolising fertility, and probably much besides. Episodes such as the disobedient modelling of a golden calf (Exod. 32: 4), with some sort of worship associated with it, illustrate this contextual world of popular religions.

Early Christianity

The birth of Christianity has to be seen against this background of Jewish religion, not least because the Jewish scriptures became part and parcel of the Christian scriptures and entered into the way Christians understood God and the world. But – and this is a crucial point – Christians came to believe that Jesus is divine. The doctrine of the Incarnation is the formal expression of this belief, and it is central to the Christian Creeds which were produced in the centuries after the earthly life of Jesus. This doctrine expressed the belief that in Jesus of Nazareth the very nature of God has come to expression in a unique human life. The creeds describe significant aspects of that divine and human existence. By the fourth and fifth centuries they were commonly used in association with baptism and acts of worship. They also included statements of belief about the Holy Spirit, about the Church, and about the salvation of humanity.

These items appear through a threefold pattern of belief. They do not simply assert a belief in God as the one and only deity; they describe God in terms of Father, Son, and Holy Spirit. Before exploring the significance of this threefoldness for picturing God, it is useful to give one of the creeds, The Apostles' Creed, in full because it has played, and continues to play, an important part in the regular worship of many Christian churches. It will also be a useful way of approaching the ways in which God has been depicted in Christianity.

The Apostles' Creed

I believe in God the Father Almighty, Maker of heaven and earth:

And in Jesus Christ his only Son our Lord, who was conceived by the Holy Spirit, born of the Virgin Mary, suffered under Pontius Pilate, was crucified, dead, and buried. He descended into hell; the third day he rose again from the dead. He ascended into heaven, and is sitting on the right hand of God the Father Almighty; from thence he shall come to judge the quick and the dead.

I believe in the Holy Spirit; the holy Catholic Church; the Communion of Saints; the forgiveness of sins; the resurrection of the body; and the life everlasting. Amen.

The Incarnation

The doctrine of the Incarnation, therefore, is a formal summary of the way Christians expressed their belief that Jesus was God in human nature. The very word 'incarnation' means 'in the flesh', and it pin-points the radical earthiness and material basis of the Christian faith.

It is difficult to exaggerate the importance of the Incarnation doctrine in Christian thinking and it is particularly important as far as picturing God is concerned. Hand in hand with the growth of belief in Jesus as divine went the writing and interpretation of new scriptures, of the Christian epistles and gospels, and of other documents that came to form what is called the New Testament. The human life of Jesus was described in the gospel stories, and further, more detailed, interpretations were provided through the epistles and other New Testament documents. Because of the Incarnation, 'picturing God' can now be, directly and simply, picturing Jesus, God in Christ reconciling the world to himself.

The crucifixion

Among the most frequently represented aspects of Christ's life stands the crucifixion. The crucifix represents the body of Christ on the cross, and it has been portrayed, both in two dimensional art and in three dimensional sculpture for centuries. The crucifixion was not portrayed in the earliest Christian art and only came into prominence from the sixth century. It is perhaps the most extensively used of all Christian symbols, not only in artistic form but also in ritual behaviour.

In many Christian traditions babies are blessed with the sign of the cross at their baptism, and priests often bless their congregations with the sign of the cross. Many of the faithful use the sign of the cross in their public and private devotions. In whatever form it is used, it reminds the Christian that the object that caused the death of Christ is the sign of life and hope for the Christian.

The resurrection

Even though the resurrection of Jesus was, obviously, a matter of belief, some writers spoke of it as a demonstrable fact. Paul outlines his own sense of the Christian tradition and message, and expresses his belief in the resurrection in I Corinthians (15: 3–8):

> For I delivered to you as of first importance what I also received, that Christ died for our sins . . . that he was buried, that he was raised on the third day . . ., that he appeared to Peter, then to the twelve. Then he appeared to more than five hundred brethren at one time . . . then to James, then to all the apostles. Last of all . . . he appeared also to me.

This factual sense of the resurrection was combined with the historical basis of Jesus's actual life in Palestine to give to all subsequent generations of Christians a firm basis for pictorial representations of Jesus. Because Jesus had been seen by his contemporaries in an ordinary way, he could be represented in paintings, pictures, and other forms of art without any sense of blasphemy or impropriety.

The Holy Trinity

Jesus came to be understood as the Son of God. The language of Son and Father grew and developed in a way that helped to interpret how Jesus could share the nature of his father. The human analogy of father and son was easily applied to the divine nature. Jesus was said to be of the same substance as the father, and this expressed the idea that Jesus was really divine. But the Christian Creeds also added a further 'person' to this group of two. This was the Holy Spirit. That sense of the power and presence of God which had been spoken of in the Old Testament came to prominence among early Christians, who no longer had the tangible presence of Jesus but who reckoned to share in the life of God through their experience of

God, the Holy Spirit. So it was that the Christian Church developed what might initially be seen as a strange teaching, the doctrine of the Holy Trinity. The three persons of this Trinity are the Father, the Son, and the Holy Spirit. Three persons but one God. Not three Gods but one God, since there can only be what there is in the case of God (namely, what God is, which must be One) but the nature of what there is is relational.

This linking of Jesus with his Father and also with the power of God the Spirit had an interesting consequence. Just as Jesus had been portrayed in artistic ways, so now the 'Father' and also the Holy Spirit came to be represented in art. The Jewish idea that God could not and should not be artistically represented was overcome through the doctrine of the Incarnation. Even if in a picture the Father is not actually portrayed, he is often symbolically represented by bright light, or surrounded by angels or cherubim, etc. Even so the very material reality of Jesus as the Son of God made it easier for artists and theologians to think of God the Father in a pictorial way.

One sculptural motif exhibits this well in a fifteenth-century limestone carving from the Netherlands, where Christ on the cross is placed immediately in front of a figure of God the Father, and with a dove, symbolic of the Holy Spirit, also as part of the total scene (Christie 1982: 482). An English example is found on an alabaster of approximately the same period in Nottingham.

Sometimes Trinitarian ideas were expressed by utilising Old Testament images and interpreting them anew in the light of Christian doctrine. A famous icon of the Holy Trinity, painted by the renowned Russian Rublev in the fifteenth century, shows three angels sitting at a kind of table and about to share a meal. It is an icon of the Holy Trinity expressed through the story of the three visitors who came to Abraham as messengers of, or as representations of, the Lord in Genesis 18. The three persons of the Trinity are reflected through these three mysterious visitors.

History and life events

The Jewish religion, out of which Christianity grew, was itself firmly rooted in history: it retained a sense of commitment to the Patriarchs, Abraham, Isaac and Jacob, to Moses who led the captive people out of Egypt, and to many judges, prophets, priests and martyrs. In Christianity this focus on history becomes even more intense through the belief that God has now, at last, fully shared in human life.

The walls, ceilings, altars and tombs of Christian churches, and in later years their stained-glass windows, not to mention painted icons and statuary, all served as media through which the story or history of salvation could be told. History itself could take shape through art, and could come to influence generation after generation of believers.

Great and little traditions in art

Christian churches provide what is probably the most extensive collection of art in the world. The catacombs of Rome with their early pictures of Jesus, magnificent cathedrals with their stained glass, and the very many ordinary churches in towns and villages from one side of the earth to the other, contain something expressing the nature of God. In many of these there is art based on Bible stories and on the tradition of Christian history.

Sometimes anthropologists and sociologists draw a distinction between what they call great and little traditions. The great tradition of a culture represents its major religion or philosophy as expressed in revered and established texts held and interpreted by trained scholars and priests. The little tradition refers to the local versions and expressions of religion, belief, and thought. The world religions as we now know them have all had complex histories, but one common feature is that they have extended into areas, societies and cultures, where once they did not belong, but from which they have derived new inspiration and forms of expression.

One interesting side of the little tradition involves the way that many stories from the Bible and wider Christian tradition have been taken up and developed by local believers from many different cultures. They have adapted them to their own cultural idiom at the same time as they have adopted them as basic elements of their faith. This process gives life and power to the stories and allows them to influence new ages and geographical regions. Images of Jesus offer one good example, as he has sometimes been portrayed with the skin colour and bodily features of Africans, Europeans, South Americans, etc.

In this way, the Bible has come to influence the artistic life of thousands of different societies across the world. Because art is visible and more durable than speech and language, this one influence upon many varied minds is a profound reminder that Christianity has become a world religion, having taken root in societies that once had their own form of religion but now possess Christianity in a way that makes it seem that they have always been Christian.

Certain works of art become so important that they also help form part of the great tradition. The growth of the media, and especially of books, film and television, means that pictures and buildings can be seen by millions of people who would not otherwise encounter them. There is a sense in which postcard pictures can take great works of art into places they would never otherwise penetrate. Similarly, visitors, tourists or pilgrims, can buy pictures of religious art and take them back to their own homes. In all these ways the great tradition penetrates the little local traditions of communities and even of individuals' private lives.[1] Some examples featuring pictures of God will illustrate this variety.

God in creation

One of the most famous pictures of God is found in the Sistine Chapel in the Vatican City in Rome. This chapel belonged to the popes, and was painted by Michelangelo (1475–1564) in the early years of the sixteenth century. The picture entitled 'the Creation of Man' depicts God as an older man of powerful build reaching out his hand to touch the extended hand of Adam. The human form of God is clear and obvious and shows that in the sixteenth century there was no problem in portraying God, or God the Father in Trinitarian language, as a man.

Many reproductions of this fine work have been made, and have found a home across the world, so that many people who have never been to Rome will be familiar with this portrayal of God. Some might even find it easier to have a reproduction of this picture on their wall than to stand and try to keep their balance while craning their necks backward in the Sistine Chapel, trying to concentrate on the original located high in the ceiling among other painted panels. But equally, many local churches have pictures that can be studied and enjoyed even though they are not regarded as world-class works of art. Similar themes and links can often be found between artistic motifs.

In Uppsala in Sweden there is, for example, an interesting mural painted high in the north transept of the Lutheran Cathedral which echoes Michelangelo's 'Creation of Man' in the Sistine Chapel. The Swedish painting is much later, coming from the 1890s. In it, God is shown as standing as a man, once more as older rather than as younger; he has slightly long hair and a white flowing robe. On the ground before him and asleep on his right side lies Adam. From Adam's left side, from a rib, Eve is emerging as the first created woman. She is depicted as actually coming from Adam, with only the top half of her body yet visible. God stands leaning slightly forward and with his left hand he holds the hand of Eve, leading her into the world. God's right hand is raised in the form of a blessing.

Through the medium of creative art, both in pictures and music, the biblical stories were given a much wider exposure than could have been achieved through the printed page alone. One good example of a work that took a biblical passage into thousands of homes is Holman Hunt's famous 'The Light of the World', painted in 1854. Hunt (1827–1910) was a founder of the Pre-Raphaelite group of painters in the mid-nineteenth century, and he travelled extensively in Palestine, getting detail for his many pictures on biblical themes. His 'Light of the World' shows Jesus as a tall man dressed in a long robe or cloak standing outside a closed door and knocking on it. In his hand he holds a lantern. This painting expresses the idea of Jesus himself being the light of the world (John 8: 12), but combines with it this text from the Book of Revelation (3: 20): 'Behold I stand at the door and knock; if anyone hears my voice and opens the door, I will come in to him and eat with him, and he with me'.

Other texts from the Book of Revelation have become widely known through being set to music by Handel in his Oratorio, 'The Messiah'. One of the best-known pieces of religious music in the western world, 'The Hallelujah Chorus' (along with 'Worthy is the Lamb that was Slain', Rev. 5: 12), comes from this source.

Both the art of painting and the creativity of musical settings of scripture provide magnificent complements to religious architecture. Sight and sound combine with the physical place of worship to furnish layers of rich symbolism for the faithful in their worship.

From catacombs to cathedrals

ROMAN CATACOMBS

Christian worship has not, however, always been conducted in the splendour of large buildings. The subterranean catacombs surrounding Rome, where the dead were often placed for burial, also became the tombs of many early Christians for about the first four hundred years of the Christian Era. Early Christians also met in these hidden places, especially during times of persecution, for worship, to celebrate the eucharist, and to remember the dead.

It was here in the catacombs that the first Christian art was developed. Pagan art had long been associated with funerary monuments, and had used figures such as Orpheus and Helios from mythology and classical authors, to express beliefs in immortality. By the third and fourth centuries Christians were also using such figures, adapting them under the control of the image of Jesus and his resurrection. Funerary art, painted both on wall panels and also on special coffins or sarcophagi, was a particularly appropriate art-form to carry the Christian message concerning resurrection and life after death. The grave, after all, had been the place of Christ's victory over death, and that was a key element in Christian thought.

The Jewish scriptures, which Christians had also made their own, gave to artists of the new faith a wealth of stories which could be used in sculpture to illustrate Christian themes. So, for example, Jonah's delivery from his 'death' in the great fish that had swallowed him, or Noah's delivery from the flood through his ark, are both used on tombs of the third and fourth century. As Sister Charles Murray (1981: 98), a specialist in Christian art, has shown, Rome is very much a centre for Noah, portrayed in his Ark, now carrying a Christian significance; these Noah sculptures start from about the year 200 CE. It is thought that the overall meaning is that the Christian, represented by Noah, has been through the water of death and rebirth in baptism, and this is a basis for life after death. It is also true that this particular biblical picture echoed some pagan mythology of Perseus.

But Christ is also an important figure, sometimes depicted through classical mythology as Orpheus or Helios, but also in more direct biblical expressions. A typical and important representation is of Christ as a young man carrying a sheep over his shoulders. This idiom of the good shepherd also has its forerunner in the art of classical antiquity, where the shepherd figure was widely used, but in Christian contexts it takes an additional significance directly from the gospels (John 10: 11; Luke 15: 4) where, in literary form, Jesus is strongly depicted as the good shepherd who loves, seeks out, and lays down his life for his 'sheep'. Once more, the human reality of a historical Jesus gives the artist a strong foundation for realistic picturing of the divine son involved in earthly activities.

From the fourth century, art becomes increasingly more plentiful and devoted to wider themes than death and baptism. Broader aspects of the life and ministry of Jesus are drawn upon. One ivory plaque from Northern Italy from approximately 400 CE shows the resurrection and ascension of Jesus. After speaking to the women who come to visit his tomb, he is seen walking up on a cloud into heaven. He has a halo painted around his head, a feature that occurs very frequently in pictures of Jesus from now on, representing his holy status. Sometimes a cross is designed into the halo to represent the form of his death and victory over sin.

THE HAND OF GOD

In this and other resurrection and ascension pictures, the right hand of God can be seen from the wrist down emerging from the cloud and taking Jesus by the right hand to receive him into heaven (Christie 1982: 60). Other pieces of art of many sorts use the hand of God to represent God, or God the Father, in relation to other activities. So, for example, some pictures of the transfiguration have the hand of God extended towards the figure of the glorified Jesus, representing, in pictorial form, the words of God on that occasion, 'This is my beloved Son with whom I am well pleased, listen to him' (Matt. 17: 5). Some scenes of the crucifixion also have the hand of God poised above the cross.

At the baptism of Jesus it is usual to have the Holy Spirit represented in the form of a dove placed above Jesus's head as he stands in the water of the river Jordan to be baptised by John, but sometimes there is an additional symbol, with the hand of God emerging from a cloud just above the dove, as represented, for example, in an illustration of an Armenian Gospel book of the sixth century (Beckwith 1970: plate 118).

This clear symbolism of God through the divine hand also occurs in some Christian art portraying Old Testament stories, as when the hand of God is shown in a mosaic of the sacrifice of Isaac in the church of S. Vitale, Ravenna, or in the hand of God delivering the tables of the Law to Moses, from an illustration in a tenth-century Bible (Beckwith 1970: plates 91, 172).

ICONS

At their simplest, icons are paintings made on wooden panels and having religious themes. They are characteristic objects within the Eastern Orthodox Churches and have a significant part to play in the history of picturing God. Icons picture the holy in a special way. The logic behind their construction and use is grounded in the assumption we have already discussed for religious art in general, namely that the incarnation of Christ gives a positive significance to the material world. Because God in Christ shared in human nature and in the material dimension of the world, that dimension is acknowledged as worthy. Then, in addition to this, it is believed that the divine essence or the divine aspect of holy persons can be encountered or experienced through their material representation. So a picture of Christ is not simply a likeness presented in paint, it is a means of experiencing and sharing in the divine attributes of the one portrayed.

In this sense icons provide a medium of contact, a channel to gain access, a kind of window or door into the divine world. They are not an end in, and of, themselves, and that is why they cannot rightly be regarded as a source of idolatry. Rather, like the sacraments in wider Christian thought, icons have an outward and visible form, but through them it is possible to encounter an underlying spiritual grace.

This idea of communicating spiritual realities to the believer becomes very evident in the architecture of many Eastern Orthodox Churches. As well as having icons around a church, the Orthodox have developed a large partition called an iconostasis which separates the altar from the rest of the church building. As its name suggests, the iconostasis is a picture stand and on it are painted or hung many large, often life-sized, icons of saints, angels and other holy persons. These structures were greatly developed in the twelfth century to reach from floor to ceiling, instead of being low walls, as they were originally.

One important feature of many Orthodox Churches is the central place given to large-scale pictures of Christ, placed at the dominant point in the building, often in its dome. This frequently takes the form of Christ as Pantokrator, the one who creates and rules over all. In theological terms, Christ stands absolutely central in these paintings, and for all practical purposes serves as the one divine referent: he stands as God and for God.

FRAMES FOR GOD

The area of the altar behind the screen is often interpreted as representing heaven, while the area where the people stand, in front of the iconostasis, represents this life on earth. During the Liturgy the priests pass through doors in the iconostasis from the altar to the people, from 'heaven' to 'earth'. In its own way this ritual passage pictures God in terms of a divine heavenly dwelling-place, in which, through worship, the believer may share. The priests serve as mediators between the two realms, and in the work of the Liturgy they bring the faithful to participate in the heavenly kingdom of God. The icons of the angels and of saints help mark out the heavenly territory, encourage the faithful in their lives and worship, and help convey to them spiritual strength and power.

In the western churches, it became usual for the long nave, where the people gathered, to be separated by a choir from the sanctuary where the altar was located. Often this separation was marked by a screen which divided the church into two major sectors. Although there was no formal theological association of these areas with earth and heaven, as in the case of Orthodoxy, in practice, the 'altar end' came to be viewed as especially sacred, while the nave might even be used for popular local activities of a much more secular type.

This distinction between holy and ordinary activities itself classifies God in the minds of worshippers, and can give the impression that God is distant, removed from ordinary life events. It may well be that the immense size of some cathedrals, especially in the light of the size of ordinary houses in the tenth to thirteenth centuries, when many of them were built, gave the impression that God was transcendent over human activities.

Objecting to pictures of God

Some modern Christians find great cathedrals a problem as far as faith is concerned. They think that immense buildings, along with their apparent wealth and richness of art and architecture, detract both from the simple teaching of Jesus, and the importance of sincere groups of believers. Slightly similar concerns were also mentioned early in this chapter when referring to idolatry as the process of making objects to represent God and then offering worship to those objects. In other words, idolatry pays to immediate objects the due that rightly goes only to the ultimate being of God. Christianity, as Judaism, has always disowned that sort of practice.

But it is very easy to misunderstand the behaviour of other people, especially when it comes to matters of religion and worship. We have already seen that Eastern Orthodox believers use icons as part of their worship of God, but they would adamantly deny that they treated icons like idols or that they practise idolatry. They would say that the icon is a medium or vehicle through which the power and grace of God come to the faithful. Some Protestant Christians would not be persuaded by this and would prefer to see icons eliminated, so that a more internalised form of piety might come to the fore. This kind of objection to the dominant force of outward objects used in worship has not only been made from Protestant quarters: one of the most important debates in the history of Eastern Orthodox religion concerned icons, with those who would have had them destroyed understanding themselves to be keeping the purity of the faith.

ICONOCLASM

From early in the eighth century a debate raged in the Eastern Church over the use of icons. The Emperor Leo III sought the destruction of icons in 726 for a wide variety of reasons, including the argument that such material representation of holy things hindered the conversion of Jews and Muslims. Theological arguments also focused on whether icons did justice to the human nature of Christ or over-accentuated the divine nature. The Iconoclastic Controversy, as it is called, involved some monks losing their lives for the cause of icons as a true form of spirituality, a position that was established by 842 CE, after which icons became a natural part of Orthodox worship.

Anthropomorphism and projection

Despite the vehemence of debates about icons and idolatry, the arguments involved are relatively simple. But there is another area that is much more complicated and perhaps even more important. It concerns anthropomorphism.

Anthropomorphism comes from the Greek and means that something is given the shape or form of man. This can apply to obvious things, such as physical objects, but it also has another sort of application, as when a dog, cat or some other animal is said to behave like a human being. We read into the animal's behaviour some of those features which are characteristic of human beings. The issue that has to be raised is whether the entire enterprise of 'picturing God' is a massive case of anthropomorphism – of projecting human ideas and ideals, and calling them 'God'. Thus, in the history of western thought on religion, some scholars have approached the whole of religion on the assumption that God does not exist and that everything said about God is really the outcome of human imagination.

A PHILOSOPHICAL VIEW

One of the best and historically most significant examples of this approach comes from the German philosopher Ludwig Feuerbach (1804–72). In his book *The Essence of Christianity* (Harper and Row, 1957; first published 1841), the idea of God as a transcendent and self-existing deity is denied. Philosophy and theology, he thought, were really about humanity and not about God. What human beings say about God are not really statements concerning a deity at all; they are statements about the human condition arising from human thought. This is why it is often said that Feuerbach wanted to replace theology as a study of God, by a philosophical anthropology which dealt with human nature.

A PSYCHOLOGICAL VIEW

From the quite different direction of psychology, though with an equally direct atheistic commitment, Sigmund Freud argued that ideas of God were the outcome of human thought and, in particular, expressed a kind of wish-fulfilment. For Freud, the pictures of God which traditional Christianity possessed were only an illusion. Men and women want to believe that there really is a 'heavenly father' because they desire a strong father figure but know that their human fathers are inadequate. Life experience shows that earthly fathers are not always dependable, and in the end they die.

But, according to Freud, the human mind was not content to accept these harsh facts of life. Instead, it constructed this image of a heavenly father to help make life bearable. Freud used the word 'projection' to describe this process through which the idea of God came into existence. For Freud, religion was an illusion, and in his suitably titled book, *The Future of an Illusion* (Hogarth Press, 1973, first published 1913), he spelled out this theory of how human beings had created the idea of God, an idea that has no future if men and women are ever fully to understand themselves and come to a mature insight into the nature of existence.

Feuerbach had also used this idea of projection in his theory of religion. He thought that the process of human self-understanding was very complex and took a long time, and he thought that religion played a vitally important part in it. Since there is no actual God, as far as Feuerbach is concerned, religion is really about human beings. What people say about God they are really saying about themselves. It is this that makes it possible for Feuerbach to believe that 'religion is man's earliest and most indirect form of self-knowledge' (*The Essence of Christianity*, p. 14).

A SOCIOLOGICAL VIEW

From Feuerbach's philosophical perspective, it is to be expected that in each society the idea of god, gods or spirits will be directly related to its values, organisation and culture. This, obviously, makes the issue open to sociological and anthropological analysis. One attempt was made by Guy Swanson who tried to relate the way different societies are organised to the way their gods are organised.[2]

One classic text on the relationship between gods and society was written by the French sociologist Émile Durkheim. In his *Elementary Forms of the Religious Life* (Allen Lane, 1976, first published 1913), he argued that what people believe to be an experience of God is really the experience of being together in a group ritual. The idea of God was 'really' a picture of society even though ordinary people were unaware of this real meaning. This kind of argument is often called a reductionist argument in that it reduces the point at issue to some underlying process which is known only to the expert.

Another expert, the sociologist Max Weber, also saw the importance of anthropomorphism in his *Sociology of Religion* (Methuen, 1963, first published in German in 1922). Having focused attention on the process of drawing analogies between things which lie behind mythology and magic, he argued that analogy also underlay the personification of gods, just as it does certain kinds of magic. Gods were regarded much as human beings were regarded, and the dynamics of human life were visible anew in the world of the gods as humanity perceived it, or reckoned it to be.

The social basis of religious ideas was extensively pursued in the twentieth century in what is called the sociology of knowledge. Peter Berger and Thomas Luckmann's book, *The Social Construction of Reality* (Penguin, 1967), gave a sociological explanation of how societies come to have a sense of meaning in life and in the organisation of culture. Berger took this further in *The Social Reality of Religion* (Penguin, 1969), where he showed how religious ideas are born out of ordinary social life. This was such a reductionist form of argument that he wrote a follow-up study called *A Rumour of Angels* (Penguin, 1971) to offset its hard-line approach and to suggest that there were certain 'signals of transcendence' to be found in play, hope, damnation, humour and the sense of good order in the world. He thought that these showed that people are not totally conditioned by their social existence.

Even so, the strictly sociological view of religion generally makes out that religious ideas are the outcome of society and are, therefore, human in origin. Pictures of God are, necessarily, human constructions and projections of the human imagination.

THEOLOGICAL VIEWS

One theological view that disagrees with this interpretation and tries to argue with it comes from John Bowker (1973, 1978). On the assumption that God exists and creates a universe in which we find ourselves, Bowker suggests that certain 'cues of meaning' are picked up by humanity and enter into ideas of God. Religious ideas are not simply the product of the human imagination but of the human imagination in relation to encounters with God. People may decide to develop and use the experience of encounter or they may decide to ignore it, but the importance of the possibility of God influencing us must not be overlooked.

The great art of the world treats physical things such as landscapes in very different ways with, for example, some Impressionists giving a sense of a scene through thousands of small dots of paint, while more traditional painters draw detailed representations of what is there to see. In each case there is an actual scene before their eyes, but their picture of it comes out in many different ways because of the difference in perspective, creativity and fashion.

This process of feedback between external source and human appreciation is evident in many aspects of daily life. In the gospels of the New Testament, for example, the disciples try to understand and form a 'picture' of Jesus, and often get it blurred through misunderstanding, as when they try to prevent Jesus being crowded by children but he calls them to him and says that the kingdom of God belongs to children (Luke 18: 16). In the end, therefore, the 'picturing of God' is always a tentative and provisional activity, open to being corrected: no one has ever *seen* God (1 John 4: 12), and therefore any imaginative representation of God must always be suggestive, pointing towards the only possible encounter with God – in prayer and worship, and above all in liturgy.

God as Christ in priests

One feature of the rise of the priesthood as a special order of leaders was the medieval doctrine that through ordination the priest was given a special character or power by means of which he could perform sacramental rituals. His key task was to celebrate the Eucharist or the Mass. In one sense the priest represented Christ. He was Christ at the altar. So in a symbolic sense it is true to say that the ritual of the Mass was a means of picturing Christ.

The Mass or Eucharist is a remarkable rite which can be understood in several different ways. At one level it is a form of memorial which simply enables people to remember the past. As such it is a kind of practical history. For many in the Protestant traditions of Christianity the memorial element predominates; it often goes hand in hand with a very simple form of ritual, in what members of those churches often call the Lord's Supper or Holy Communion.

By contrast, in the Orthodox traditions of Greece and Russia, the church on earth comes to share in the eternal kingdom of God through the worship of the Eucharist. In the Roman Catholic Church the doctrine of transubstantiation (which became popular in the twelfth and thirteenth centuries), asserted that through the prayer of consecration the body and blood of Christ came to replace the inner substance of the bread and wine. This brought the real presence of Christ into the Mass as a focus for devotion and worship, and also as the basis for a constant re-presenting and sacrificial offering to God.

These rites can often be complex, involving the priest and other clergy and assistants wearing special clothes or vestments which carry a heavy weight of symbolism. One interpretation sometimes given for the eucharistic vestments is that they blot out the personal identity of the ordained individual to emphasise the role and nature of the priest. This is all the more significant when the priest is believed to represent Christ, for not only is the Mass a kind of representation of the Last Supper, but it also represents the sacrificial death of Christ, with the priest being a symbol of Christ. As such this ritual offers a way of portraying and depicting Christ through a ritual act rather than through art.

Christ pictured by faith

Whether at its simple or most elaborate level, this ritual of taking bread, blessing, breaking, sharing and eating it with others links the present with the past. The historical Jesus and the original Passover meal become intimately bound up with the present moment of faith. The past mixes with the present. Just as believers are taken in heart and mind back to events recorded in the Bible, so they feel the effects of those events in their life today. For many believers, their experience of God, focused in Jesus and active in their personal faith, is nurtured and fostered through the Holy Communion.

Changing times and changing images

These images of Jesus cover a wide spectrum of belief. As both artistic and verbal images, they move from a picture of Jesus as the mighty conqueror mirroring the Old Testament idea of God as the warrior, through the image of the dying saviour sacrificed for sin, to the gentle carer concerned for those he loves.

Christian doctrine is intimately associated with these images of Jesus, because they are deeply influenced by the theological meaning that a tradition wants to express. This makes Christian art in the widest sense a useful key to the belief of Christian groups at different times and places. This includes the images of God and of Jesus Christ which theologians construct in their writing.

One very explicit example of this can be found at the end of Albert Schweitzer's *The Mystery of the Kingdom of God* (A&C Black, 1914), which was itself part of a longer study of the Holy Communion in Christianity. His work was very influential at the beginning of the twentieth century, not least because he sought to explore the life of Jesus in a historical and critical way. He wrote a very telling postscript saying that the aim of his book was,

> to depict the figure of Jesus in its overwhelming heroic greatness and to impress it upon the modern age and upon modern theology.
>
> (1914: 274)

Schweitzer thought that the modern world-view had taken the heroic aspect away from the picture of Jesus, and because of this had 'humanised and humbled him'. Referring to two philosophers of religion of his day, he went on to say what he thought about the verbal pictures of Jesus they had painted in their work:

> Renan has stripped off his halo and reduced him to a sentimental figure, coward spirits like Schopenhauer have dared to appeal to him for their enervating philosophy, and our generation has modernised him, with the notion that it could comprehend his character and development

> psychologically. We must go back to the point where we can feel again the heroic in Jesus. Before that mysterious Person, who, in the form of his time, knew that he was creating upon the foundation of his life and death a moral world which bears his name, we must be forced to lay our faces in the dust, without daring even to wish to understand his nature. Only then can the heroic in our Christianity and in our world-view be again revived.
>
> (1914: 274)

As we shall see in a later section, Schweitzer was committed to this heroic aspect of Jesus and to a degree reflected it in his own life. In the mid-twentieth century the picture of Jesus as deeply socially involved helped fire a series of theological views focused on political and social theology aimed at justice for oppressed people. This made him more of a revolutionary than a hero, but the general trend was similar. For others, it is the humility of Jesus, or Jesus as the key to the mystery of the universe, or as a miracle worker, which stands to the fore.

So it is that sometimes these pictures are images for the mind to dwell on in an intellectual and poetic kind of way. But they may also be more three-dimensional and tactile, for it is equally possible for a tradition to stress that we 'see' God at work today through the lives and service of faithful followers of Jesus. The following section is devoted to this idea because it plays an important part in the total picture of Christian living.

God depicted in people

Christians sometimes stress the fact that the true faith has more to do with people than with buildings. They emphasise the idea of the faithful gathered together as the body of Christ more than they do the building where they gather. Following the biblical point that where two or three are gathered together in his name, there Christ is in their midst (Matt. 18: 20), such Christians see themselves as the dynamic expression of God's activity. Where the Christian community is active, there God can be 'seen'. This is an ethical expression of God's nature and though it may seem far removed from artistic pictures of God or Christ, yet, in its own way, it can be a powerful expression of the divine nature.

A charity such as the Mission to Lepers provides an obvious link between what Jesus did in his earthly life and what Christians should do today. Movements like Christian Aid, and many other charities, provide a kind of moral sketch of the divine nature through human activity.

CHRIST-LIKE LIVES

And as with groups of people so, too, with individuals. In most generations church historians can point to particular individuals who have been regarded by others as examples of a Christ-like life. The martyrs, or witnesses as the word means in Greek, of the early church were typical examples of lives in which the divine power was expressed. And such martyrdom continues today, especially in South America, as Christian leaders advocate justice and freedom in the face of hostile political regimes.

Many others live less dramatically but also furnish examples to their generation of what Christian life should be. We have already talked about Albert Schweitzer as a New Testament scholar. He was also a fine musician as an organist, conductor and historian of J.S. Bach. While at the peak of his influence in Europe, he decided to train as a doctor to serve as a medical missionary in Africa and went to Lambarene in French Equatorial Africa (as it then was) in 1913.

When the influential Dutch phenomenologist of religion Gerardus Van Der Leeuw wrote his classic study, *Religion in Essence and Manifestation*, in 1933, he included Schweitzer in the category of 'The Exemplar'. An anecdote explains why Schweitzer was included in this category of those whose faith is seen through the example of the life lived. An ordinary workman who attended one of Schweitzer's organ recitals, given to raise money for Africa, was asked why he had come to the concert. He said he had come to hear the one who had done something while everybody else talked.

THE GENDER OF GOD IN HUMANS

Another twentieth-century example of a life that expresses the life of Jesus through service to others is that of Mother Teresa of Calcutta. Throughout the 1980s and 1990s she has gained wide public recognition for her work and that of the sisters of her religious order who serve the destitute not only in India but in many parts of the world.

Mother Teresa is, obviously, a woman. Although this point may sound absurd, it raises a most interesting question for religious studies in relation to picturing God. There is a great tradition in Christianity of nuns living lives of service to others, and there is no practical problem interpreting this as Christ-like behaviour.

It is all the more interesting, then, when the question of gender emerges in relation to the priesthood. The Eastern Orthodox, Roman Catholic, and some Anglican Churches have argued against the ordination of women on the assumption that because priests are today's representatives of Christ and are, in a symbolic sense, a kind of Christ when they celebrate the Eucharist, they must be male to represent fully Jesus who was male.

This is a good example of how Christ is pictured in different genders. It also raises another key, yet subtle, point which needs to be spelled out with care.

CHRIST IN HELPER OR HELPED

In the case of Schweitzer, Mother Teresa and many hundreds of saintly people of both genders, the picture of Christ that comes through them is as individual servants of God. Christ is seen in the helper. This has a firm biblical basis in the idea that whoever listens to or rejects Christ's disciple listens to or rejects Christ (Luke 10: 16). But it is equally possible to focus on Christ in the person who is helped. In the gospels this emerges in a discussion about who is the greatest in the kingdom of God. Jesus tells his disciples that whoever receives a child in his name receives Jesus (Matt. 18: 5). This insight has been taken up in a radical way by one of the most influential of all twentieth-century theological explorations, that of Liberation Theology. Gustavo Gutierrez wrote *A Theology of Liberation* in Spanish in 1971. At its heart is the practical concern to love through living by becoming a neighbour to those suffering injustice. Here theology, ethics and spirituality lie close together and are combined on the assumption that God is best seen today in the lives of other needy individuals:

> God is revealed in history, and it is likewise in history that men encounter his Word made flesh. Christ is not a private individual. . . We find the Lord in our encounters with men, especially the poor, marginalized, and exploited ones. An act of love towards them is an act of love towards God.
>
> (Gutierrez 1974: 201)

SOURCE OF CHRIST'S IMAGE

Yet another angle on picturing Christ in other people comes from the Russian Orthodox Archbishop Anthony Bloom. Speaking of the 1960s, he reflected on how popular it was to 'look for God in one's neighbour', and noted that the third- and fourth-century desert fathers used similar language. But he went on to make the very important theological point, that:

> In order to see the features of Christ in our neighbour's face, which is sometimes very difficult to read, we have to have in us the vision of Christ so as to be able to project it on to them.[3]

For Bloom the source of Christ's image first lies within the Christian, within the helper. It is there because of God's grace which enables the life of faith to learn about Christ through the scriptures, the tradition of the church and worship. In Christian living this internal sense of Christ is then 'projected', as he puts it, on to those who are served and helped. It is interesting to see him use the idea of projection in this way. It takes into account the fallenness of people, which makes the image of God difficult to read or to perceive, something the Orthodox speak of as the 'coats of skin' which cover humanity after the Fall (Yannaras 1991: 87); but it also shows the importance of the process of being made new in the image of God, which is an important feature of Orthodox theology and belief.

The marks of Christ in the believer

St Paul speaks of bearing in his body the marks of Jesus (Gal. 6: 17). Whatever he meant by that, some Christian saints have spoken of receiving in their bodies the marks of the passion and crucifixion of Christ. These marks, or stigmata as they are called, were quite uncommon until the thirteenth century, a period when devotion to the sufferings of Christ became common. More than three hundred cases are referred to by the Catholic Church, notably St Francis of Asissi, who is said to have been the first to have been granted these signs of Christ's suffering. These marks are dramatic 'pictures' of Christ within the life of a faithful devotee.

This brings us full circle, from the ethical reflecting of God in the Old Testament, through the actual manifestation of God in Christ of the New Testament, to the representing of Christ in the sacred buildings and ritual of the medieval period, to the modern world where God is reflected in the moral behaviour of believers, and in marks on the actual bodies of a few select individuals.

NOTES

1. See Bethell, D. (1972) 'The Making of a Twelfth Century Collection', in G.J. Cuming and D. Baker *Popular Belief and Practice*, Cambridge, Cambridge University Press.
2. Swanson, G. (1960) *The Birth of the Gods*, Ann Arbor, University of Michigan.
3. Bloom, A. (1971) *God and Man*, Darton, Longman & Todd, p. 112.

FURTHER READING

Baggley, J. (1987) *Doors of Perception*, London, Mowbray.
Beckwith, J. (1970) *Early Christian and Byzantine Art*, Harmondsworth, Penguin.
Berger, P. (1971) *A Rumour of Angels*, London, Penguin.
Bowker, J. (1973) *The Sense of God*, Oxford, Oxford University Press.
—— (1978) *The Religious Imagination and the Sense of God*, Oxford, Oxford University Press.
Christie, Y. et al. (eds) (1982) *Art in the Christian World: A Handbook of Style and Forms*, London, Faber and Faber.
Colvin, H. (1991) *Architecture and the After-Life*, London, Yale University Press.

Gutierrez, G. (1974) *A Theology of Liberation*, London, SCM Press.
Murray, Sister Charles (1981) *Rebirth and Afterlife*, Oxford, British Archaeological Reports.
Stevenson, J. (1978) *The Catacombs*, London, Thames and Hudson.
Yannaras, C. (1991) *Elements of Faith: An Introduction to Orthodox Theology*, Edinburgh, T & T Clark.

3. Hinduism

Sharada Sugirtharajah

The Hindu tradition is replete with a wide variety of images of the Divine. The Supreme is seen as a personal God, as a transcendent Being, as immanent within each person as *Antaryāmin* ('inner Controller'), and in all creation. Images of the Divine as lord, king, judge, master, father, mother, husband, friend, beloved and as creator, preserver and destroyer of evil, find expression in scriptures, mythology, art, iconography, music, dance and worship. The Divine is also described in terms of its plethora of attributes, such as love, wisdom, knowledge, beauty, power, and also in abstract categories such as pure consciousness, pure Being.

Monistic and theistic images of the Divine.

BRAHMAN

Ultimate Reality is conceptualised in many different ways in the Hindu tradition. The Sanskrit term *Brahman,* which is used for the Ultimate Reality, is seen as the one eternal, all-pervading and all-transcending principle of the universe and all creation (*Śvetāśvatara Upaniṣad* 6.11). There seems to be more than one linguistic derivation of the term. In the Veda it denotes the cosmic or sacred power contained in the vedic chants, and the priest who chanted the sacred verses was called *brāhman* (a member of the priestly class). In the *Upaniṣads* the term Brahman comes to refer to the impersonal transcendental principle, the first cause of the universe. Hindu monists see *Brahman* as being identical with the inner self or *ātman,* the spirit dwelling within us. For Hindu theists, *ātman* is only partially identical with *Brahman*.

Brahman is described as *Sat-cit-ānanda* (Truth, Consciousness and Bliss). It is conceived as both one and many, form and formless, immanent and transcendent, male and female, benign and terrible – not so much opposites as complementary aspects of the One Being (*Śvetāśvatara Upaniṣad* 4.1–3).

Brahman is perceived and experienced as both *saguṇa* (with qualities, personal) and *nirguṇa* (without qualities, non-personal). The image of the Divine as a personal god is central to the theistic tradition, whereas the image of an impersonal Absolute is central to the monistic tradition. While the former affirms the infinite attributes of the Absolute, the latter does not deny such qualities in a preliminary way, but sees *Brahman* as being beyond all thought and speculation. Both positive and negative categories are used to affirm the reality of the Supreme. The Absolute is affirmed as *iti iti*, meaning that all this is *Brahman* – emphasising the immanental dimension (*Chāndogya Upaniṣad* 3.14.1) – and *neti neti*, implying that *Brahman* is 'not this, not that' – emphasising that *Brahman* is more than what we perceive and experience (*Bṛhadāraṇyaka Upaniṣad* 4.5.15). Both conceptions of the Divine are equally valid, though there has been a tendency to exalt one over the other.

In the *Ṛg-veda*, there is a trend towards monotheism – all the different vedic gods are seen as manifestations of the One Reality. The *Upaniṣad*s affirm both the personal and non-personal dimensions of the Supreme, with the latter being predominant, but the Epics, the *Purāṇa*s and the *Bhagavadgītā* (secondary scriptures) focus on the personal dimension of the Supreme in the form of *avatāra*s, 'descents' of Viṣṇu (one of the vedic gods) into humanity in various animal, semi-human and human forms, at times of crisis to conquer evil and restore harmony (See Viṣṇu pp. 79–81 below). Some Śaiva texts speak about the *avatāra*s of Śiva but these have not played a central role in Śaiva thought.

The Absolute in its formless aspect is far removed from the experience of most people, but the experience of the Absolute in its personal aspect/form is within the reach of all. The Supreme is conceived of as having many attributes, functions, forms, manifestations and names but, at the same time, oneness is seen as the basis of all multiplicity. The Hindu concepts of *Trimūrti* and *avatāra* illustrate the point.

THE DIVINE AS *TRIMŪRTI*

In the Epics, the transcendent Being becomes a personal, living God. Images of the Divine, such as creator, sustainer and destroyer of evil, are dominant in the epic literature. The One Reality is seen as having three different but complementary aspects or functions – that of Brahmā who creates, that of Viṣṇu who preserves, and that of Śiva who destroys evil. In the *Upaniṣads*, *Brahman* is the cause of the endless cyclic process of creation, preservation, and destruction of evil, but in the Epics it is attributed to the three gods of the Hindu Triad. Although each of these gods is assigned a specific role, their functions are not mutually exclusive; they overlap with one another. Though Śiva is primarily the destroyer of evil, he is also seen as Śiva Trimūrti – manifesting the triple aspects of creation, preservation and destruction of evil. Viṣṇu, too, represents all the three functions, though his primary role is the preservation of *dharma*. Though Brahmā is the Creator, he is shown in popular iconography as emerging forth from a lotus flower which grows out of Viṣṇu's navel (see Brahmā, Viṣṇu and Śiva below). Each of these gods has a consort who is worshipped in her own right (see Feminine Images of the Divine, pp. 98ff. below).

AVATĀRA, 'DESCENT' OF THE DIVINE

Although the Ultimate Reality is seen as being formless (*nirākāra*), and beyond all thought and speculation, it is seen as assuming forms. The idea of oneness as the basis of the multiplicity of forms is illustrated through the concept of *avatāra*, which literally means 'descent' of the Divine into the world. The Divine takes different forms whenever there is a decline of righteousness, in order to restore harmony and peace (*Bhagavadgītā* 4.7). The significance of the *avatāra* is two-fold: the descent of the Divine into the world, and the rise of humanity to a divine consciousness. This concept is particularly applied to Viṣṇu, who has taken various forms to conquer evil (see Viṣṇu pp. 79–81 below). Of all the *avatāra*s of Viṣṇu, Rāma and Kṛṣṇa are the most popular and have become the object of devotion and worship. The plurality of forms of the Divine does not diminish the oneness of the Divine; rather it enhances it. As Sri Aurobindo states:

> The Divine Being is not incapable of taking innumerable
> forms because He is beyond all form in His essence,
> nor by assuming them does He lose His divinity,
> but pours out rather in them the delight
> of His being and the glories of His godhead;
> this gold does not cease to be gold because it shapes itself
> into all kinds of ornaments . . .
>
> (Sri Aurobindo 1955: 765)

In contrast, a monist Hindu philosopher like Śaṃkara may accord only a secondary status to the various forms; they are seen as being relatively real – as having an empirical appearance of reality which is finally negated when one experiences the formless *Brahman* or Absolute. But both theist and monist Hindus acknowledge the different approaches to the Divine, although each may look upon their conception as having greater validity.

MANY NAMES OF THE DIVINE

In Hindu worship the Supreme is affirmed through names and forms. The idea of giving many names to the One Reality finds expression in the *Ṛg-veda*, where names of vedic deities such as Indra, Mitra, Varuṇa and Agni refer to the Divine. 'Truth is one but the sages call it by manifold names' (1.164.46). Each of the gods and goddesses has more than one name, each signifying one of the various attributes of the deity. Chanting the name of one's chosen deity (*iṣṭa devatā*) and worshipping God in embodied form are seen as strengthening the personal bond between God and the worshipper. For example, Viṣṇu is known by names such as Nārāyaṇa, Hari and Padmanābha, and Kṛṣṇa is known by names such as Madhusūdana, Gopāla and Janārdana (see Viṣṇu, Kṛṣṇa and other gods).

There are masculine and feminine forms of addressing the Divine. Expressions such as *Paramātman* (the Supreme Self), *Parameśvara* (the Supreme Lord), *Īśvara* (Personal Lord), *Bhagavān* (God), indicate different ways of addressing the Divine. Feminine forms of address such as *Devī* (Goddess) or *Mahādevī* (the Great Goddess) are used in prayer, meditation and worship. Village deities are addressed as *amman*, mother (see Village deities, pp. 109–10 below).

ICONIC IMAGES OF THE DIVINE

The variety of names and forms of the Divine is affirmed in worship, dance, music, art, iconography, literature, mythology, folklore and philosophy. In Hindu worship, images play a central role. The Sanskrit word that is commonly used for an iconic image is *mūrti*, but *mūrti* is more than an iconic representation of the deity; it is an embodiment or form of the Divine itself. It suggests more than what one can readily perceive and experience. The infinite attributes and aspects of the Divine, which may appear contradictory to the uninitiated beholder, for instance, are reflected in the four-armed dancing Śiva with a third eye in the middle of his forehead; Gaṇeśa, the elephant-headed deity with four arms; Subramaṇya with six faces; and Kālī with a garland of skulls around her neck and dancing on her husband Śiva.

The Divine is represented in a variety of ways: fully human (e.g., Rāma); half-human and half-animal (e.g., Gaṇeśa and the Narasiṃha *avatāra* of Viṣṇu); half-male and half-female (e.g., Śiva as Ardhanārīśvara). All are shown holding various emblems in their hands, symbolising their power and authority. They are depicted in standing, sitting or dancing positions, with their hands held in *abhaya mudrā* (protective gesture). They are usually shown with their mounts. Animals and birds are associated with various deities as their vehicles, *vāhanas*. For instance, a bull is seen with Śiva, an elephant with Lakṣmī, a swan with Sarasvatī, a peacock with Subramaṇya, a garuḍa with Viṣṇu, a cow with Kṛṣṇa.

Iconographical representations of various gods and goddesses adorn the temple towers (*gopurams*) and walls within the temples of India. Some of the North and South Indian temples are known for their splendid sculptural representations of the deities and of stories from the Epics and the *Purāṇas*. The *sanctum sanctorum* (*garba gṛha*), womb of the temple, houses the images, made of stone, metal or wood, to whom worship is offered. Domestic shrines may contain a variety of images made of brass or copper and framed calendar pictures. Even a road-side tea or coffee shop will have a picture of a deity. In the work-place, whether it be school, factory or hotel, one can see calendar pictures of the deities. Most Indian film producers include an invocation to a deity before the actual film is shown. Most drivers of cars, buses, trucks and other vehicles will have pictures of their chosen deities, to whom they offer incense and pray for safe travel. Images made of clay are used on festival occasions, after which they are ceremoniously immersed in a river (see Feminine images of the Divine, pp. 98ff. below).

ANICONIC IMAGES OF THE DIVINE

Images such as *liṅga* (Śiva) and *śālagrāma* (Viṣṇu), which do not have any anthropomorphic shape or form, are also the focus of worship in the Hindu tradition. As Diana Eck points out, 'the aniconic images are those symbolic forms which, although they refer to a deity, do not attempt any anthropomorphic form or any representational likeness' (Eck 1985: 32). The aniconic symbol of Śiva, the *liṅga*, has a central place in Śaiva worship. The word *liṅga* means both 'sign' and 'phallus'; it has various levels of meanings, such as procreation and fertility (see Śiva). Śaiva homes may have a small stone image of Śiva *liṅga* and small smooth polished stones known as *bāṇaliṅga*s in their *pūjā* (worship) room. Vaiṣṇavas may have small rounded river-worn ammonite stones, *śālagrāma*s, symbolising Viṣṇu. Other aniconic representations, such as geometrical diagrams called *yantra*s and *maṇḍala*s, which function as sacred symbols, are used in *tantric* worship and meditation. Wayside shrines may have a symbol such as a spear or a stone representing a particular deity. Even a tree or a particular spot is invested with religious significance as all forms of life are seen as sacred. The manifold aspects of nature such as rivers, mountains, trees, plants and flowers are seen as embodiments of divinity. For example, Śiva is associated with the sacred river Ganges; *tulsī* (basil) leaves are offered to Viṣṇu in worship, and *bilva* (wood-apple tree) leaves to Śiva. Of the trees, pipal and banyan are considered particularly sacred.

VEDIC IMAGES OF THE DIVINE

The vedic tradition has a variety of aniconic images, affirming the presence of the Divine in all creation – the sun, moon, sky, fire, storm and various other manifestations of nature. Most of the gods of the vedic pantheon are personifications of nature, such as Sūrya the sun god, Indra the storm-god, Agni the fire-god, Vāyu the wind god and Uṣā the goddess of dawn. The central focus of the vedic tradition was not the image but *yagña* or fire sacrifices (see Agni and p. 77 below) which were offered to the gods, and hymns were chanted during the performance of the ceremony.

THE DIVINE AS *ŚABDA-BRAHMAN*

In the vedic ritual tradition the emphasis was not on visual representation of the gods, but sound (*śabda*). Accurate chanting of hymns and *mantra*s during the performance of sacrificial rituals was important. It is for this reason that the Veda (*śruti*, 'hearing') was transmitted orally and preserved in the form of sound before it came to be written down. Of all sounds, *Auṁ* (OṀ) is the most sacred sound – the primordial sound from which all other sounds have emerged. Therefore the Divine is also seen as *Śabda-Brahman* ('the *Brahman*-sound, revealed aspect of *Brahman*'). In meditation, prayer and worship, sound plays an important part.

THE DIVINE AS AGNI

Agni, the fire-god is one of the important vedic deities to whom a great number of hymns are addressed. He is described as a friend and companion. He symbolises warmth, protection and purification. He figures as the messenger of gods and mediator between the gods and humanity. Vedic worship centred on Agni, the divine minister of sacrifice, who received sacrificial offerings and carried them to the gods, and thus sanctified them.

Although Agni as fire is an aniconic image, he is represented in sculpture as a three-legged deity riding on a ram. The three legs stand for three sacred fires: marriage, ceremonial and sacrificial. He is depicted with one or two faces and seven hands. The two faces symbolise two fires, solar and terrestrial. The seven hands may indicate the all-pervasive quality of Agni. From his mouth emerge flames which receive the sacrificial offerings.

Agni is of central importance in the religious practices of the Arya Samaj, a modern Hindu reform movement founded by Swami Dayananda Sarasvati (who believed in the absolute authority of the Veda and aimed at purifying Hinduism from within). Followers of this sect do not use images in their worship. They perform *havan* or *homa* (fire-offering) instead of *pūjā*. Fire continues to play a central role in most Hindu ceremonies, particularly marriage and death. For both the sanctification of marriage and the purification of death, Agni is essential.

THE DIVINE AS SŪRYA

Sūrya, the sun god, is seen as dispeller of darkness, both physical and spiritual. He is the source not only of light and warmth, but also of knowledge. In time, other solar divinities, such as Vivasvat and Savitṛ, were merged with Sūrya, and he has many other names which affirm his various attributes. In the *Ṛg-veda* he figures riding across the sky in a golden chariot drawn by splendid horses. Sūrya is represented in this form in the sun temple in Koṇārak, Orissa, where worship is offered to him. He may be depicted standing on a lotus pedestal and holding two lotuses, with a halo round his head. In South Indian representations he is bare-footed, whereas the North Indian images show him wearing knee-high boots.

The *Gāyatrī mantra* in the *Ṛg-veda* (3.62.10), in honour of the sun god, is the most sacred *mantra* of the Veda and is repeated by orthodox brahmans each day at sunrise and sunset. The officiating priest whispers this *mantra* in the ear of the initiate at the sacred thread ceremony, and this marks the beginning of new birth:

> tat savitur vareṇyaṃ
> bhargo devasaya dhīmahi
> dhiyo yo naḥ pracodayāt
>
> ('We meditate upon the glorious splendour of the Vivifier divine. May he himself illumine our minds!').
>
> (Panikkar 1989: 38)

This *mantra* is uttered in almost all Hindu rites and ceremonies. There are many sacred verses in honour of Sūrya, whose blessings are invoked. Sūrya-namaskāra (prostrations to the Sun god) are performed in the morning by some Hindus. It is seen as promoting the physical and spiritual well-being of those who perform it.

In South Indian temples, worship offered to Sūrya, along with other planets such as Mars, Jupiter and Mercury, known as *Navagraha*(s) (nine planets), is common. Hindus light a *diva* (small clay lamp) and place it before the shrine. It is commonly believed that the position of the planets can have adverse effects on people and therefore they are worshipped.

It is said that Sūrya's wife, Samjñā, had to leave him because she could not bear the intense blazing light of her husband. Leaving behind her shadow (*chhāyā*), she departed for the colder regions in the north. The desperate Sūrya went in search of her and found her. The architect of the gods, Viśvakarma, expressed his desire to refashion Sūrya and urged him to accept his proposal. Viśvakarma created a magnificent and luminous form of Sūrya but his legs remained untouched.

Masculine images of the Divine

THE DIVINE AS CREATOR: BRAHMĀ

Brahmā was originally an important member of the Hindu *Trimūrti* or Triad. Brahmā is the creator and lord of the world and all creatures. In popular art and iconography Brahmā is usually shown with four heads (sometimes five; the fifth was burnt off by Śiva's third eye) and four arms, indicating that he is the creator – the cause and source of all creation. The four heads are also seen as representing the four Vedas (sacred scriptures), the four *varṇa*s (classes), the four *āśrama*s (the four stages of life) and the four *yuga*s (epochs of time). In his hands he is seen holding the sacred scriptures (as the author of sacred knowledge), a string of prayer beads (representing time), a ladle (a sacrificial spoon), and a water jug (symbolising the water from which all creation has evolved. Brahmā's bearded face shows him as a venerable sage and god of wisdom. He is usually depicted wearing a white garment and his mount is a goose (*haṃsa*), a symbol of discrimination and creative power.

In the Veda Brahmā figures as the creator, the Lord of sacrifice and father of gods. In the *Purāṇa*s he is conceived of as having sprung from the golden cosmic egg. In mythology he is subordinated to Viṣṇu and Śiva, whose help he often seeks. He is represented as emerging from a lotus which sprang out of Viṣṇu's navel.

Although he is the creator, Brahmā occupies a less prominent place when it comes to worship. Unlike Viṣṇu and Śiva he has no devotees. He figures in temple sculptures but there is perhaps only one temple in India dedicated to Brahmā, at Puskara in Rajasthan.

THE DIVINE AS PRESERVER AND SUSTAINER: VIṢṆU

Viṣṇu, the preserver and sustainer of the world, is the second member of the *Trimūrti*. He is conceived of as the cosmic god, Nārāyaṇa, 'moving in the waters', pervading the whole universe. He is often shown in iconography seated or reclining on a seven-headed snake called Śeṣa, or Ananta ('the Endless'), floating in the middle of an ocean, signifying a state of complete absorption before creation begins. In this representation he is also known as Ananta-śāyana ('who sleeps on the serpent Ananta'), and is seen with his consort Lakṣmī massaging his feet with devotion, and Brahmā (Creator) seated in a lotus emerging from his navel. Viṣṇu in this reclining posture is worshipped in the Southern Indian Vaiṣṇava temple at Srirangam.

Viṣṇu is also shown in standing posture. The symbols he carries in his four hands are of enormous significance. The white conch shell (*śaṅkha*) signifies the primeval sound of creation and victory over the demons, the rotating wheel (*cakra*) which he uses to confront and conquer adverse forces shows him as a sustainer of the world and represents the cycle of time, the golden mace (*kaumodakī*) is a symbol of his royal power and authority, and the lotus flower (*padma*) symbolises purity, perfection and the unfolding of forms (also associated with other gods and goddesses). The Vaiṣṇava sign of three vertical lines is worn in the centre of the forehead by the followers of Viṣṇu. Viṣṇu's *vahana*, or vehicle, is Garuḍa, an enormous bird, partly human and partly eagle. Garuḍa, the king of the birds, is seen as the destroyer of evil and is one of the manifestations of Viṣṇu himself (see Lakṣmī, pp. 101–4 below).

Viṣṇu is also represented in the form of a *śālagrāma*, a river-worn ammonite shell which is spiral or rounded in shape. It is seen to be a 'natural form' (*svarūpa*) of Viṣṇu. It is said that Lord Viṣṇu appeared in the form of *śālgrāma* stones on the Gaṇḍakī river bed in answer to the prayer of the river goddess, Gaṅgā, who desired that

Viṣṇu be born in her womb. Viṣṇu is worshipped in this form along with his other *avatāra*s, especially Rāma and Kṛṣṇa.

Viṣṇu has a thousand names (*sahasra-nāma*), each of which affirms one of his attributes. It is a common practice among Hindus to chant the manifold names of their chosen deities. Chanting the thousand names of Viṣṇu is seen as purifying and awakening one's spiritual consciousness. In Vaiṣṇava and other temples, chanting is done in the early hours of the morning.

Viṣṇu, as his names suggest, is one who pervades and sustains the world. As Nārāyaṇa, he is associated with water; as Hari, with saving activity; and as Padmanābha, with creation. As Nīlameghaśyamā, the blue sky, he signifies the all-pervasive nature of being.

Viṣṇu's love and compassion are manifested in his *avatāra*s, ('descents' into the world whenever righteousness declines, to restore harmony and peace – *dharma*). Of the three gods of the Hindu Triad, Viṣṇu alone assumes various forms – animal, semi-human and human – to conquer evil. According to the *Bhāgavata Purāṇa*, Viṣṇu's *avatāra*s are twenty-two but the standard list is ten. The myths surrounding these *avatāra*s are many. Viṣṇu incarnated himself as a fish (*matsya*), to save Manu, the first ancestor, from a flood; as a tortoise (*kūrma*), to support a mountain on his back so that the gods and demons could churn the ocean to retrieve the lost divine treasure, the nectar of immortality, *amṛta*; as a boar (*vārāha*), to raise on his tusks the earth, which had been pushed down into the depths of ocean by a demon; as a man-lion (*narasiṃha*), to destroy the demon king Hiraṇyakaṣipu (who could not be killed either by a man or a beast) who inflicted untold suffering on his son, Prahlāda, who was an ardent devotee of Viṣṇu; as a dwarf (*vāmana*), to restore the harmony of the earth (which was threatened by King Bali; when Bali granted Viṣṇu's request to take the space covered by his three steps, the dwarfish *avatāra* assumed a gigantic form and took three steps – two covering the earth and the third being placed on Bali). As Paraśurāma, Viṣṇu appears as militant brahman who destroys the *kṣatriya*s; as Rāma, the seventh incarnation of Viṣṇu, he restores the ideal of *kṣatriya* (warrior) and justice. Viṣṇu in the form of Rāma figures as the ideal prince, ruler, husband, son. Viṣṇu in the form of Kṛṣṇa is perhaps the most complete expression of God's humanity and divinity. The Buddha, who opposed brahmanical orthodoxy and ritualism, is the ninth *avatāra* and the tenth, *Kalkin*, is yet to come. The anthropomorphic and other images of Viṣṇu are usually represented on the walls of a Vaiṣṇava temple. The saving activity of Viṣṇu through his ten *avatāras* (*Daśāvatāra*) is given a significant place in the South Indian classical dance, *Bharatanatyam*.

In Viṣṇu, one finds the most complete expression of a loving and compassionate god. In the *Ṛg-veda* he is a minor god, but he becomes an important member of the Triad in the Epics and the *Purāṇas*. In the *Padma Purāṇa* Viṣṇu represents all the triple aspects (creation, preservation and destruction of evil), although his primary function is the preservation of the Divine Order.

RĀMA AS SUSTAINER OF *DHARMA*

Rāmacandra, or Rāma, the seventh incarnation of Viṣṇu, is the subject of the epic, the *Rāmāyaṇa*. In some iconographical representations he is shown standing with a bow (*śārṅga*) in his left hand. The bow symbolises valour and strength. Rāma succeeded at a contest in breaking the bow of Śiva given to Sītā's father, King Janaka, and thereby won the hand of Sītā. In popular art and temples Rāma is usually shown with his wife Sītā, his brother, Lakṣmaṇa, and the Monkey God, Hanumān.

Rāma emerges as a son obedient to his father (going willingly into exile), as a husband devoted to his wife Sītā, as a valiant prince who rescues Sītā from the hands of the demon king Rāvaṇa, and as an ideal ruler. The purpose of Rāma *avatāra* was to establish *dharma*, justice and peace in society. Gandhi used the concept of *Rāma Rājya* (kingdom of justice on earth) in his non-violent struggles against all forms of oppression and injustice.

Rāma's wife, Sītā, figures as a devoted and faithful wife who follows him into the forest. Both Rāma and Sītā are seen as ideal partners in marriage, embodying all the ideal qualities of manhood and womanhood (see 'Hinduism' in *Women in Religion* in this series). The Hindu festival *Daśarā* (also known as *Navarātri* and *Durgā-pūjā*) is associated with the victory of Rāma over the demon Rāvaṇa. It is said that Rāma prayed to the Goddess Durgā before embarking on his expedition to defeat Rāvaṇa. On this day effigies of Rāvaṇa are burned and the story of the *Rāmāyaṇa* is enacted on the stage. Some Hindus associate *Diwālī* with the return of Rāma and Sītā to their kingdom Ayodhyā, to be crowned as king and queen after vanquishing Rāvaṇa. The festival of *Rāma Navamī* commemorates the birth of Rāma. It is celebrated by Hindus in most parts of India, especially by Vaiṣṇavas.

In personal devotions, meditations and prayers, names of gods and goddesses are used as *mantra* (sacred word) to attain peace. Gandhi believed in the efficacy of the Rām *mantra*.

HANUMĀN AS AN IDEAL DEVOTEE

Hanumān, the monkey-god, the friend and devotee of Rāma and Sītā, figures in the Epic, the *Rāmāyaṇa*. In popular representations he is shown kneeling at the feet of Rāma, showing his devotion and love. Another popular representation shows Hanumān flying through the air, carrying a mountain containing medicinal herbs to cure Rāma's brother who was wounded in the battle against Rāvaṇa. He helps Rāma to recover his wife Sītā from Rāvaṇa's captivity. Being the son of the wind god, he leaps into the air, travels swiftly and performs extraordinary feats, to vanquish Rāvaṇa. He is known for his agility, strength, valour, steadfastness and devotion to Rāma. The relationship between Rāma and Hanumān is one of mutual affection. The Epic has scenes where Rāma demonstrates his love for his devotee by embracing him. In some representations Hanumān is shown tearing open his chest with both his hands, revealing Rāma and Sītā. This picture shows Hanumān's devotion to Rāma, as well as the idea that God resides in our hearts. Hanumān is worshipped in his own right, and his *mantra* is said to help one overcome fear of any kind. The birthday of Hanumān (*Hanumān Jayanti*) is celebrated especially in Delhi and in certain parts of South India.

Kṛṣṇa

Kṛṣṇa, the eighth *avatāra*, is considered the most complete incarnation of Viṣṇu. Kṛṣṇa is pictured as divine child, friend, beloved, teacher, master and so on. *Smṛti* literature (the *Mahābhārata*, the *Bhagavadgītā* and the *Bhāgavata Purāṇa*) offers splendid insights into the many-faceted personality of Kṛṣṇa. There is only passing reference to the name Kṛṣṇa in the *Ṛg-veda* and the

Upaniṣads. It is in the Epic, *Mahābhārata*, that Kṛṣṇa assumes a central role as a god in his own right.

Kṛṣṇa means 'the dark one' or 'black'. The colour is seen as indicating his non-Aryan origins. In popular pictures he is blue – the colour of the sky and oceans – symbolising the endless and infinite nature of the Supreme.

KṚṢṆA AS DIVINE CHILD

Kṛṣṇa figures as a mischievous child yet an enchanting one. His early youth and adult years are the subject of classical and popular music, dance, art and literature. His miraculous birth and early years are recorded in the *Purāṇas*. As divine child he evokes maternal love in mothers, who find it emotionally and spiritually satisfying to worship Kṛṣṇa in that form. This kind of relationship between God and his devotee is known as *vatsalya bhava*. In popular pictures he may be shown eating butter or stealing it, along with his friends. He may also be seen in a crawling position or holding a sweet cake in one of his hands. On Kṛṣṇa's birthday, a picture or an image of the infant Kṛṣṇa becomes the focus of devotion and worship. Sometimes a bronze or silver image of Kṛṣṇa in a swing may be used. That the idea of God as divine child appeals to the Hindu mind is evident from the way Kṛṣṇa's *janamaśtamī* (birthday) is celebrated by Hindus in their homes and temples, especially at Mathura (the birthplace of Kṛṣṇa) and Vrindavan (where Kṛṣṇa is said to have spent his early years). Tiny foot-prints of baby Kṛṣṇa are drawn with white or coloured powder all along the hallway leading to the *pūjā* (worship) room.

Hindus are fond of listening to stories about Kṛṣṇa's childhood or watching them being enacted on the stage. One of the most delightful and awe-inspiring stories is about Kṛṣṇa eating clay. Kṛṣṇa's friends report it to his foster mother, Yaśodā. Kṛṣṇa convinces his mother that he has not eaten clay and opens his mouth to show that he is not up to any mischief. Yaśodā sees the whole universe in Kṛṣṇa's mouth and herself with Kṛṣṇa on her knee. Yaśodā is as awe-struck as Arjuna is in the *Bhagavadgītā* when Kṛṣṇa reveals his cosmic form, *viśvarūpa* (see Kṛṣṇa as the Immanent and Transcendent God, pp. 86–8 below).

The image of divine child helps one to approach God with the freedom and spontaneity of a child. A mother's love for her child is uninhibited and the child is not bound by social norms or conventions; it responds to its mother's love in a spontaneous manner. Kṛṣṇa in the form of an infant and a child invites devotees to abandon all formalities and approach him openly.

KṚṢṆA AS A YOUNG COWHERD

In the *Purāṇa*s Kṛṣṇa emerges as cowherd (Kṛṣṇa Gopāla), playing melodious music on his flute, thus ravishing the hearts of the *gopī*s (cowherd girls), and even peacocks are said to dance to his music. He is sometimes shown standing beside a cow, playing the flute and surrounded by birds and animals. In this form he is also known as Veṇugopāla ('cowherd with flute'). Popular and miniature paintings portray Kṛṣṇa in his pastoral setting, and his childhood and boyhood days offer an endless variety of images. Kṛṣṇa dancing on the poisonous snake, Kāliya, shows him as a conqueror of evil. The snake has poisoned the holy river Yamunā with its venom, making the water lethal and unfit for consumption. He fights with the snake in whose coils he becomes enmeshed, but frees himself and takes hold of the tail of the snake and stands on its hood and dances. He does not kill the snake but pushes it into the ocean where it can harm no one.

Another popular image of Kṛṣṇa Gopāla shows Kṛṣṇa lifting the mountain Govardhana (near Mathura) with one hand, and sheltering the inhabitants from angry thunder storms, severe winds and rain unleashed by the god Indra. In both these representations Kṛṣṇa is seen as a protector and sustainer.

KṚṢṆA AS BELOVED

Kṛṣṇa is also seen as the eternal beloved, inspiring intense devotion and the longing of the soul to merge with him. In popular iconography and Rajput miniature paintings, Kṛṣṇa is seen dancing with the *gopī*s, who long to be united with him. Kṛṣṇa's dance with the *gopī*s is known as *Rāsalīlā*. *Rāsa*, in this context, refers to 'emotional delight' and *līlā* to 'play' or 'sport'. Kṛṣṇa's sport with *gopī*s symbolises the soul's deep yearning to be united with the

Divine (Kṛṣṇa). He multiplies himself innumerable times to make himself accessible to each of the *gopīs*; each is led to believe that she alone is dancing with Kṛṣṇa.

Kṛṣṇa is usually shown with his favourite *gopī*, Rādhā, playing on a swing. Kṛṣṇa is also depicted sitting on a high branch of a tree, having stolen the garments of the *gopīs* while they are bathing; they have come to him to fetch their clothes. This highly erotic scene is interpreted as meaning that one has to be spiritually naked, to abandon all shame and honour in the presence of the Divine.

In the *bhakti* tradition, the image of the Divine as beloved has a central place. Senses are not rejected but turned towards the Divine to experience mystical love, as in the amorous *Rāsalīlā* dance where Kṛṣṇa makes himself available to each of his devotees. Even male devotees need to suspend their masculinity to relate to Kṛṣṇa as their eternal beloved (see 'Hinduism' in *Women in Religion* in this series). Bengali *bhakti* poets such as Jayadeva (twelfth century) and Chandi Das (fifteenth century) were inspired by the divine–human love expressed in the relationship between Kṛṣṇa and Rādhā, and their poetry is replete with such images of passionate love. The South Indian devotional hymns of Āḷvārs are known for their intense devotional fervour. The hymns of the Āḷvār saint, Andal, who looked upon herself as one of the *gopīs*, express her intense devotion to Kṛṣṇa. They are sung by women, especially young girls who look forward to happy marriages.

It is not uncommon to find the concept of God as the husband and the devotee as bride (*mathura bhava*). This is best exemplified in the relationship of the sixteenth-century Rajput saint, Mirabai, to Kṛṣṇa. Her intense spiritual yearning and love for Kṛṣṇa come alive in her devotional songs.

> Come to my house, O Krishna,
> Thy coming will bring peace.
> Great will be my joy if I meet Thee,
> And all my desires will be fulfilled.
> Thou and I are one,
> Like the sun and its heat.
> Mira's heart cares for nothing else,
> I want only the beautiful Shyām.
>
> (Alston 1980: 80)

KṚṢṆA AS FRIEND, TEACHER AND LIBERATOR

While in the *Purāṇas* Kṛṣṇa emerges as a delightful and energetic youth, in the *Mahābhārata* he assumes the stature of an epic hero. In the *Bhagavadgītā*, which is part of the *Mahābhārata*, Kṛṣṇa figures as a divine teacher and friend to Arjuna in the guise of a charioteer. Kṛṣṇa takes the side of the Pāṇḍavas, who were unfairly cheated in a game of dice by their cousins, the Kauravas. In his dialogue with Arjuna, Kṛṣṇa addresses him as a friend and instils confidence in the warrior Arjuna who is reluctant to fight against his cousins. As a *guru*, or spiritual teacher, he shows the path that is appropriate for Arjuna but does not force it upon him. The opening chapter of the *Bhagavadgītā* offers us a visual image of the divine–human encounter – Kṛṣṇa and Arjuna in a chariot in the middle of a battlefield. The iconographic representation of this scene has become popular since the last century, when the *Bhagavadgītā* was used (to encourage selfless commitment to the cause of freedom) during the struggle for Indian Independence.

Kṛṣṇa's role as a gracious lord and liberator is pronounced in the *Bhagavadgītā*. One of his names is Janāradana, meaning liberator. Kṛṣṇa tells Arjuna:

> Even if a man of the most vile conduct worships me with undistracted devotion, he must be reckoned as righteous for he has rightly resolved.
>
> (*Bhagavadgītā* 9.30)

> And whoever, at the time of death, gives up his body and departs, thinking of Me alone, he comes to My Status (of being); of that there is no doubt.
>
> (*Bhagavadgītā* 8.5)[1]

KṚṢṆA AS THE IMMANENT AND TRANSCENDENT GOD

The *Bhagavadgītā* affirms the immanental and transcendental dimensions of Kṛṣṇa. The tenth chapter gives a vivid picture of Kṛṣṇa as both the Eternal and Personal Lord. Although 'unborn', the

Supreme is seen as the source of all forms. Kṛṣṇa tells Arjuna that he is the beginning and end of the entire universe and that the world is strung on him like pearls on a string (7.7). He is the nucleus of all things, both animate and inanimate. Things of beauty, strength and spiritual power have sprung from a fragment of his Splendour (10.41):

> [I am] the goal, the upholder, the lord, the witness, the abode, the refuge and the friend. [I am] the origin and the dissolution, the ground, the resting place and the imperishable seed.
>
> (*Bhagavadgītā* 9.18)

> There is no end to My divine manifestations. . . . What has been declared by Me is only illustrative of My infinite glory.
>
> (*Bhagavadgītā* 10.40)

The eleventh chapter of the *Bhagavadgītā* presents us with a glorious and terrifying cosmic form or *viśvarūpa* of Viṣṇu. The immanence and transcendence of Kṛṣṇa are revealed to Arjuna, who seeks to know the truth. Kṛṣṇa discloses his infinite forms, with innumerable mouths, arms, thighs, feet, bellies – all blazing with glory. Kṛṣṇa emerges as the Supreme Person, who is both divine and human. Arjuna, who grasps this truth, utters:

> I behold Thee with Thy crown, mace and discus,
> glowing everywhere as a mass of light, hard to
> discern, (dazzling) on all sides with the radiance
> of the flaming fire and sun, incomparable.
>
> Thou art the Imperishable, the Supreme to be realized.
> Thou art the ultimate resting-place of the universe;
> Thou art the undying guardian of the eternal law.
> Thou art the Primal Person, I think.
>
> (*Bhagavadgītā* 11.17 & 18)

Kṛṣṇa in the form of Jagannāth ('Lord of the Universe') is the focus of worship in Puri, Orissa. The large wooden images of Jagganāth, his sister, Subdharā, and brother, Balarāma, are taken out yearly in a grand ceremonial procession in three beautifully decorated *rath*s, chariots, on the festival of *Rathayātrā*. This festival is also celebrated in a grand manner by the International Society of Krishna Consciousness (also known as Hare Krishna).

The Kṛṣṇa temple at Guruvayur in the south-western state of Kerala is also one of the major pilgrim centres. It is known for the healing powers of Kṛṣṇa, and even today many visit the temple to seek the grace of the lord of Guruvayur. The central shrine contains the image of Kṛṣṇa standing with a crown and four arms: holding a conch, a *cakra*, a club and a lotus, symbols often shown in images of Viṣṇu. The temple is open to Hindus of all castes, and many Hindus wish to be married in the Guruvayur temple.

Śiva

If Viṣṇu has many *avatāra*s, Śiva has many aspects, and is more complex than Viṣṇu. Śiva's origins go back to the pre-Aryan period. The images of Śiva as father-god, lord of animals and ascetic are seen to be pre-vedic. One of the Harappan seals depicts a three-faced deity seated cross-legged and deep in meditation, surrounded by animals. This yogic figure corresponds with the later conceptions of Śiva as a Mahāyogin (the great ascetic), as Pāśupati (lord of the beasts), and as having three eyes and a trident. Śiva is identified with the Rudra of the Veda, who is both a destructive and a beneficent deity. The vedic storm-god, Rudra, has developed into a great god, Śiva, merging with pre-vedic god-concepts.

ŚIVA AS *TRIMŪRTI*

Śiva seems to hold together all opposites, tensions and contradictions in a variety of ways. Although he is primarily the destroyer of evil, he is also portrayed in the three-fold form, *Trimūrti*, as creator, preserver and destroyer of evil. The Mahādeva image in the Elephanta Caves in Bombay shows Śiva representing these triple aspects. The three faces also represent the masculine and feminine aspects – the face to the left shows Śiva in his terrifying aspect (*bhairava*) and the face to the right shows his gentler nature. The silent and serene face in the centre harmonises the two aspects of terror and love – the Supreme that transcends all contradictions.

The elaboration of this concept of *Trimūrti* is seen as an attempt to harmonise Vaiṣṇavism and Śaivism. Vaiṣṇavas look upon Viṣṇu as the supreme god and Śiva as an emanation or creation of Viṣṇu, while Śaivas regard Śiva as the high god and Viṣṇu as an emanation of Śiva. They were occasionally at loggerheads over this issue, but generally Vaiṣṇavas and Śaivas have lived together without friction, acknowledging that both Viṣṇu and Śiva are manifestations of the same Divine Being. Another significant attempt at such a synthesis is seen in the representation of Śiva as Harihara, Hari being a title of Viṣṇu and Hara of Śiva. In Sangameshvara temple in Mysore, Śiva is depicted in sculpture as Harihara. The holy city of Hardwar is associated with both Śiva and Viṣṇu. The holy river Ganges flows through the hair of Śiva and the feet of Viṣṇu, so it is sacred to both Śaivas and Vaiṣṇavas.

ŚIVA AS NAṬARĀJA

Śiva has many names and one of the best-known is Naṭarāja, the Lord of the Dance. In this aspect Śiva is associated with the arts. Exponents of Indian classical dance look upon him as the supreme dancer who revealed the rules of the sacred dance to men and women. As Lord of the Dance, Śiva symbolises the cosmic energy that flows through and sustains the world and the universe. The eternal dance involves the destruction of evil, which brings about new creation. In this form he performs all the three functions – creation, preservation and destruction of evil. Unlike the ascetic Śiva, whose hair is collected in a top-knot, the dancing Śiva has his hair loose. It symbolises power, strength and energy. While the ascetic Śiva conserves his energy, the dancing Śiva releases it – and both for the good of the world. All apparent tensions are held in a harmonious unison.

The four-armed dancing Śiva in the renowned South Indian temple at Cidambaram holds a drum and a fire-ball in two of his hands (Figure 1). The drum symbolises rhythm and sound – both are associated with creation. Sound is associated with ether, one of the five elements of the universe (the others being air, fire, water and earth). The fire-ball and the circle of flames around Śiva symbolise the destruction of the world. He is the symbol of life and death and the renewal of life. The hand in upright gesture, *abhaya mudrā*,

Figure 1 Śiva as Naṭarāja, Lord of the Dance
(By Kathy Wedell)

signifies grace and protection, and the one pointing to his feet signifies that liberation is open to all those who seek refuge in him. He has one foot on a demon, symbolising the triumph over evil, ignorance or ego. The dynamic movements of his body stand in sharp contrast to his serene yogic face.

An invocatory hymn in praise of Lord Naṭarāja precedes any South Indian classical dance. All fine arts, including dance, have a spiritual dimension to them. *Devadāsīs* ('servants of God') were married to the gods, and they sought union with God through dance. Even today a devoted dancer sees her dance as a spiritual journey leading to the Divine (see 'Hinduism' in *Women in Religion* in this series).

ŚIVA AS *YOGI* AND *GṚHASTHA*

Śiva figures as a great *yogi* (ascetic) and a *gṛhastha* (householder). He symbolises both renunciation and affirmation of life. Both as ascetic and householder he is the source of life. The ascetic Śiva is represented seated in a yogic posture (cross-legged) on a tiger-skin, with prayer beads and a mendicant's bowl. The third eye in the middle of his forehead is interpreted as the eye of wisdom and enlightenment. The snake around his neck shows his association with death and his power to retain sexual energy. He holds in his left hand a trident (symbol of power) which represents the triple aspects of Śiva as creator, preserver and destroyer. His right hand is held in *abhaya mudrā* (upright position) assuring protection. The three horizontal marks in the middle of his forehead also indicate the three functions of Śiva. Śaivas may wear this mark on their foreheads. His long matted hair, raised up in a top-knot with a crescent moon on it (symbol of creation) and water flowing from it, brings out the dual nature of Śiva: serenity and dynamism. Śiva retains and releases his energy for the benefit of the world. Sometimes a small figure of the goddess Gaṅgā is seen on his top knot, showing Śiva's close association with the river Ganges. In order to reduce the forceful impact of the flow of the river Ganges upon the earth, Śiva allows the river to flow smoothly through his hair, thus fertilising the earth. The river Ganges is *śakti*, or the feminine aspect of Śiva.

In the South Indian Mīnākṣī temple in Madurai, Śiva is known as Sundraeśvara and his consort is Mīnākṣī. In popular art Śiva is seen with his wife, Pārvatī, and their children, Gaṇeśa and Kārttikeya (also known as Skanda or Murugan). Śiva nourishes and sustains the world, both as a householder (*gṛhastha*) and as an ascetic (*sannyāsin*); these two stages being the second and fourth in the pattern of Hindu life.

ŚIVA AS DAKṢIṆĀMŪRTI

As a universal guru or spiritual teacher Śiva is known as Dakṣiṇāmūrti. As expounder of sacred knowledge he is known as Jñāna Dakṣiṇāmūrti (*Jñāna* means 'knowledge', *dakṣiṇa*, South, and *mūrti*, image of the deity). He is depicted seated facing south, his right foot resting on the demon (symbolising ignorance), and his left foot on his right thigh and his right hand in a *mudrā* (gesture) of explanation. Śiva's various other names, such as Vīṇādhara Dakṣiṇāmūrti (teacher of music), Yoga Dakṣiṇāmūrti (teacher and master of *yoga*), show him as the patron of all the arts.

ŚIVA AS MASCULINE AND FEMININE

Śiva is also depicted iconographically as *Ardhanāri* (half-female and half-male), symbolising the union of the feminine and masculine. One of the myths in the *Śiva Purāṇa* tells that Śiva assumed this form to help Brahmā complete the task of creation. Brahmā created a number of males to begin the work of creation but his mission was unsuccessful. Hearing his prayers, Śiva appeared in the androgynous form of *Ardhanārīśvara*. On seeing Śiva in this form, Brahmā realised that without the creation of the female, he could not complete his task. Without the activating power of the feminine principle (*śakti*) creation will remain incomplete. This myth conveys the upaniṣadic idea of the divine being both male and female (*Bṛhādaraṇyaka Upaniṣad* 1.4.3).

In Śaiva temples Śiva is worshipped in the form of *liṅga* (a phallic symbol) in association with *yoni* (womb). It is cylindrical in shape with a rounded top rising out of a horizontal base, the *yoni*. This symbol lends itself to a variety of interpretations. It is seen as symbolising the union and co-existence of the male and female principles. The *liṅga* represents creativity at all levels: biological, psychological, spiritual and cosmic. In some of the temple sculptures, the *liṅga* is depicted with the face of Śiva (*Mukhaliṅga*) or four faces (*Caturmukha*) – and the fifth face represented by the *liṅga*. The five-faced *liṅga* represents the five elements of the universe.

Liṅga is the most important symbol of Śiva and the main object of Śaiva worship. The holy city of Kāśī, meaning 'luminous' or 'shining' (also known as Banaras or Varanasi), is dotted with *liṅga*s and numerous shrines to Śiva. The city itself is seen as a *liṅga* of light. It is said that Śiva's *liṅga*, a fiery column of light, arose from the netherworlds, piercing the earth and sky at Kāśī. Here the Divine has manifested itself in the form of *liṅga*, so the city is seen as the very embodiment of Śiva himself. To die in Kāśī is seen as being sanctified and purified of all sins.[2]

On the festival of *Śivarātri*, Hindus fast and sing hymns in praise of Śiva. Śaiva temples all over India are crowded with devotees who come to offer their devotions and have a *darśan* (view or glimpse) of Śiva and receive *prasāda* (blessed food).

Śiva's mount, the sacred bull, Nandi, is found in Śaiva temples, usually at the entrance, facing the shrine. It is Śiva in his animal form, symbolising fertility.

The veneration of the *liṅga* was common among non-Aryan peoples and later became the most important form of worship among the Śaivas.

Gaṇeśa

GAṆEŚA AS REMOVER OF OBSTACLES

Gaṇeśa is one of the most popular Hindu deities worshipped all over India. He is represented as a pot-bellied deity with four (or more) arms and the head of an elephant, but with a single tusk, and accompanied by a mouse (see Figure 2). The elephant-head is seen as signifying macrocosm, and his body, microcosm. In other words, the half-elephant and half-human form of Gaṇeśa stands for the cosmic and human dimensions of existence. His large belly is seen as containing within it the entire created world. It also signifies prosperity.

Gaṇeśa may be shown in various postures: sitting, standing or dancing. In some iconographical representations he may be shown with two tusks (one whole and one broken), and holding in his hands a goad, noose, rosary and the broken tusk. The unbroken tusk symbolises the unmanifest Truth and the broken one represents the manifest world. Both the abstract and manifest world are two aspects of the One Reality. The noose indicates the need to restrain desires and passions, the goad is a symbol of authority and the rosary is associated with Śaiva meditation and mendicants. In some representations Gaṇeśa may be shown holding a sweetmeat in one of

Figure 2 Gaṇeśa as remover of obstacles
(By Usha Azad)

his hands, indicating his fondness for sweets, and his right hand is usually in *abhaya mudrā*, assuring protection. The swastika is a symbol also associated with Gaṇeśa, and it represents good luck. His large fan-like ears signify his willingness to listen to problems. The elephant trunk symbolises Gaṇeśa's role as remover of obstacles, and his mount, a mouse, is seen as performing the task of removing obstacles by drilling holes and finding its way to its destination. Both the elephant and the mouse, in different ways, remove obstacles on the way. On the other hand, the mouse is also an obstacle to our undertakings. Gaṇeśa's task is to create and remove obstacles. His association with the mouse shows that he cares for even the most ordinary creatures.

Gaṇeśa is also represented as the master of the arts. He is depicted in a graceful dancing pose. In this form he is called Nṛttagaṇapati (dancing Gaṇeśa). He is also worshipped in aniconic forms such as *yantras* (geometrical diagrams), *liṅgas* and *kalaśas* (pots of water).

Gaṇeśa is sometimes shown with his two wives, Siddhi and Ṛddhi. Siddhi symbolises success, and Ṛddhi, prosperity. Gaṇeśa is known by many names but most commonly called Piḷḷaiyār ('the son or the young elephant') or Gaṇapati ('lord of the group'), especially in South India. Some of his names give a visual picture of the deity. He is called Gajānana ('elephant-faced'), Ekadanta ('single tusked'), Lambodara ('pot-bellied'), Vighneśvara ('Lord of obstacles'), Vināyaka ('leader'). He is also known as lord of learning or wisdom. The Gāṇapatyas sect (South and Western India) look upon him as their supreme deity and offer special devotions to him.

As Gaṇeśa is the remover of obstacles, his blessings are invoked before embarking on any new venture, whether it be buying a house, or applying for a job or going on a journey. Most Śaiva temples in India have shrines to Gaṇeśa. Both rural and urban India have countless shrines to Gaṇeśa. Sometimes he is comfortably seated under a banyan tree. Most students pay a visit to his shrine just before exams to pray for success, and offer coconuts to Gaṇeśa on passing their exams.

GAṆEŚA AS GUARDIAN DEITY

There are many legends associated with the birth and beheading of Gaṇeśa. According to one of them, Pārvatī created Gaṇeśa from the scurf of her body. She asked him to guard the house while she had her bath. In the meantime, Śiva arrived but was refused entry into the house by Gaṇeśa. A quarrel ensued between the two and Śiva cut off Gaṇeśa's head. Pārvatī was annoyed and demanded that her son should be brought back to life. Śiva replaced Gaṇeśa's lost head with the head of an elephant with a single tusk, as this was the first one his attendants chanced upon, and made Gaṇeśa the lord of his attendants. Gaṇeśa's role as a guardian deity and remover of obstacles is further enhanced by his newly acquired elephant-head which has close associations with the elephant symbolism in Indian culture. Elephants are associated with Hindu deities and guard the door of temples, and lead religious and royal processions.

The festival of *Gaṇeśa Caturthī* celebrates the birth of Gaṇeśa and is popular in most parts of India, particularly in western, central and southern India. Small and large clay images of Gaṇeśa are made for the festival and worship is offered to them. This festival is celebrated in a grand style in and around Bombay. Large clay images of Gaṇeśa are carried out in a ceremonial procession through the crowded streets and eventually to the seashore in Bombay and immersed in the sea.

Skanda as Devasenāpati, Subramaṇya and Saṇmukha

Skanda, the second son of Śiva and Pārvatī, is a complete contrast to his brother, Gaṇeśa. He is young and handsome. He is usually depicted (see Figure 3) with two (or four) hands, holding a sword and a spear, symbolising his triumph over the demons. In other words, it signifies the destruction of ignorance. He may be shown standing by, or seated on, a peacock, on whose legs a snake lies entangled. The snake symbolises time and the peacock the transcendence of time and all dualities. The peacock also signifies the beauty and splendour of all creation. Skanda is sometimes seen with his two consorts, Vallī and Devasenā.

Skanda figures as Devasenāpati, the god of war and a military commander. He was born in order to destroy the demon Tārakā. He is more popular in South India than in the North. He is known as Subramaṇya ('one who tends the spiritual growth of the aspirants') and more popularly as Murugan in the South. He is also known as Kumāra (Prince). Most temples to Murugan in South India are

Figure 3 Skanda and his vehicle, the peacock
(By Usha Azad)

situated on a hill-top. The Murugan temple in Palani in South India is a well-known pilgrimage place. The Skanda Vale ashram in rural Wales is a place of spiritual retreat and worship. It has become an important pilgrimage centre for Hindus in the United Kingdom.

It is said that Skanda was brought up by six divine mothers of the star, Kṛttika (Pleiades), and therefore came to be called Ṣaṇmuka (six-faced) and Kārttikeya. In this form he is shown with six faces and twelve arms. The six faces of this deity symbolise six divine attributes and six seats of spiritual consciousness. The twelve hands indicate his power and capacity to accomplish all kinds of tasks.

Feminine images of the Divine

The Divine is perceived and experienced as both male and female. The *Upaniṣads* affirm the masculine and feminine dimensions of the Divine and the spiritual equality of both male and female (see 'Hinduism' in *Women in Religion* in this series). The Divine feminine is seen as *śakti* or energy (see below and p. 99) and is of central importance in *tantric* tradition. Feminine images of the Divine such as virgin (*kumārī*), consort, mother, daughter, warrior, sustainer, and as both love and terror, are represented in worship, art, literature and iconography. The female counterparts of the male gods Brahmā, Viṣṇu and Śiva are Sarasvatī, Lakṣmī and Pārvatī (and her other forms, Durgā and Kālī), are associated with wisdom, wealth and power respectively, and are worshipped in their own right.

THE DIVINE AS VIRGIN

The image of the Divine as a virgin, or *kanyā kumārī*, is represented in a South Indian temple in Kanya Kumari (formerly Cape Comorin). Although Kanyā Kumārī is unmarried, she is said to answer the prayers of those who wish to be married. She is an embodiment of *śakti*, or divine energy, and her virgin status signifies her creative power.

THE DIVINE AS *ŚAKTI*

The many goddesses are seen as many aspects or manifestations of the one supreme principle or energy known as *śakti*, the feminine power, usually addressed as Devī (Goddess) or Mahādevī (the Great Goddess) – the ground and centre of all creation and existence. The well-known text, *Devi-māhātmya* ('The Exaltation of the Goddess'), of the sixth century CE, affirms the primacy of the feminine power or *śakti*. *Śakti* is known by various names. She is linked to the masculine as *śakti*, or power inherent in it, without which the male principle is incomplete. Without the activating power of *śakti*, Śiva is said to be incomplete. In her gracious form she is Mahālakṣmī and Mahāsarasvatī, and in her terrible form she is Mahākālī. As Mahāsarasvatī she is the goddess of supreme knowledge, as Mahālakṣmī she is the goddess of supreme love and grace and as Mahākālī she is the goddess of supreme strength who conquers evil and is the embodiment and reconciliation of all apparent opposites. Both in her benign and terrible forms she offers comfort and solace (see 'Hinduism' in *Women in Religion* in this series).

Sarasvatī as bestower of knowledge and wisdom

Sarasvatī, the consort of Brahmā, is the goddess of wisdom and fine arts. She is usually depicted with four arms, holding a stringed musical instrument called *vīnā* with two hands (symbol of arts), and manuscripts (symbol of wisdom and learning), and a string of prayer beads (see Figure 4). Her vehicle, a swan, symbolises spiritual perfection and transcendence. Sometimes she is seen with a peacock, or standing or seated on a lotus flower (symbol of purity), which also symbolises the transcendence of all imperfections. She is usually draped in a white sari and her face is calm and benign, signifying the quality of *sattva guṇa* (goodness and purity). Although Brahmā is associated with sacred rituals and knowledge, it is Sarasvatī who plays an active role in imparting wisdom and perfecting every mode of expression. She symbolises all forms of artistic and intellectual knowledge and expression.

Sarasvatī is popular among all classes of people and is worshipped on her special day by students, teachers, scholars and others. Most Hindus perform Sarasvatī-*pūjā* in their homes during the festival of *Navarātri*. Sacred books, academic texts and musical instruments are placed before the image of the goddess and her blessings for the growth of knowledge and wisdom are sought.

As well as through stories and festivals, Hindu children learn about their tradition through dance and music. There is no strict demarcation between the sacred and secular areas of life and activity. Dance, music, knowledge, wealth are very much intertwined

Figure 4 Sarasvatī, goddess of wisdom and fine arts (By Usha Azad)

with the sacred dimension of life. Lord Naṭarāja is the patron of dance and all forms of art (see Śiva pp. 89–91 above), and Indian classical music is seen as having its origin in one of the sacred texts of the primary scriptures, *Sāma-veda*, which was chanted during the vedic fire-sacrifice (*yagna*) ceremony. Music plays an important part in worship, and on religious occasions women are expected to chant or sing devotional hymns. Most Hindus start the day listening to devotional music. Audio-cassettes of Sanskrit *slokas*, sacred verses in praise of various deities and their attributes, are easily available and they are also played on special occasions such as Sarasvatī- or Durgā-*pūjā*, when the goddesses are honoured in a special way.

The Goddess Sarasvatī was originally associated with a river in the Vedas, and with the goddess of speech, *Vāc*. Later, she came to be associated with wisdom, learning and all forms of creative art. As the goddess of creative speech or sound, Sarasvatī embodies the power of the sacred *śabda* (sound). The conception of the Divine in the form of sound (*Śabda-Brahman*), from which all creation proceeds, finds expression in Hindu sacred literature and in some iconographical representations, especially in the dance of Śiva who holds a drum in one of his hands, symbolising the origin of sound.

There are many accounts of Sarasvatī's origin. It is said that Brahmā divided himself into two halves – male and female – in order to create the world but fell in love with the female half and she became his consort. In some myths Sarasvatī's origin is associated with Viṣṇu and Kṛṣṇa.

Lakṣmī

LAKṢMĪ AS GODDESS OF WEALTH AND PROSPERITY

Goddess Lakṣmī (consort of Viṣṇu) symbolises wealth, prosperity and good luck. In popular iconographical pictures Lakṣmī is shown with four arms (see Figure 5). In two of her hands she holds a lotus flower (symbolising purity), her right hand is held in an upright gesture (*abhaya mudrā*), symbolising assurance, and from her lower left hand fall gold coins, symbolising wealth and prosperity. As Gaja-Lakṣmī, she is depicted standing on a lotus flower, which is her main symbol, with a white elephant (*gaja*) on each side, representing royalty. She is shown holding a lotus flower, a fruit, pot of *amṛta*, or nectar, and a conch shell (*śaṅkha*), symbolising protection and liberation.

In mythology Lakṣmī is said to have emerged from the primeval ocean with a radiant lotus in her hand, along with the other divine treasures which the gods were trying to rescue. Śiva desired Lakṣmī

Figure 5 Lakṣmī, goddess of wealth, prosperity and good luck (By Usha Azad)

as his wife, but since he had already taken possession of the crescent-moon, she became the consort of Viṣṇu. It is said that Śiva's disappointment at the loss distracted him and led him to hold in his throat the poison emitted by the serpent so that he came to be called Nīlakaṇṭha, the 'Blue-necked One'.

Earlier associated with kingly power and royal authority, Lakṣmī is known as *śrī* ('beauty' and good fortune) and worshipped along with Viṣṇu. The couple symbolise marital harmony, prosperity and stability. She is shown seated on Viṣṇu's right thigh, with his left arm around her waist and her right arm around Viṣṇu's neck.

Lakṣmī is worshipped on various occasions during the year. Women perform Vara Lakṣmī-*pūjā* in the month of August. In this form she offers boons and assures prosperity and long life. The Hindu festival *Diwālī* is particularly associated with the worship of Lakṣmī. For Gujarati Hindus *Diwālī* is beginning of the New Year and the financial year. Business men and women place their account books before the image of Lakṣmī and have their books blessed by the priest. The pursuit of wealth (*artha*, one of the four aims of Hindu life) is seen as legitimate as long as one acquires it by proper means and for useful purposes, such as providing for the needs of family, society and community.[3]

Lakṣmī plays an important role in Śrī Vaiṣṇava philosophy and devotion. She figures as an intercessor between Viṣṇu and his devotees. She has a central place in the Vaiṣṇava Pāñcarātra school of philosophy. She is associated with the cosmic functions of Brahmā, Viṣṇu and Śiva. As the female counterpart of Viṣṇu she is linked with the creation and evolution of the universe. When worshipped on her own, Lakṣmī is regarded as 'Lokamātā', mother of the world.

LAKṢMĪ AS DEVOTED WIFE

Lakṣmī is sometimes shown with two arms when she is seen with Viṣṇu, massaging his feet with devotion. In popular iconography Lakṣmī is often shown with Viṣṇu, riding on Garuḍa, the divine eagle in whose claws a snake lies entangled. Both the animals are representations of Viṣṇu and Lakṣmī – symbols of opposite forces harmonised in Viṣṇu. The eagle, which symbolises the sky and the sun, is at constant war with the snake, which symbolises the watery-element (the source of life). Unless a balance of opposites is maintained, the harmony of the world and the universe is believed to be at risk.

Lakṣmī figures as the consort of Viṣṇu in each of his incarnations.

When Viṣṇu took the form of Vāmana, the dwarf *avatāra*, Lakṣmī emerged from the waters, gliding on the flower of a lotus, and hence came to be called Padmā (lotus) or Kamalā. When Viṣṇu assumed the form of Paraśurāma, Lakṣmī came down to the earth as his wife, Dharanī. When Viṣṇu appeared as Rāma, Lakṣmī was Sītā and when he came as Kṛṣṇa, she appeared as his favourite *gopi* Rādhā and as his wife, Rukmiṇī.

The Divine feminine as Mahādevī

The many feminine forms of the Divine are seen as embodiments of the Great Goddess (Mahādevī), who is manifest in all creation as *śakti* or divine energy. Mahādevi has many names, forms and attributes and has a central role in some myths. She is known as Umā (knowledge), Satī (virtuous wife), Haimavatī (the daughter of Himavan, god of the Himalayas), Pārvatī ('from the mountains'), Durgā ('inaccessible') and Kālī ('black' and 'time'), originally associated with the vedic fire-god Agni.

SATĪ AS VIRTUOUS WIFE

Each of the names throws light on her various functions. As Satī, she attracts Śiva into marriage by her devotion and ascetic practices, and marries him against her father's wishes. To save the honour of her husband (who was not invited to the sacrificial ceremony), she burns herself on the sacrificial fire. The grief-stricken Śiva carries Satī in his arms. In order to end Śiva's grief, which causes cosmic imbalance, Viṣṇu relieves Satī's body from Śiva's arms by slicing it until nothing is left. The various places where the pieces of Satī's corpse fell became sacred. The grief-stricken Śiva retreats to the mountains, though in some myths he goes in search of Satī. He eventually finds her in the form of *yoni* and he takes the form of the *liṅga* and enters into her and thus the two remain united forever. The underlying theme of Satī's myths shows the tension between, and reconciliation of, asceticism and love. Satī, in the form of *yoni*, attracts the ascetic Śiva from his seclusion and thus makes him accessible to the world in the form of *liṅga*.

The Goddess Satī is also associated with the practice of *satī*, widows immolating themselves on the funeral pyre of their husbands (see 'Hinduism' in *Women in Religion* in this series). However, it is not clear whether the death of the goddess is seen as a mythological model for *satī* (Kinsley 1987: 40).

Pārvatī as spiritual partner

As with Satī, Pārvatī's main role in mythology is to draw the ascetic Śiva into marriage so that the stored-up energy of Śiva is released for the benefit of the world. She even goes to the extent of performing severe austerities (*tapas*) to win the hand of Śiva and thus make him fulfil the role of a householder. Śiva is impressed by her ability to do *tapas* to win him, and thus considers her a worthy partner. The tension between the householder ideal and the ascetic ideal is the underlying theme of myths concerning Śiva and Pārvatī. The reconciliation between the two finds expression in mythology and iconographical representations of Pārvatī and Śiva. The Śiva–Śakti dance, Śiva as Ardhānarīśvara (half-man and half-woman), and *liṅga* and *yoni* are some of the best examples.

The marriage of Śiva to Pārvatī is the subject of popular iconography. They are shown walking round the sacred fire, Agni, and receiving blessings from Brahmā, Viṣṇu and Indra. Śiva marries Pārvatī in his ascetic garb (clad in a tiger skin). In popular art they are depicted as a happy couple with their two children, Gaṇeśa and Skanda. In the *Purāṇa*s they are shown seated upon the mountain Kailāsa, engrossed in either love-making or philosophical debate. In the southern school of Śaiva Siddhānta, Pārvatī figures as Śiva's 'embodied grace'. Pārvatī and Śiva are also depicted dancing together and this dance is called *Umā-tāṇḍava*. *Tāṇḍava* is a vigorous type of dance associated with Śiva who performs the cosmic dance of creation and destruction of evil.

Durgā

DURGĀ AS WARRIOR AND SUSTAINER

Durgā, the fierce form of Pārvatī, figures as a warrior and mother goddess. She is the feminine energy or power, *śakti*, of Śiva. In iconographical representations Durgā is depicted with eight or ten arms, each holding a weapon given by the male gods (symbolising divine power), riding a tiger or lion, *siṃha*, (symbolising power and authority), and in the act of destroying the demon who was invulnerable to all enemies except a woman. She is also known as Daśabhujā ('the ten-handed One') and Siṃhavāhinī ('the one who rides the lion'). She is both fierce (as her name suggests) and beautiful, and is usually dressed in red.

The gentle Pārvatī assumes the form of a warrior goddess to slay the buffalo demon, Mahiṣāsura, who threatened the balance of the world. From then on she came to be called Durgā. She destroys Mahiṣāsura, who attacks her unsuccessfully, by changing his form quickly into a lion, elephant, etc. In this form Durgā is known as Mahiṣāsuramardinī, the slayer of Mahiṣāsura. She acts independently on the battlefield to vanquish the demon. She does not seek the support of the male gods who created her. Instead she fights with the help of female assistants whom she creates from herself.

During the festival of Durgā-*pūjā* in Bengal, beautiful clay images of the warrior goddess are housed in temporary shrines built for the purpose and at the end of the festival the images are taken on a truck to be immersed in the river Hooghly.

The worship of Durgā as a warrior goddess was common among kings and rulers who sought success in battle. The Hindu festival *Daśarā* (also known as *Navarātri*) is associated with Durgā, to whom Rāma prayed for victory in his battle against Rāvaṇa, who had abducted his wife Sītā. The success of the Pāṇḍava brothers in their fight against the Kauravas in the *Mahābhārata* is also associated with Durgā. Arjuna, one of the five Pāṇḍava brothers, sings a hymn in praise of Durgā's military valour, seeking her help in overcoming their opponents.

Durgā departs from traditional norms of womanly behaviour. Her place seems to be not so much in the home as on the battlefield. She, like Kālī, is associated with blood, death and destruction of evil. Durgā, originally associated with the tribal non-Aryan peoples who offered her animal sacrifices, assumes a central role in medieval and later Hinduism. Durgā plays a similar role to that of Viṣṇu, as sustainer and preserver of *dharma*. She intervenes when order and harmony are threatened and restores peace.

DURGĀ AS MOTHER AND DAUGHTER

Although Durgā is often portrayed as an independent deity, she assumes a domestic role in her later history. She is motherly and is fondly called Ambā (mother) or Durgā Ma. In this role she is associated with Pārvatī who represents the domestic ideal (marriage and family). In popular pictures she is shown as the mother of Gaṇeśa and Kārttikeya, Lakṣmī and Sarasvatī.

In Bengal, the Durgā-*pūjā* has a special significance. Durgā figures in the role of a daughter returning to her family during the festival (as is the custom) and departing to her husband's home after the festival. The festival re-enacts the joy of parents who eagerly look forward to their daughters' arrival and their sadness at their departure. The festival is also associated with agriculture and fertility of the crops. In the North Indian tradition, Durgā's role as mother and daughter is far more pronounced than in the South Indian tradition, where she is depicted as a fiercely independent deity whose sexuality is said to be dangerous.

The Divine feminine as love and terror: Kālī

KĀLĪ AS CONQUEROR OF EVIL

Śiva's *śakti* in terrifying form is Kālī. She is the goddess of destruction of evil but at the same time she initiates new creation. Kālī is depicted with four arms (sometimes ten) holding in three hands, a sword, a trident, and the severed head of a demon, while the fourth one offers protection to her devotees. She is seen wearing a garland of skulls around her neck, almost naked except for a belt made of the severed hands of the demons, and dancing on the prostrate body of her husband Śiva. She is dark blue (*shyma*) or sometimes black (*kālī*), as her name indicates, and Kālī also means 'time'. Her hair is dishevelled and her tongue, dripping with blood, hangs out.

In mythology, Kālī kills the demon Raktavīja who had been granted a boon of being born several times and of becoming more powerful each time a drop of his blood was shed. In fact, Kālī drinks the blood that gushes forth from his wound to the last drop, to conquer evil. She becomes blood-thirsty and goes about killing all the demons. Realising that this frenzied cosmic dance of destruction would threaten the universal balance, Śiva throws himself down at the feet of Kālī to calm her fury. When Kālī discovers that she is dancing on her husband, she stands aghast with her mouth wide open and her long red tongue jutting out. In this pose she is known as Daksiṇakālī ('south facing'). In the South Indian tradition, however, both of them perform the vigorous *Tāṇḍava* dance in which Kālī is subdued. This myth has also been interpreted in more philosophical categories. The passive Śiva under the feet of Kālī and the dynamic activity of Kālī are seen as two different but complementary aspects of the Absolute. Kālī's fierce nature is also evident in her other forms as Caṇḍi ('the fierce') and Bhairavī ('the terrible'). Here Kālī is the female counterpart of Śiva as Bhairava.

Kālī is both attractive and repulsive. In her terrible and ghastly form she is associated with the battlefield or the cremation ground. She is very popular among tribals and others, who offer her blood offerings. She takes life to feed herself and at the same time gives life. Like Śiva, she is the embodiment and reconciliation of apparent contradictions. Kālī plays a central role in Tantrism and popular worship. She is seen as the principal divine energy or force, *śakti*, from whom all else unfolds. She challenges conventional patriarchal standards and traditional norms of purity and pollution. While Pārvatī's role is to attract the ascetic Śiva into the world of domesticity, marriage and love, Kālī's role, on the contrary, is to drag Śiva into vigorous activity – annihilating forces of evil and ignorance and initiating new birth. It is not surprising that contemporary Hindu women look to Kālī as their model. The publishing house Kālī in Delhi was set up by two women. They chose the name Kālī as she stands for the destruction of ignorance.

KĀLĪ AS MOTHER

In Bengal, Kālī is worshipped as the Divine Mother, and the festival, *Diwālī*, is associated with her. Although blood-thirsty and far removed from conventional norms of behaviour, Kālī also assumes a maternal role. She is associated with death but at the same time she is the source of all life. Great Bengali saints of the last two centuries, such as Ramprasad and Sri Ramakrishna and his disciple Vivekananda, were ardent devotees of Kālī and looked upon her as mother. They longed to have her *darśan*, to see her face to face (see below p. 110). Vivekananda's disciple, Margaret Noble (Sister Nivedita), an Irish woman, speaks fondly of Kālī in her book, *Kālī the Mother*. At the end of her book is a poem on Kālī written by Swami Vivekananda.

> For Terror is thy name,
> Death is Thy Breath,
> And every shaking step
> Destroys a world for e'er.
> Thou 'Time' the All-Destroyer!
> Then come, O Mother, Come!
>
> Who can misery love,
> Dance in destruction's dance,
> And hug the form of Death, –
> To him the Mother comes.
>
> (Nivedita 1983: 111)

The image of the Divine as Mother is far more dominant than other feminine images at the popular level. Pre-Aryan beliefs seem, to a great extent, to have been centred on feminine imagery, and female divinities rose to prominence again in post-vedic and classical times. The sacred river Ganges is also personified as Mother (Gaṅgā Ma). A holy dip in her waters is seen as purifying one of all impurities. As mother, she nourishes and sustains those who come seeking her. *Mokṣa*, or salvation, is granted by her. The image of mother goddess became far more pronounced during the Indian struggle for independence, especially in Bengal. Kālī was seen as Bengal personified. Legend has it that while Śiva was carrying the dismembered body of Satī, the toe of her right foot fell on earth near the river Ganges, where a temple to Kālī was built. It came to be known as the Kālīghāt temple, and Calcutta derives its name from a neighbouring village Kalikata. In some parts of India Kālī is symbolised by a black or dark-blue stone.

Village deities as both malevolent and benevolent

The village deities, *grāma devatās*, are predominantly female and they are perceived as both malevolent and benevolent. The villagers are less directly concerned with the deities of the Hindu pantheon than with the *grāma devatās*, which are far more involved in the day-to-day life of the villagers. They bring death, disease and famine, and at the same time protect villagers from them. The village goddess in the form of mother is known as *amman* in South India. There are many *amman*s such as Kanaka Durgamman and Māriyamman (bringer of small pox). The fiercer goddesses, called *śakti*s, have no specific temples or image. It is doubtful whether they have any links with Durgā or Kāli who, as *śakti*s of Śiva, manifest the energy of the male gods.

Darśan of the Divine

Hindus go to a temple to have a *darśan*, or glimpse or vision, of the deity. The word means 'seeing'. Hindus consider it a blessing to behold the image of the deity beautifully adorned with ornaments and flowers and to witness the *āratī*-light being waved before the deity. This 'seeing' is auspicious and brings blessings of the deity to the beholder.

For most Hindus the image is more than a symbol. Once the image of the deity is consecrated in a temple, in a rite called *prāṇa-pratiṣṭhā* ('putting in the breath'), it becomes sacred. The officiating priest implores the deity to come and dwell in the image. From then onwards, the image becomes the living presence of the deity. The Divine is seen as making itself accessible through the image to its worshippers. This communion between the deity and the worshipper is of supreme importance to most Hindus. Worship involves seeing, touching, offering fruits, flowers and incense to the deity, and this helps the worshippers to develop a close relationship with their chosen deities. A deep yearning for the divine finds expression in *bhakti*, devotional literature. In worship *Saguṇa Brahman* (with attributes) is the object of devotion.

For Hindu monists the images have only a symbolic value. They are no more than aids to meditation and worship. They aim at experiencing *Nirguṇa Brahman* (without attributes), who is beyond all thought and speculation. The monist Hindu, who sees *Brahman* as non-personal, and the theist Hindu, who sees *Brahman* as personal, are seeing the same Reality but in different ways and are emphasising the two different but complementary aspects of

Brahman. The conceptions and experiences of *Brahman* as utterly transcendent and as personal lord and creator are seen as equally valid. The paths of *karma-yoga* (selfless action), *bhakti-yoga* (love and devotion) or *jñana-yoga* (knowledge and contemplation) merge with one another without losing their distinctiveness. Together they lead to an integral vision and experience of the Divine as both matter and spirit, form and formlessness, male and female, love and terror, immanent and transcendent, finite and infinite.

NOTES

1. All quotations from the *Bhagavadgītā* are taken from Radhakrishnan, S. (1971) *The Bhagavadgītā* (First Indian Reprint), Bombay, George Allen & Unwin. For other scriptural references see Zaehner, R.C. (trans) (1966) *Hindu Scriptures*, London, J.M. Dent.
2. See Eck, D.L. (1982) *Banāras, City of Light*, New York, Alfred A. Knopf.
3. The other three aims are *kāma* (artistic and sensual fulfilment), *dharma* (righteousness) and *mokṣa* (salvation). It is important that one's actions and goals in life are guided and governed by *dharma*.

FURTHER READING

Alston, A.J. (trans) (1980) *The Devotional Poems of Mīrabāi*, Delhi, Motilal Banarsidass.

Aurobindo, Sri (1955) *The Life Divine*, vol. 111, Pondicherry (India), Sri Aurobindo Ashram.

Coomaraswamy, A.K. (1982) *The Dance of Śiva* (2nd edn), New Delhi, Munshiram Manoharlal.

Coomaraswamy, A.K. and Sister Nivedita (1967) *Myths of the Hindus and Buddhists*, New York, Dover.

Courtright, P.B. (1985) *Gaṇeśa: Lord of Obstacles, Lord of Beginnings*, New York, Oxford University Press.

Eck, D.L. (1985) *Darśan: Seeing the Divine Image in India* (2nd revised and enlarged edn), Chambersburg, Anima Books.

Gupte, R.S. (1980) *Iconography of the Hindus, Buddhists, and Jains* (2nd edn), Bombay, D.B. Taraporevala.

Harshananda, Swami (1981) *Hindu Gods and Goddesses*, Mysore, Sri Ramakrishna Ashrama.

Ions, V. (1967) *Indian Mythology*, London, Paul Hamlyn.

Kinsley, D. (1987) *Hindu Goddesses: Visions of the Divine Feminine in the Hindu Religious Tradition*, Delhi, Motilal Banarsidas.

Mookerjee, A. (1988) *Kālī: The Feminine Force*, London, Thames and Hudson.

Moore, A.C. (1977) *Iconography of Religions: An Introduction*, London, SCM Press.

Nivedita, Sister (1983) *Kālī The Mother* (2nd edn), Mayavati, Himalayas, Advaita Ashrama.

O'Flaherty, W.D. (1981) *Śiva: The Erotic Ascetic* (first published in 1973 under the title *Asceticism and Eroticism in the Mythology of Śiva*), London, Oxford University Press.

Panikkar, R. (1989) *The Vedic Experience: Mantramañjarī* (2nd edn), Pondicherry, All India Books.

Stutley, M. (1985) *The Illustrated Dictionary of Hindu Iconography*, London, Routledge and Kegan Paul.

4. Islam

Clinton Bennett

Muslims picture God conceptually, not artistically or visually. Muslim theology paints word pictures to describe the nature of the divine being, or reality. Islamic mysticism has produced beautiful and eloquent poetry, full of metaphors that vividly portray the mystics' understanding and experience of God, and of the soul's search for, and final absorption into, the divine unity. All Muslim thinking, and writing, about God begins with the concept of *tawḥīd*, unity, or oneness, but the word also denotes harmony, balance, integration of all divine attributes and of all reality into the one ultimate being. An early chapter of the Qur'ān, Islam's scripture, is *sūrah* 112, *Tawḥīd*. Popularly, this *sūrah* is known as the 'essence of the Qur'ān', which indicates how crucial this short chapter of only four verses is as a foundation for almost all Islam's theological thinking. Muslims believe that the Qur'ān is God's final, complete revelation of his straight path for all people; containing no element of human thought whatsoever, it is word for word God's *kalām* (speech).

The scriptural origin of Islam's conceptual world

This definitive revelation of God's will was revealed chapter by chapter to the prophet Muhammad (570–632), at different times during his life. The process began with Muhammad's call to prophecy in 610 and continued until his death. Thus the Qur'ān is the most authoritative source of knowledge about God, supplemented by the inspired life, and sayings, of its prophetic messenger. This *ilhām* (inspiration) makes the prophet's example in the moral, legal, political as well as in the devotional aspects of Islam authoritative for all Muslims, second in importance only to the Qur'ān. In this chapter, we shall discuss how Muslims conceive, or mentally picture God, beginning with the qur'anic material and with Muhammad's interpretation and understanding. Next, by visiting some of the classical debates between different schools of thought, we shall survey how Islamic theology developed these early concepts. Then we shall visit the language world of the Ṣūfīs, the Muslim mystics, who use poetry as skilfully as any artist uses the brush to picture God with their imageless imagery. Finally, we shall add a brief word about the relationship between Muslim concepts of God and abstract and calligraphic art forms in Islam, and also about mathematics as a science predicated, like so much else in Islam, on *tawḥīd*.

Qur'anic imagery

Muhammad himself described *sūrah* 112 as 'equivalent to one-third of the Qur'ān' (quoted in Zakaria 1991: 341). With the first *sūrah*, *Fātiḥah*, *sūrah* 112 is the most frequently recited chapter, always recited during prayers as part of the prescribed ritual. *Sūrah Tawḥīd* announces that God is indivisibly One, and that neither he, nor his power, can be compared with anything else: 'Proclaim to all: God is One; He is the only one. He is the eternal, the absolute. He has begotten none and of none has he been begotten. There is, indeed, none to compare with him.'

Tawḥīd

When Muhammad began his preaching, popular religion in Arabia, where he lived, was polytheistic and his city, Makkah, was a pilgrim centre adorned with countless idols, images of the Arabs' many gods and goddesses. Many of these surrounded the ancient shrine known as the *Ka'bah*, which local legend associated with the patriarchal figures of Abraham and his son, Ishmael. The Arabs believed that Ishmael had settled in Arabia after being banished from Abraham's family home, and that Abraham had visited his son there. Together, they built (or rebuilt) the *Ka'bah*. Originally, worship offered there had been to the One God, but generations later, Ishmael's descendants fell into superstition and polytheism. In fact, at Makkah, three goddesses were especially popular, al-Lāt, al-'Uzzā and Manāt, who were thought to be daughters of the supreme God, Allāh, a somewhat distant, remote God. Many thought that human fate was actually controlled by *zamān*, time, an impersonal and quite arbitrary power. Although less powerful, the three goddesses could, if placated, exercise some beneficial influence over the affairs of women and men.

Muhammad's message, as succinctly contained in *sūrah* 112, rejected all these popular religious myths except the name of the one, all powerful God. This God is Allāh, but he, not some arbitrary, impersonal time, controls human destiny and, unlike the Allāh who had fathered al-Lāt, al-'Uzzā and Manāt, the real Allāh has no children. Nor does he have a consort (*sūrah* 6: 102). As Muhammad's preaching developed, the association of any partner with God became known as *shirk*: God is Complete, God is Totality, he is One and Indivisible. To associate anything with God denies that God is who he is, and therefore equals disbelief. Other *sūrah*s also warn against *shirk*: 'God forgives not anyone who sets up partners with him. Everything else can be forgiven, but not this. It is the most heinous sin' (*sūrah* 4: 48). Elsewhere, the Qur'ān explicitly criticises Christian belief in Jesus as God's son, and in the Trinity: 'Say not Three – Cease. It is better for you! Allāh is only One God. Far be it removed from his transcendent majesty that he should have a son' (*sūrah* 4: 171). To 'associate a partner with God', says *sūrah* 7: 33, trespasses against reason. Belief in *tawḥīd* is the first article of faith (*īmān*), and forms the opening statement of the *shahādah*, the first pillar of Islam: 'I testify that there is no God but God'. The second part of the declaration is: 'and I testify that Muhammad is the messenger of God'. Muhammad himself said that he had brought nothing more important than the *shahādah*.

Muhammad's preaching at Makkah denounced both the Arabs' association of goddesses with Allāh as his children and their worship of images and idols. Tradition says that when Makkah finally fell to the followers of Muhammad, three hundred and sixty idols were destroyed, although the *Ka'bah*, purified, remains Islam's most sacred symbol. 'Truth has come and falsehood vanished', said the prophet (quoted in Ahmed 1988: 20), as he reclaimed the ancient House of God for Islam as the restored faith of Adam, Moses, David and Jesus, of all who had refused to worship the many, instead of the one. As described at *sūrah* 2: 125, the *Ka'bah* is seen to fulfil for Islam the function of the Holy of Holies in the Jerusalem temple. As the *shekhinah* represented God's 'shadow', not his presence in any physical sense, but the place towards which his face shone, so the *Ka'bah* is the place from where the divine reality radiates out in every direction. For this reason, Muslim prayer faces the *qiblah* (direction) of Makkah. Any attempt, however, to picture God visually is anathema. God is incomparable. Even if human disposition towards idolatry was not itself sufficient reason to oppose iconography, no object could possibly represent God's infinite, absolute power.

Tawḥīd and the social order

As Muhammad's preaching developed, the social and political implications of *tawḥīd*, as well as its theological significance, quickly became apparent. Muhammad's mission was not only to call people to worship the one God as God demanded to be worshipped, forsaking all other false deities, but to order society so that it functioned as God wanted it to function. The Qur'ān contains God's ideal blueprint for human behaviour. This governs not only women's and men's relationship with their creator (the Qur'ān states that God created everything, and that everything is sustained by his power) but also their relationship with each other. This social blueprint begins with *tawḥīd*. God is One, therefore all people are created equal and stand as one in his sight. No one, high born or low born, is inherently superior, or inherently inferior. Society, then, should treat everyone equally. No one should be treated unfairly because of their social status, just as no one should be privileged because of their rank. Justice must be fair. Extremes of wealth and poverty are unacceptable. Society should strive (a fundamental concept in Islam) to achieve a balance between wealth and poverty: 'The good is of steep ascent. It consists of freeing slaves. Of feeding the deprived. Of being kind to orphans. And to do so with patience and compassion' (*sūrah* 90: 13f). Perhaps not surprisingly, since much of this went against the received wisdom of his day, certainly against the ethos of the blood-proud Arab nobility, Muhammad's egalitarian message won, initially, more enemies than friends. However, success followed, and *tawḥīd* became the foundation principle of the whole Islamic social and political system, as well as the foundation and first pillar of faith (*īmān*).

More colours to the qur'anic picture

We have, so far, focused on *tawḥīd* in order to underline its importance as the concept from which most others develop. However, we must be careful to avoid suggesting that the Qur'ān's imageless imagery of God is monochrome. The opposite is true. The God of the Qur'ān is described by so many images that ninety-nine names are traditionally derived from its text. These were recited by Muhammad himself. *Sūrah* 7: 180 says: 'Allah's are the fairest names. Invoke him by them. And leave the company of those who blaspheme his names.' *Dhikr*, remembrance (by recitation) of these names has always played an important part in popular Muslim piety. In the mosque, often using prayer beads as aids to devotion, perhaps before, or after formal prayers (*ṣalāt*), countless Muslims around the world perform *dhikr*, which, in a very real sense, helps them form word-pictures of God.

The most frequently used names for God in the Qur'ān refer to his Mercy: he is *a-raḥmān*, *a-raḥīm*, 'The Merciful Lord of Mercy'. Every chapter except chapter nine begins with the invocation, 'In the Name of God, the Merciful Lord of Mercy'. These names, like all ninety-nine, describe God's nature, his attributes (*ṣifah*). As we shall explore below, much debate took place about how these attributes should be understood, but the word *ṣifah* entered Muslim theological discussion quite early, and originally derives from the Arabic verb 'to describe'. At first, the term was used to denote no more than descriptions of what God was actually like: he sees everything, hears everything, is full of mercy, and is supremely powerful. He is generous, and also just. He looks to see that justice is upheld in society, to safeguard the poor, the widows and the orphans. 'He is Cherisher and Sustainer of the Worlds' (*sūrah* 7: 54). Chapters such as 57 are especially rich in *ṣifah*: 'He is the First, the Last. He is the Transcendent, the Immanent. He is the possessor of all knowledge. He is the knower of all things'. A particularly beautiful description of God is found in *sūrah An-Nūr*, 'Light':

> Allāh is the Light of the heavens and the earth. The similitude of his light is as a niche wherein is a lamp. The lamp is in glass. The glass is as it were a shining star. This lamp is kindled from a blessed tree, neither of the East nor of the West, whose oil would almost glow forth of itself though no fire touched it. Light upon light, Allāh guideth whom he will. Allāh speaketh to mankind in allegories, for Allāh is knower of all things.
>
> (*Sūrah* 24: 35)

This vivid imagery helps Muslims picture how God's mercy, and power, and concern for justice, permeate the world as light-rays radiate out from their source, illuminating, touching, penetrating even the darkest corners. Al-Maqtul (*d.* 1191) developed this imagery in his two treatises, *The Philosophy of Illumination* and *The Temples of Light*. He wrote:

> The essence of the First Absolute Light, God, gives constant illumination, whereby it is manifested and it brings all things into existence, giving life to them by its rays. Everything in the world is derived from the Light of His Essence and all beauty and perfection are the gift of His bounty, and to attain fully to this illumination is salvation.
>
> (Quoted in Smith 1950: 79)

We shall explore later how the Ṣūfīs elaborated still further this concept of the Divine Light. Many of these attributes, or qualities (*awṣāf*), like *tawḥīd*, both describe what God is like, and also the type of behaviour he expects from Muslims as those who have submitted to his will. However, we should note that although technically correct, this English rendering of the Arabic word 'Islam' as 'submission' inevitably misses the nuance of the original. Derived from the root *slm* (peace), Muslim, the participle, and Islam, the noun, both carry the meaning of tranquillity as well as of 'obedience'. The 'obedience' implied here requires active commitment, not a passive, fatalistic acceptance.

The development of Islamic law and theology

After Muhammad's death, the leaders and scholars of the rapidly expanding Islamic empire, dedicated to governing newly won territories according to God's will, devoted much intellectual energy to codifying the tradition, or blueprint, they had received. First, the verses of the Qur'ān were carefully collected into a definitive edition. Muhammad had not recorded, or written down, the verses himself but had dictated them to various scribes. The process of collecting the *sūrahs* was supervised by Zayd ibn Thabit, who had served as one of Muhammad's amanuenses, and was completed in about 653 CE. Next, the *Ḥadīth* (words and deeds of Muhammad) were collected and a science – the infant science, or *fiqh*, of jurisprudence – developed to distinguish authentic from fraudulent traditions. As the best guide to the Qur'ān, the example of the prophet in every sphere of life was of critical concern for Muslims as they strove to order their common, and personal, lives. The majority of Muslims, the Sunni, who derive their name from the *Sunna* (or tradition) of the prophet, recognise six sound collections of *Ḥadīth*, those of al-Bukhari (*d.* 870), Muslim (*d.* 875), Abu Dawud (*d.* 875), at-Tirmidhi (*d.* 892), an-Nasai (*d.* 915) and ibn Maja (*d.* 886).

If either the Qur'ān or the *Ḥadīth* contained explicit guidance, specific rules of conduct, or prescriptive punishments for certain crimes, the *qāḍi*s (jurists) of the *Khalīfahs*, who succeeded to the temporal leadership of the Muslim community, could pass immediate judgement. Soon, however, situations occurred about which there was no explicit rule but to which the principles that underlay both Qur'ān and *Ḥadīth* could be applied. *Fiqh* thus developed methods to extend the scope of what technically became known as the *Sharī'ah*, divine law, literally 'a path leading to a watering hole', or guidance. By the tenth century, the content, or corpus, of this law, covering every aspect of life, had more or less reached its definitive version, and the work of four famous scholars emerged as final: Imam Malik (*d.* 795), Imam Hanifa (*d.* 767), Imam Shafi (*d.* 820) and Imam Hanbal (*d.* 855). Hereafter, jurisprudence – now known simply as 'the science' (*fiqh*) – interpreted, and commented on, their work. Until now, scholars had tended to concentrate on legal questions. For example, they discussed how literally they should understand the Qur'ān. How should: 'The life for the life, and the eye for the eye, and the nose for the nose, and the ear for the ear, and the tooth for the tooth, and for wounds, retaliation' (*sūrah* 5: 45) be understood? Literally, or as allegorical language (and see *sūrah* 24: 35 quoted above)? It soon became apparent, though, that this very issue – must the Qur'ān be understood literally, or were allegorical and metaphorical interpretations valid – had profound theological as well as legal consequences. It impacted directly on how Muslims were to conceive of God, how they might picture his essential qualities.

The beginning of *kalām* (theology)

The debate that developed as a result of this discussion is of immediate relevance to the concern of this chapter, since it focused on some of the Qur'ān's descriptions of God. We visit this debate below, but before we do so it is necessary to add a brief word about how *kalām* (theology) emerged from out of its roots in *fiqh*, becoming a separate, although parallel, discipline. *Tawḥīd* itself implies that Islam seeks to hold the affairs of *dīn* (religion) in balance with those of *dunyā* (world). One mechanism for handling this interaction was to view *fiqh* as primarily concerned with 'practice', sometimes technically referred to as '*Islam*', while *fiqh-al-akbar* (the greater science, but by the tenth century known as *kalām*, speech, or discourse, hence discourse about God, theology) was developed to focus on *īmān* (faith). These distinctions were drawn by Muhammad himself, in a conversation with the Archangel *Jibrā'īl* (Gabriel), who once asked the prophet to define Islam. Muhammad replied, 'To bear witness that there is no God but God and that I am the messenger of God, that one should perform the prayers, pay the legal alms, fast in the month of Ramadan and make pilgrimage to the House, if possible'. *Jibrā'īl* then asked, 'What is *Īmān*?' The Prophet replied, 'That you should believe in God and His Angels, and His Books, and His messengers, and in the Last Day, the Resurrection from the tomb, and the decreeing of good and evil' (quoted in Glassé 1991: 88). Islam is thus defined primarily in terms of practice, what you do, while Muhammad's definition of *īmān* focuses less on what you do, more on what you believe. In fact, his definition extended the basic declaration of faith, the *shahādah*, into the beginning of a systematic statement of belief, a creed (*'aqīdah*).

Later, the need for more doctrinal clarification arose as an empire that was also a religious, political and social unit found it convenient to define who was, and who was not, a good Muslim. Were sinners still Muslims? Who were worthy enough to serve as *qāḍis*? Could a bad Muslim, whether deviant by practice or by unorthodox belief, rule as *khalīfah*, or as his representative? Did the *khalīfah*s (originally chosen by a process of consultation and consensus, but after 661 CE, hereditary) rule by virtue of birth, or could they be legitimately removed by virtue of their unworthiness? One group, the Kharijites (seceders) totally opposed the Umayyad *khalīfah*s, for whom power alone mattered, and whose Islam was little more than a convenient smokescreen to help consolidate their empire. According to the Kharijites, any righteous Muslim could rule, but corrupt sons of former rulers had no divine, automatic right to be *khalīfah*. It was as a direct result of the political implications of these questions that *kalām* developed. *Khalīfah*s wanted creeds to define orthodoxy. Several demanded that civil servants sign them as qualification for holding office. Indeed, as we shall see below, as *kalām* developed it was used as a tool not only by the *khalīfah*s, but also by those who opposed the political *status quo*.

The verses of likening

The issue, however, on which the first theologians (*mutakallimūn*) focused was how should Muslims understand the 'verses of likening' (*āyāt-al-tasbih*) which appear to ascribe human, or anthropomorphic, characteristics to God? This directly relates to how Muslims are, within acceptable parameters, to picture or conceive of Allāh who, according to the Qur'ān, sees, hears (*sūrah* 17: 1), and sits on a throne (*sūrah* 57: 4); but how? Does he see as people see, through eyes, or hear as they hear, through ears, or sit, as they sit? Yet is Allāh not incomparable? How, then, should these qur'anic verses be understood? Should Muslims picture God literally sitting on a throne, or is this mental idolatry? Very quickly, discussion about these verses developed into another debate – about the nature of the divine being itself, especially about the relationship between the One, and the many qualities, or attributes, which the ninety-nine names suggest. As scholars discussed these verses, different interpretations were favoured by different schools. Some scholars declared that both the clarity, and number, of anti-anthropomorphic verses (warning against *shirk* and idolatry) cancelled out the verses of likening. Therefore, they should be ignored. Some, probably a minority, professed outright anthropomorphism. If the Qur'ān said that Allāh sat on a throne, Allāh indeed did just that. Another school drew on *qiyās* (deduction by analogy), one of the methods developed by *fiqh* to extend the *sharīʿah*. This illustrates the interaction between the two disciplines. An example of how *qiyās* was used in *fiqh* is the extension of the qur'anic prohibition against drinking grape-wine to include any alcoholic drink or substance. Many intoxicating substances are very different from grape-wine. They are made from completely different fruits, or grains, taste differently, and may be said to share relatively little in common with grape-wine. The jurists, though, pointed out that, although in many respects unlike grape-wine, they were similar in their intoxicating potential.

Some *mutakallimūn* applied this reasoning to the anthropomorphic verses. Allāh, they said, does see and hear, even as people see and hear, but any likeness with human seeing and hearing is not a physical likeness. There is a likeness, but only a partial likeness, just as the likeness between grape-wine and beer is only partial. They are similar but different. On the other hand, the apparent contradiction between the anthropomorphic and the anti-anthropomorphic verses could also, by this means, be reconciled. Just as God's seeing and hearing, and sitting on his throne, was only in some respects the same as human seeing, hearing and sitting, so the qur'anic prohibition against comparing God with anything can be understood as prohibiting comparison in some respects, but not in all respects. Indeed, were this not so, it would be quite impossible to speak about God at all, even to conceive of him mentally, let alone visually. In this view, then, God sees, but not as we see, and hears, but not as we hear.

Two schools, respectively the Muʿtazilites and the Asharites, opposed each other as diametrically on this issue as they did in several other important debates. For about a century, they competed for political influence by attempting to define orthodoxy, once and for all, according to their views. For a while, Muʿtazilites dominated. Between 827 and 850, during the reigns of three ʿAbbāsid *khalīfah*s, their version of the creed was imposed on all state officials, under their *miḥnah*, inquisition into belief, but by the end of the tenth century the Muʿtazilites had all but disappeared. In 1017, and again in 1049, the *Khalīfah* al-Qadir demanded a profession of faith explicitly rejecting the Muʿtazilites' dogmas (see Rippin 1990: 69). Since then, the Asharites have represented Sunni orthodoxy. Both schools were much influenced by Greek philosophy, especially by

Platonic realism, the concept that immutable ideals form a hierarchy of forms below the 'Form of the Good'.

Islam's Golden Age

This period of Islamic history, the early centuries of the 'Abbāsid Khalifate, is often described as the Golden Age of Islamic civilisation. Perhaps the excitement of success, perhaps the Qur'ān's high regard for knowledge and Muhammad's saying 'seek for science, even if it be in China', combined with its geographical location at the crossroads between the Occident and the Orient, made Baghdad not only capital of the empire, but a centre of medical, philosophical and scientific discovery and excellence as well. Greek texts were translated into Arabic and a third Muslim discipline, *falsafah* (philosophy), emerged alongside (but also interacting with) *fiqh* and *kalām*. Some Muslim philosophers greatly influenced European thought; most noteworthy among them were al-Farabi (870–950), ibn Sina (980–1037) and ibn Rushd (1126–1198), whose reputations were such that they acquired Latin names, respectively Avennasser, Avicenna and Averroes. Ibn Rushd, a serving *qāḍi* in Seville, was master of all three disciplines. In Islamic thought, especially in the writings of these philosophers, Aristotle's 'Prime Mover' became the one absolute, ultimate reality, Allāh. This is the level of real existence, more real than the material level. Matter, though, is a manifestation of the ultimate reality, and dependent on it for its derived existence. Were matter to exist in and of itself, the ultimate reality would cease to be absolute. Typically, their metaphysics saw existence as hierarchical, beginning with the 'necessary existent', God, and descending through various 'forms', or spheres, to the material world. Below, we shall see how this conceptual image of the relationship between God and creation was developed by the Muslim mystics.

Immediately, armed with Platonic ideals as a conceptual tool, some scholars associated the qualities of God implied by the ninety-nine names, as manifestations, or attributes, of God's essence. Allāh's essence is one but the divine unity manifests its qualities through many attributes (*ṣifāt*). The logic went like this: the name '*a-raḥmān* (Mercy) is, first, a name of the Divine Being but, secondly, since it bestows mercy, it is also an act of that being. Thirdly, for those who experience God's mercy, it is also an event. As name, act and event, it is distinct from God's other attributes. For example, it is not the same as *al-Ghafūr* (forgiveness), or as *Qudrat* (power). All describe, and are names of, God's one being, yet each exists as a separate reality. They are also experienced by people as separate and as distinct acts or events. Thus the orthodox doctrine developed of belief in seven divine attributes, derived from those qualities considered most crucial for an adequate understanding of God's nature. They are: Life (*Ḥayāt*), Knowledge (*'Ilm*), Power (*Qudrat*), Will (*Irādah*), Hearing (*Samā'*), Seeing (*Basr*) and Speaking (*Kalām*). The last, as we shall see, was closely associated with the qur'anic revelation. Ibn Kullab (*d.* 854), an early *mutakallim*, elaborated the doctrine of *ṣifah*, as eternal, uncreated attributes within the divine being, which indicates how early this belief became part of orthodox teaching.

The Mu'tazilites

The Mu'tazilites completely opposed the doctrine of attributes, and their creed demanded a repudiation of belief in *ṣifah*. Their political agenda will become apparent below but their starting point was theological jealousy for *tawḥīd*. The Mu'tazilites, themselves profoundly influenced by Greek philosophy, regarded themselves as champions of God's Unity:

> Muslims enumerate ninety-nine 'beautiful names' (*al-asma al-husna*) of God mentioned in the Qur'ān, and of these seven received special attention from the early theologians. . . . Some theologians held that God had attributes (*ṣifah*) corresponding to these names, such as knowledge, power, will. To the Mu'tazilites, however, this was seen as introducing an element of multiplicity into the unity of God's nature or essence (*nafs, dhāt*), and in insisting on 'unity' they were asserting that these attributes had no sort of independent or hypostatic existence, but were merged in the unity of God's being.
>
> (Watt 1985: 48f)

The existence, or non-existence of attributes had far-reaching consequences for understanding the nature of the qur'anic revelation, indeed, for understanding scripture. Popularly, the Qur'ān as word for word God's speech, or *kalām*, was associated with *kalām* as an uncreated, eternal attribute of God. In this view, the Qur'ān was not composed or created by God at the moment of *tanzīl* (sending down), but had always existed in God's mind, to use anthropomorphic language. In fact, several verses in the Qur'ān seem to refer to some type of pre-existence: *sūrah* 85: 21–22 refers to a 'Glorious Qur'ān on a heavenly table' (*lawḥ*), or 'guarded tablet' in some English renderings. This (and other verses) was interpreted to mean that the Qur'ān was uncreated. It may, though, have existed – and may still exist – as a heavenly reality created outside of God's divine being before it was 'sent down' to Muhammad, but this heavenly book is an exact replica of that which had eternally existed within God.

The Mu'tazilites rejected the uncreatedness of the Qur'ān, arguing that a verse such as, 'we have made it an Arabic Qur'ān' (*sūrah* 43: 3) clearly indicates that God made or created it. Some political consideration may have influenced their theological affirmation of the Qur'ān's createdness. The Mu'tazilites wanted to give more scope to reason, which (admiring Aristotle) they revered highly. They believed that human reason, or logic, could deduce 'the good life' without the aid of divine revelation. Even without their belief in the created Qur'ān, their insistence that logic and reason alone were sufficient to guide human affairs, challenged the authority of the jurists who claimed 'sole possession of the right interpretation of all Muslim dogma' (Rippin 1991: 69). When the Qur'ān's createdness was added to this confidence in human reason, its authority was also reduced. Since it was created, God may, presumably, have created it other than

> it is, whereas, if it is uncreated it presumably expresses something of his own being which is unchangeable. If the Qur'ān could have been created other than it is, the work of the *'ulamā'* in interpreting it loses much of its authority; and a divinely inspired *imām* (caliph) would be entitled to say how the law was to be changed. In practice this would almost certainly mean more power for the caliph's ministers and secretaries.
>
> (Watt 1985: 35).

Thus the Mu'tazilites enjoyed the support of at least three 'Abbāsid *Khalīfahs*. However, their theological argument was again predicated on *tawḥīd*. The idea of an uncreated Qur'ān, perhaps transcribed on to a heavenly tablet, suggested that both God, and God's book, existed separately. This not only compromised *tawḥīd*, but verged on associating a partner with God, albeit an inanimate partner. The Mu'tazilites challenged their opponents to explain what happens when someone recites the Qur'ān. Are the words, as uttered, created or uncreated. As we shall see, orthodoxy, as represented by the Asharites, affirmed the Qur'ān's uncreatedness. Their reply to the Mu'tazilites' challenge went like this:

> The Qur'ān is the speech of Allāh . . . uncreated, that is his revelation and what he has sent down. It is not he, but neither is it other than he, but in a real sense it is one of his attributes. . . The ink, the paper, the writings are created things, for they are the work of men, but the speech of Allāh . . . is uncreated. The writing, the letters, the words, the verses, are an adaptation of the Qur'ān to human needs, but the speech of Allāh . . . exists in itself, though its meaning comes to be understood through these things.
>
> (Imam Hanifa, cited in Zakaria 1991: 89f)

The Asharites

The Asharites regarded themselves as people of the *ḥadīth* (tradition) and, in *fiqh*, identified with Imam Hanbal (780–855). Al-Ashari (873–935), who developed his theological thought within the Hanbalī tradition, began his career as a Mu'tazilite but abandoned their views in about 912. Legend has it that Muhammad appeared to al-Ashari in a series of dreams and challenged him to use his skills to defend those doctrines that he, the Prophet, had taught, but without abandoning reason as an intellectual tool. Al-Ashari thereafter aimed to use reason in support of revelation, but, unlike the Mu'tazilites, not at the expense of revelatory authority (Watt 1985: 65). Much of his thinking is reflected in his lengthy creed, which affirmed attributes as eternal and, in some sense, as distinct from God's essence. However, God, his essence, his names, and his qualities, have 'been from eternity, and will be to eternity . . . none of his qualities or names has come into being; from eternity he knows by virtue of his knowledge; he is almighty by virtue of his power' (from the Asharite creed, *al-fiqh-al akbar* 11). With Imam Hanifa, al-Ashari affirms that the Qur'ān is uncreated. Our pronouncing, our reading the text, is created but the Qur'ān itself is uncreated. This means that when Muslims hear the words of the Qur'ān recited aloud, they are, in a real sense, hearing God's *kalām*. This is why the science of qur'anic recitation developed, *tajwīd*, literally, the science of 'making beautiful', or of 'striving for excellence'. Artists may not have liberty to represent God visually, but famous *qāri'* (reciters) can skilfully and beautifully chant his *kalām*.

As for the 'verses of likening', these, said al-Ashari, must be accepted without asking 'in what sense?': 'God's place is on his throne, as he has said. God has two hands, as he has said – we do not question: in what sense? God has two Eyes, as he has said – we do not question: in what sense?' (Glassé 1991: 88f). Al-Ashari thus preferred a literal interpretation of the Qur'ān, although his refusal to ask 'in what sense' such descriptions of God should be understood suggests that he thought the answer lay beyond the grasp of the human intellect. In explaining a verse such as *sūrah* 75: 23: 'That day will faces be resplendent, looking toward their Lord', which describes how believers will see God in Paradise, he resisted metaphorical or allegorical interpretations and insisted that people will 'see' in the normal sense of seeing, but stated that we cannot understand how this will happen. God, though, he also insisted, does not have a body. Al-Ashari's scepticism about human ability to 'know' was not shared by the philosophers, whose interest in epistemology led them to develop what became known as the theory of the 'unity of the intellect'. Put simply, in answer to the questions, 'how can we know?', or 'how are we capable of cognition?', their reply was: 'we know because we already contain what we know'. There is Cosmic Intellect (God), and there is that intellect which extends into the centre of our being. We 'know' when we realise that the distinction between Cosmic Intellect , and our intellect, is an illusion. Al-Farabi spoke of three types of intellect: active, the world of immutable ideas, or universal forms; potential, the latent capacity to acquire eternal truths about God; and acquired intellect, or learned knowledge.

This metaphysical description of God (ontological being) as the Cosmic, uncreated Intellect complete our survey of how the Muslim theologians discussed and elaborated the Qur'ān's multi-coloured verbal picture of God. In summary, orthodoxy begins with belief in *tawḥīd*, in God's unity, but also believes that the divine being is a complex, and not a simple, reality. Manifesting many qualities,

God's outward plurality of attributes does not compromise his internal oneness. God is one, not many, and, as al-Ashari says: 'It is not to be said that God's names, or attributes, are anything other than himself' (Glassé 1991: 89).

This survey, however, represents but the beginning of Islam's imageless imagery: the mystic poets and theologians, to whom we now turn, developed even more complex doctrines. To enter the world of the Muslim mystic is to enter a world rich in metaphysical thought, as well as in poetic expression and literary analogy. The mystics, too, do not confine themselves to words, but employ music and dance to depict the ultimate reality and the soul's quest for union with reality.

Ṣūfī imagery: the metaphysical framework

Muslim mystics emerged very early in Islam's historical development; Hasan of Basra (642–728), for example, was an early exponent of mystical thought. Often cited as an authority in the *isnād*, or chain of *ḥadīth* transmission, he provides an important link with the Prophet himself. He also contributed to the theological debates we have described above, and the Mu'tazilites are said to have originally broken away from his school. The mystics became known as Ṣūfīs, from *ṣūf* (wool) because they apparently wore distinctive woollen clothes. However, a device of the mystics is to see inner (esoteric) and outer (exoteric) layers of meaning in qur'anic verses, ritual acts and technical and theological terms. Later, they spoke of a secret identity between the word 'Ṣūfī', and the word '*ṣāfī*' (pure). Bishr al-Hafi, an early Ṣūfī of Baghdad, said: 'The Sufi is he who keeps his heart pure' (Lings 1975: 77).

However, our concern must be with Sufism's conceptual and metaphysical framework. Its history will only be referred to in order to illustrate this. That framework begins with an interpretation of the doctrine of *tawḥīd*, as contained in the first statement of the *shahādah*: 'I testify that there is no God but God'. Martin Lings explains:

> Every Muslim is obliged to believe in theory that there is no Reality but the Reality, namely God; but it is only the Sufis . . . who are prepared to carry this formulation to its ultimate conclusion. The doctrine which is based on that conclusion is termed 'Oneness of Being', for Reality is that

which is, as opposed to that which is not; and if God alone is Real, God alone is, and there is no being but His Being.

(Lings 1975: 65)

The mystic's concern is to journey from asserting self-existence, to a conscious merging of self with the ultimate, and only, reality. The goal is *fanā'*, the passing away of self – a type of death – resulting in *baqā'*, or union with the one reality – a type of re-birth, or *tawḥīd*, 'making one'. While travelling, the mystic is a *sālik* (traveller) and his journey takes him or her along the *tarīqah*, or path. Along the way, the *sālik* is guided by a teacher, usually known as a *shaikh*, or a *pīr*, who is believed to stand in direct initiatic succession (*silsilah*) with Muhammad, usually through Hasan of Basra. Thus, the mystics do not neglect the significance of the second statement of the *shahādah*, and, indeed, believe that their doctrines originate from Muhammad's esoteric teaching. Before the goal of union with reality can be realised, various stages (*maqāmāt*) and states of perception (*aḥwāl*) mark the Ṣūfī's journey along the path. Their *niyyah* (intent or desire) must also be pure, which marks the beginning of the journey towards what is sometimes called 'perfection', although the goal itself is not earned. 'The thing we tell of', said Persian mystic al-Bistami (*d.* 874), 'can never be found by seeking, yet only seekers find it' (Glassé 1991: 377). Selflessness, renunciation of extreme wealth (*faqr* – hence fakir), love of others, all help to purify the Ṣūfī but the goal can only be realised through God's love (*ḥubb*) and grace (*karāmāt*). Ibn Sina, one of Islam's most distinguished philosophers, whom we met above, also a renowned physician and an acclaimed Ṣūfī writer, wrote, 'Every created thing, by its nature, longs for the perfection which means its well being, and the perfection of the created being is brought about by the grace of that One who is essentially perfect. The most perfect object of love is the First Cause of all things' (quoted in Smith 1950: 47). This reference to Aristotle's 'First Cause' clearly illustrates the connection between ibn Sina's metaphysical and mystical thought.

The 'perfect man'

One other allusion in our quotation from ibn Sina should be explained; his reference to 'perfection'. Frequently, Ṣūfīs refer to one who has realised union with God, or who has experienced *baqā'*, as a 'perfect man'. This term, though, is generic and includes women:

> He to whom this supreme happiness has been granted has become a perfect man and the most exalted of creatures, for his own existence has become merged in that of the Absolute Being. . . . Whether woman or man, such a one is the most perfect of human beings. This is the grace of God which He gives to whom He will.
>
> (The Mughal princess Jahanara (*d.* 1681), quoted in Smith 1950: 133)

Since human intellect is but the cosmic intellect within, and since the object of both normative and of Ṣūfī Islam is to achieve a complete identification between an individual and the divine will, it follows that human perfection is an inherent possibility. In a real sense, the Ṣūfīs are saying that if you want to picture God, picture the perfect man, picture the individual whose life is so tuned into the will of God, whose life so reflects the qualities of God, that duality between creature and creator is annihilated. 'Every man', says al-karim Jili (*d.* 1428), 'is a copy of God in His perfection; none is without the power to become a perfect man' (quoted in Smith 1950: 119).

The lover and the beloved

The mystics often use the metaphor of human love, between the lover and the beloved, to describe their goal of *baqā'*:

> I am He whom I love and He whom I love is I,
> We are two spirits indwelling one body.
> When thou seest me, thou seest Him,
> And when thou seest Him, thou dost see us both.
>
> (Al-Hallaj (*d.* 922), quoted in Smith 1950: 37)

As we shall see below, al-Hallaj was executed for heresy because of his ecstatic utterances declaring that he was one with God. Al-Ghazali (*d.* 1111), however, who did much to accommodate Ṣūfī thought within Sunni orthodoxy, could also write:

> When He admits you to His Court, ask from Him nothing but Himself.
> When your lord has chosen you as his lover, your eye has seen all things;

> the world of love allows of no duality – what talk is this of 'me' and 'you'? When you come forth from life and your dwelling place, then through God you will see God.
>
> (Quoted in Smith 1950: 77)

Sometimes, this language of love was expressed in passionate terms. Islam's pre-eminent woman mystic, Rab'ia (*d.* 801) wrote: 'The groaning and yearning of the lover of God will not be satisfied until it is satisfied in the Beloved' (quoted in Smith 1950: 12).

The Five Presences of God

Below, we shall return to some of the images used by the Ṣūfīs to illustrate, and to teach, their doctrines. First, however, brief reference should be made to their complex doctrine of the Five Presences which built on the metaphysical framework we have already described. This doctrine is associated especially, although by no means exclusively, with ibn 'Arabi (1165–1240). Born in Spain, ibn 'Arabi travelled widely throughout the Khalifate and died in Damascus. He is often accused of monism, of denying any distinction between God and creation, because he taught the doctrine of the 'unity of being'. In fact, his metaphysical thought built directly on the concept of God's attributes emanating out in act, and event, from the divine presence. Neo-platonic influence is easily identified. If there is no reality other than the Reality, what is the exact nature of the relationship between created objects, and God? Clearly, a stone, or a tree, or even a human being, shares few of God's qualities. This question was answered by the doctrine of divine presences: a complex word picture not only of God, but of the interrelatedness of everything that exists, a total cosmology, which conceives of five different dimensions, or degrees, of reality. *Sūrah* 2: 115 says: 'Everywhere you turn, there is the face of God'. These degrees are usually listed in descending order. They are: 1. God's Essence; 2. God as Divine Being; 3. the world of angels; 4. the subtle world; 5. the material, and human world. Each degree manifests God, radiates, or emanates out from God, and returns towards God. Lings explains:

> The Fiveness of the Divine Presence does not contradict its Oneness, that is, the Oneness of Being, for it is always the Same Presence. Nonetheless, from the point of view of Absolute Reality, the fiveness is an illusion since from that point of view the hierarchy has 'already' been folded up: like the rolling of a written scroll, the ice has 'already' melted. . . . The 'eye of ice', that is, the eye of illusion, can see nothing but ice. Only the Eye of Water can see Water . . .
>
> (Lings 1975: 71, see also *Sūrah* 21: 104)

Architecture as a picture of God and his universe

This metaphysical scheme finds physical expression in the architectural heritage of the Ṣūfī tradition. Since Ṣūfī masters, the *shaikh*s, are believed to have completed the mystical journey through these degrees of existence, to union with God, the architectural style of their tombs, or shrines, reflects this cosmology. When a Ṣūfī looks at the shrine of the founder of his *tarīqah*, he or she is actually looking at an architectural representation of the hierarchy of existence. Thus, the dome represents the angelic sphere, the heavenly zone, while the octagonal drum and square base on which this rests represents the *shaikh*'s transformation through the various states of perception, from the material world, to perfection. Both tomb, and occupant, are bridges between heaven and earth. They thus become sources of *karāmāt* (grace) and of *barakah* (blessing), and many miracles and wonders are associated with the great Ṣūfī centres. These *shaikh*s, often called *awliyā'*, singular *walī*, are themselves believed to play an important part in the cosmological order, forming an invisible hierarchy in descending grades of sanctity, and, headed by the *quṭb* (centre, axis), help to maintain cosmic balance. Many scholars have compared the Ṣūfī goal with the Buddhist *nibbāna*.

Whether Buddhist influence can be proven is probably debatable (and such comparisons may not be very helpful), but it is not insignificant that, in India, Ṣūfī Islam quickly took root and flourished in some areas where Buddhism had previously dominated, such as East Bengal, where it still maintains an ancient presence in the Chittagong Hill Tracts. I worked for several years in Bangladesh, and observed how similar such Ṣūfī practices as garlanding shrines with flowers were to Buddhist customs. The comparison, too, between the role of the *walī*, who, having gained perfection, continues to assist those who are still seeking it, with the *bodhisattva*, who, having achieved *nibbāna*, delays his final liberation for the sake of other beings, should be noted. Certainly, for Ṣūfīs, the *awliyā'*, or friends of God, mediate something of divine grace and blessing to those who are still travelling along the path.

The music of angels

For his imagery, there are few better Ṣūfī masters to visit than Jalal ad-Din ar-Rumi (1207–1273). His *tarīqah*, the 'whirling dervishes', employ music and dance in their Ṣūfī litanies (*samā'*), which enables us to introduce some rare, but significant, non-conceptual Muslim pictures of God. Rumi himself explains the meaning of the flute's music:

> Hearken to this Reed forlorn,
> Breathing, ever since twas torn
> From its rushy bed, a strain
> Of impassioned love and pain.
>
> The secret of my song, though near,
> None can see and none can hear,
> Oh, for a friend to know the sign
> And mingle all his soul with mine!
>
> Tis the flame of Love that fired me,
> Tis the wine of Love inspired me.
> Wouldst thou learn how lovers bleed,
> Hearken, hearken to the Reed.

(From the *Mathnawi*, quoted in Glassé 1991: 268)

Here, as well as such typical metaphorical allusions to God as the 'Beloved' with whom the 'Lover' wishes to mingle his or her soul, the flute's Reed is seen yearning to return to the rushes where it grew. Its music signifies nostalgia for this lost existence. Rumi also describes music as a bridge between the earthly and the heavenly spheres. The flute's melodies are melodies we once heard in paradise. Although material things have cast their 'veil upon us we retain faint reminiscences of these heavenly songs' (quoted in Nicholson 1975: 64). 'At one time our home was in heaven, there we had companionship with the angels. Let us go back to our abode, O Lord, for that is our dwelling place' (Rumi, quoted in Smith 1950: 105). Al-Ghazali similarly describes music as emanating from 'the mystic relationship which God has ordained between the rhythm of music and the spirit of man' (Smith 1950: 64). Some orthodox Sunnis opposed the use of music, believing that it lures the soul into such a state of repose that it can easily be stolen away.

Picturing God in dance and movement

Perhaps the most unusual and vivid imagery is that of the Ṣūfī dance. The following description and interpretation is based on Lings' account (1975) of one of the dances of Rumi's disciples. As flutes play and drums beat, the *shaikh* occupies a central position. The dancers, arms folded, process solemnly past him. As they pass the *shaikh*, each dancer unfolds his arms and pivots around on the spot, at first slowly, then with faster and faster tempo. Arms are stretched out to their full extent on both sides, with the right palm pointing upwards, the left palm downwards. Lings interprets this choreography as follows: the dancers' bodies symbolise the Axis of the Universe, which, he says, is none other than The Tree of Life, introducing another Ṣūfī concept. This is a vertical dimension that passes through each of the five horizontal degrees of existence, connecting each to the highest degree. Traditionally, the connecting point on earth is believed to have been the Garden of Eden, sometimes identified with the *Ka'bah* at Makkah, which, long before its rebuilding by Abraham and Ishmael (see above) had been Adam's shrine. The palm raised upwards is 'as receptacle of Heaven, and the left palm downwards to transmit Heaven to earth' (Lings 1975: 84).

The dance therefore portrays how God's vertical presence permeates the material, horizontal world. In order to journey along the axis (as the Ṣūfī masters have journeyed before them) the *sālikūn* must be open to receive God's love and grace. They must also be willing to communicate this to others. Ṣūfīs also speak about a spiritual axis, or *quṭb* which can 'reside in a human being' but which is 'at the same time a celestial reality' (Glassé 1991: 327). The greatest spiritual master of each age, who heads the heavenly hierarchy of saints, is known as the *quṭb*. In a real sense, however, all people have the potential to recover this 'lost centre', for it resides in every human heart: 'The high road to God for your spirit, by which your prayers can reach God, is the polishing of the mirror of the heart' (San'ai (*d.* 1150), quoted in Smith 1950: 75).

Ṣūfī writing has many descriptions of the soul's ascent, replete with accounts of the mystical journey through the seven heavens to the very throne of God. Such descriptions recall Muhammad's 'Night Journey', or *mi'rāj*, when, in the Divine Presence, he received the instructions on prayer. The soul's journey, however, is both a vertical ascent, and a horizontal journey within the heart itself: 'The heart is the dwelling-place of that which is the essence of the universe, within the heart and soul is the very Essence of God. Like the saints, make a journey into your self; like the lovers of God, cast one glance within' (ad-Din Attar, quoted in Smith 1950: 89). As the dancers dance, says Lings, they also perform *dhikr*, repeating the name of God. In fact, they breathe his name,

> for even if the dancer has not consciously the name Allāh on his tongue, he has another Name of the Essence in his breath, and that is *Huwa* (He) which, as the Sufis know, transforms the very act of life into a perpetual invocation.
>
> (Lings 1975: 85).

Dhikr aims to achieve a state of consciousness in which the heart itself says 'God, God, God', so that awareness of self ceases, and, as a window to the lost centre within opens up in his heart, the Ṣūfī becomes aware only of God.

Popular Ṣūfī imagery

Other popular Ṣūfī images also attempt to convey the sense of the soul's yearning to return to its origin, in God. Several metaphors try to explain how the apparent duality between creatures, and the Creator, is both a real distinction, since people are clearly not the same as God, yet, at the same time, also an illusion. For example, Farid ad-Din Attar (*d.* 1229) wrote:

> The Presence of God Most High is as a Mighty Ocean, and the Gardens of Paradise, with all their joys, are but as the least drop in it. He who possesses the Ocean possesses the drop also. All that is not the Ocean is mere vanity. Since thou art able to find the way to the Ocean itself, why dost thou hasten to seek a single drop of dew? Can he who shares in the secrets of the Sun dally with a mote in its beams? When a man has become one with the Whole, what concern has he with the part? What need has he who has found his soul of the members of his body? If thou, O man, hast found thy reality to be one with the Whole, then contemplate the Whole, seek out the Whole, become one with the Whole, and choose for thyself the Whole.
>
> (From *Mantiq al-Tayr*, quoted in Smith 1932: 58)

Note again the reference to the 'Presence of God'. Attar also tells the famous story of the Phoenix, the mythical bird, who, after a thousand years, lights its own funeral pyre, dies and then rises again from the fire's last spark. Both these metaphors suggest that Ṣūfīs do not necessarily believe that the individual personality is totally annihilated. Rather, as a water drop that has joined the Ocean remains part of that Ocean, although indistinguishable from the Whole, and, as the last spark of the funeral fire gave birth to the new Phoenix, we die (*fanā'*) in order to live, but to live within the being of God from which we originally emanated (*baqā'*). Princess Jahanara wrote: 'He has become a drop in the ocean, a mote in the rays of the sun, a part of the whole' (quoted in Smith 1950: 131).

Language of intoxication

Some Muslims have always regarded Sufism with suspicion as compromising *tawḥīd* and, at times, Ṣūfīs have suffered persecution. Some of their more ecstatic utterances, expressing feelings of absorption, almost of 'God intoxication', led to charges of heresy. The most famous example of this was al-Hallaj's 'I am Truth'. '*Ḥaqq*' (truth) is one of the Names of God, and, therefore, in orthodox understanding, indistinguishable from that which it names. Al-Hallaj's ecstatic cry was 'taken to mean that he felt himself actually to be God incarnate in the world' (Rippin 1991: 123). To put it crudely, it sounded as if he was saying, 'Look at Me, I'm God'. This was idolatry since God cannot be pictured visually, and al-Hallaj was executed in 922, becoming a Ṣūfī martyr. In fact, he had spoken the language of intoxication, of complete 'at oneness with God', which usefully introduces another favourite Ṣūfī aphorism: 'love as the wine of life' – 'I am that which is drunk and he who gives to drink'(al-karim Jili (*d.* 1428), see Smith 1950: 119); 'Drink for a while the wine of ecstasy: perhaps it will save you from the power of self. Yes, I tell you, drink this wine that it may save you from yourself and lead the essence of the drop into the ocean' (Shabistari (*d.* 1320), see Smith 1950: 111). Criticised for heterodoxy, the Ṣūfīs, for their part, accuse those who insist on saying 'I exist' and 'God exists', of polytheism.

The 'divine light'

In addition to many references, inspired by Qur'ān *sūrah* 24, to God as the 'Light of the heavens and of the earth', the Ṣūfīs developed a doctrine of the light within each individual woman and man, the 'divine light'. The *Ikhwān al-ṣafā* (Brethren of Purity), a Ṣūfī order dating from the tenth century, taught that all souls contain within them the 'divine light', planted there before birth by God. Souls, the Ṣūfīs believe, pre-exist birth and, as Rumi said, lived with God and his angels in paradise. Indeed, says Rumi, without this 'light' knowledge and perception would be impossible, 'everyone who perceives must have some relationship to the light, by which he is able to perceive, and everything which is perceived has a relationship with God, who is Light, that is, all which perceives and all which is perceived' (quoted in Smith 1950: 98). This is the Muslim philosophers' epistemology expressed in different words. Many Muslims also believe in what is called 'the light of Muhammad'. This pre-existed his birth, and was God's creative instrument. It was also the light within that inspired and illuminated Muhammad's prophetic activities. The Shi'ah believe that this same light inspired their *imāms*, while some Ṣūfīs identify this light with the grace that is conveyed from Muhammad, through the initiatic chain, to their *shaikhs*.

Islamic art as mediating divine reality

Islam's conviction that God cannot be pictured visually, because nothing can compare with his omnipotent reality, also forbade any artistic representation of the human form. Sometimes, especially in Persian art, very stylised human figures were painted and there are even some representations of Muhammad, although always with his face obscured. Instead, Islam developed its own distinctive tradition of calligraphic, and of abstract, art. Given the Qur'ān's status, not only as the primary source of all Islamic teaching, but also as the vehicle for God's own *kalām*, not surprisingly, copies were beautifully written and decorated. While this art form falls far short of offering Muslims a picture of God, it nevertheless symbolises God's presence: as an attribute of God, *kalām* is also no other than God. Understood crudely, this might imply that Muslims worship a book, which was one reason why the Mu'tazilites opposed the doctrine of its uncreatedness. Properly understood, it means that the Qur'ān mediates God's word, so even its physical, created cover, should be treated with reverence. Muslims rarely handle the Qur'ān without first washing their hands.

God is believed to be 'Beautiful'. How, since Muslims cannot picture him, is not known but this conviction led to the idea that mosques and public buildings, and also private homes, should be beautiful. Al-Ghazali wrote: 'It cannot be denied that where beauty is perceived, it is natural to love it and if it is certain that God is beauty, he must be loved by that one to whom his beauty and majesty are revealed' (quoted in Smith 1950: 66). Just as God's qualities of Justice and Mercy impact on how he wants people to live, so does his love of Beauty. In a sense, then, the whole of Islamic architecture says something about God. In fact, its use of geometric pattern, of arches and domes, is said to derive from *tawḥīd*. If 'only absolute reality is absolutely real', then the Ṣūfīs are right to say that God is simultaneously both everywhere and also nowhere, in as much as his totality cannot be said to reside in any single place. Thus, geometric shapes, which have no obvious centre, or an arch with no obvious 'point', points to the Point that is, at one and the same time, everywhere yet also nowhere.

Space and light also depict God's nature; his limitlessness, his permeating presence. This is clearly reflected in the architectural style of 'places of prostration', or mosques. Huge, often unvaulted roofs suggest the metaphorical presence of an infinite God, while open access to external courtyards proclaims that this God can never be contained. He is within the world of nature as much as he is within a place of prayer. Originally, mosques were built to imitate the building in which Muhammad had lived, and led ritual prayer, at Madinah. That was a simple, insubstantial structure little more than a series of roofs resting on tree trunks, with a stone to mark the *qiblah* (direction of prayer) and a stool, or perhaps a wooden platform, from which Muhammad delivered the Friday *khuṭbah* (sermon). As the Muslim empire expanded in the centuries after Muhammad's death, more sophisticated and elaborate mosques were built to reflect the power and prestige of the *khalīfah*, to whom allegiance was pledged each Friday from the *minbar*, or pulpit, which replaced the humble stool of Muhammad's mosque. City status was conveyed by possession of such a mosque, rather as cathedrals carried city status in Christian Europe. Huge, monumental mosques proclaimed not only the success of the khalifate, but also the sovereignty and majesty of God. Muslims did not hesitate to interpret Islam's phenomenal spread as proof of God's favour and blessing. City mosques were also multi-functional, as Muhammad's had been. Many became famous seats of learning. Located at the centre of city life, often next to the bazaar, they also served to remind good Muslims that their God was as concerned with the correctness of their business transactions in the market-place, or with their leisure activities in the adjoining coffee-shops, as he was with their prayers and doctrinal orthodoxy. The conviction, too, that prayer can be offered anywhere, within or without a mosque, also encouraged the building of countless smaller mosques throughout the city, which served to remind citizens that there is no hiding from the eyes and ears of the all-seeing, all-knowing God. The ubiquitous presence, too, of qur'anic calligraphy as an art form, not only on the walls of mosques but also of private homes and public buildings, similarly says 'God sees everything you do'. The precision and beauty of such calligraphy, the sheer harmony of its visual impact, also bears witness to the orderliness, harmony and balance of God's creation.

Mathematics: theology in number

Finally, mathematics, which underpins Islam's abstract art, is, like music and colour and beauty, also said to begin in the heavenly or angelic sphere. It is itself part of the vertical axis that communicates God's qualities, and grace (*karāmāt*), in the horizontal spheres. This was one reason why mathematics, algebra and astronomy received particular attention during Islam's Golden Age of scientific discovery and development. Heaven touches earth in mathematical precision, and in the beautiful mosaic pattern. Mathematical equations, shapes and patterns represent God symbolically. They do not employ any visual form that can encourage idolatry, yet succeed in conveying something of God's essence to the onlooker. As the circumference of a circle has no beginning or end, as 'number' cannot be visually conceived, so Allāh has neither beginning, nor end, nor tangible form.

Conclusion

Muslims do not picture God visually, but they have created their own rich tradition of literary and metaphysical descriptions. Beginning with the concept of *tawḥīd*, that there is no reality but the reality, there is a real sense in which, if a Muslim wants to look at God, he, or she, needs only to look at the world. Its beauty, its laws of physics and of motion, the fixture of stars in the firmament, all contain God yet God is beyond what is seen, for God is the unseen cause, the invisible ground of all being. Muhammad himself said 'Revile not the world, for God is the world' (quoted in Smith 1950: 99). Picture God, says the Muslim, by picturing creation.

FURTHER READING

*Ahmed, A.S. (1988) *Discovering Islam*, London, Routledge.

Glassé, C. (ed.) (1991) *The Concise Encyclopaedia of Islam*, London, Stacey International.

***Lings, M. (1975) *What is Sufism?*, London, George Allen & Unwin.

***Nicholson, R.A. (1975) *The Mystics of Islam*, New York, Schocken. (First published in 1914)

**Pickthall, M.M. (original ed.) (1930) *The Meaning of the Glorious Koran*, London, Ta Ha Press.

*Rippin, A. (1990–91) *Muslims: Their Religious Beliefs and Practices* (2 vols), London, Routledge.

**Smith, M. (1932) *The Persian Mystics*, London, John Murray.

**Smith, M. (1950) *Readings from the Mystics of Islam*, London, Luzac and Co.

***Watt, W.M. (1985) *Islamic Philosophy and Theology*, Edinburgh, Edinburgh University Press.

Wolfson, H.A. (1976) *The Philosophy of the Kalam*, Cambridge, Mass., Harvard University Press.

**Zakaria, R. (1991) *Muhammad and the Quran*, Harmondsworth, Penguin.

Note: Books marked * are good introductory texts on Islam; those marked ** contain primary sources; those marked *** are especially recommended for material relevant to the focus of this chapter.

5. Judaism

Norman Solomon

Picturing God in words

Judaism allows no visual representation of God, no image, icon or symbol. The understanding of God is conveyed through verbal imagery and through reflection on experiences. As we cannot 'see' God, how do we learn to talk about him? How do we learn to use the word 'God' correctly?

In the following sections we explore several of the contexts in which, in traditional Jewish sources, the word 'God' or any of its equivalents has been used. This is a highly appropriate way to understand Jewish 'imagery' of God, for on the whole the Jewish sources do not theorise about the nature of God, but talk about situations in which God acts, or is perceived to be present.

At all stages there have been questionings, as if to say that talk about God is at best incomplete, inexhaustive, and often misleading. Already in biblical times there was unease about 'anthropomorphism', the use of human terms to describe God. Moses, sternly warning Israel against the manufacture of images, reminds them, 'The Lord addressed you from the midst of the flame. You heard the sound of words, but saw no appearance, only a voice' (Deut. 4: 12). Deutero-Isaiah proclaimed, 'To whom will you compare God; or what likeness will you compare with him?' (Isa. 40: 18). The most intense questionings were formulated by the medieval philosophers, who wrestled to interpret biblical anthropomorphism in the light of the firm denial to God of any bodily attributes.

Bible

The Hebrew scriptures present God through experience, both national and individual. We now review some of the biblical 'images' of God, noticing what sort of experiences they refer to. The selection is not biblical theology *per se*, but focuses on those elements which most strongly influenced the formation of rabbinic Judaism.

The most decisive experience of God in Israelite/Jewish history was his self-revelation at Mount Sinai, as he proclaimed the Ten Commandments to the whole people. Why, asked the rabbis, did he open the Commandments with the statement, 'I am the Lord your God'? Surely, his identity was evident to all?

> 'I am the Lord your God . . . ' Why is this said? Since he revealed himself to them at the Red Sea as a mighty man of war, as it is said, 'The Lord is a warrior, the Lord is his name' (Exodus 15: 3); then as an elder, replete with mercy, as it is said, 'They beheld the God of Israel, and beneath his feet was a pavement of sapphire, (and, referring to their redemption) blue as the very heavens . . . ' (Exodus 24: 10); and 'I kept looking, and then thrones were set in place and one ancient in years took his seat, his robe was white as snow and the hair of his head like cleanest wool (Daniel 7: 9–10)' – so, to allow no pretext to the nations to say 'There are two powers', (he declared) 'I am the Lord your God; It is I who am on the sea and the dry land, in the past and in the future, in this world and in the next . . . .
>
> (*Mekhilta* on Exod. 20: 2)

Clearly, the rabbis understood that biblical talk about God consisted of images, not definitions. Each image (warrior, elder and so on) might correspond to some aspect of our experience of God's work, but no image, not even all the images together, could possibly exhaust the theme, nor does any image attempt to convey anything about God 'in himself'. Moreover, images do not have to be mutually consistent, for they are no more than pointers, from different locations, to the one ultimate which cannot be formulated in words.

The image of God at Sinai, God the 'lawgiver', is of a compelling presence; yet the voice is not stern, but that of a gentle and compassionate 'elder'. The *mitzvot* (commandments) of the Torah are the embodiment of his love for Israel. The 'Pharisaic' Psalm 119 encapsulates this equation of Torah and love. Nothing could be further from rabbinic Judaism than the Pauline concept of law as a burden (2 Cor. 3: 6), and the distorted image of God to which this gives rise.

God the Creator is majestically presented in the opening chapter of Genesis. Note the insistence on the 'rightness' of natural order, each species created in ascending order 'according to its kind'; likewise, at the Flood, Noah must save a viable population of each species.

Several Psalms (29, 104) attest to God's wisdom in governing nature. That is, the experience of the 'harmony' of nature is translated into God-talk. The most powerful biblical testimony to the natural order as witness to God is Job 38–41. Nature is never confused with God, though. A comparison of Psalm 19 with the Egyptian Hymn to Ikhnaten shows how the Psalmist reworked his Egyptian source to demote nature (the sun) from being God to being testimony to God.

God who made the world becomes God who governs it – the experience of history, particularly the Exodus, becomes a story of God:

> Hear me, Jacob,
> and Israel whom I called:
> I am He; I am the first,
> I am the last also,
> With my own hands I founded the earth,
> with my right hand I formed the expanse of sky;
> when I summoned them,
> they sprang at once into being.
> Assemble, all of you and listen to me;
> which of you has declared what is coming,
> that he whom I love shall wreak my will on Babylon
> and the Chaldeans shall be scattered?
>
> (Isa. 48: 12–14)*

In determining the fate of nations, God is Warrior and Saviour (as

* Biblical references in this chapter are taken from the *New English Bible*.

God was not confused with nature, he is not confused with Messiah):

> 'Who is this coming from Edom,
> coming from Bozrah, his garments stained red?
> Under his clothes his muscles stand out,
> and he strides, stooping in his might?'
> It is I, who announce that right has won the day.
> I, who am strong to save . . . .
>
> (Isa. 63: 1–2)

These more violent images of God arise from the ascription to him of hatred of injustice and zeal against idolatry.

'Wherever you find God's power mentioned, you find also his humility'.[1] Side by side with pictures of God as Almighty Creator and director of history are pictures of him as healer and comforter:

> The Lord is my shepherd; I shall want nothing.
> He makes me lie down in green pastures,
> and leads me beside the waters of peace;
> he renews life within me,
> and for his name's sake guides me in the right path.
> Even though I walk through a valley as dark as death
> I fear no evil, for thou art with me,
> thy staff and thy crook are my comfort.
>
> Thou spreadest a table for me in the sight of my enemies;
> thou hast richly bathed my head with oil,
> and my cup runs over.
> Goodness and love unfailing, these will follow me
> all the days of my life,
> and I shall dwell in the house of the Lord
> my whole life long.
>
> (Ps. 23)

Elijah, the fearless prophet, scourge of kings and vanquisher of the prophets of Baal, discerned God not in the raging thunder but in the 'still, small voice':

> . . . the Lord was passing by: a great and strong wind came rending mountains and shattering rocks before him, but the Lord was not in the

> wind; and after the wind there was an earthquake, but the Lord was not in the earthquake; and after the earthquake fire, but the Lord was not in the fire; and after the fire a low, murmuring sound. When Elijah heard it, he muffled his face in his cloak and went out and stood at the entrance to the cave. Then there came a voice: 'Why are you here, Elijah?'
>
> (1 Kgs 19: 11–13)

To complete this section, here, with sample references, are some of the metaphors that contribute to the biblical picture of the relationship between God and people:

METAPHOR	COMMENT
King and client state (Isaiah 43: 15)	The suzerainty treaty as model 'covenant'
King and subject (Judges 8: 23)	Individual allegiance in return for royal protection
God and special people (Exodus 19; Amos 3)	A double-edged metaphor, of favour and responsibility
Shepherd and flock (Psalm 23)	
Master (Mistress) and servant (Psalm 123: 2)	
Owner and possession (Exodus 19: 5)	
Lover and beloved (allegory of Song of Solomon) Husband and wife (Hosea 3) Bride and groom (Isaiah 62: 5)	
Doctor and patient (Psalm 147: 3; Exodus 15: 26)	
Judge and plaintiff (Job 9: 15)	
Father and child (Deuteronomy 14: 1)	

Theologians often generate confusion by taking one or another of the metaphors too literally. A common candidate for preferential treatment is the covenant (king and client) relationship. So-called 'covenant theology' sets up 'the covenant' as an objective entity which defines people and obligations, and to which groups – Jews and Christians – can lay competing claims. 'Covenant' is not an objective entity. It is just one of several alternative biblical metaphors for the relationship between God and people, and no contradiction is involved in using it for different groups.

On *Yom Kippur*, just prior to an abject confession of sin, the congregation bursts into a song which celebrates several biblical metaphors:

For we are your people	and you are our God
We are your children	and you are our father
We are your servants	and you are our master
We are your congregation	and you are our portion
We are your inheritance	and you are our lot
We are your sheep	and you are our shepherd
We are your vine	and you are our keeper
We are your work	and you are our maker
We are your beloved	and you are our lover
We are your treasure	and you are our God
We are your people	and you are our king
We recognise you	and you have recognised us

Talmud

Like the Bible, the Talmud on the whole refrains from doctrinal formulations, and from definitions of God. Faith, *emunah*, is trust in God, not assent to propositions about his nature. Trust in God includes trust in the wisdom of his commandments. Faith and deeds are one (see Urbach 1987: Ch. 2).

The Talmud is on occasion provocatively anthropomorphic:

> Rav Judah said in the name of Rav: The day has twelve hours. For the first three, the Holy One, blessed be He, sits and studies the Torah. For the second three, he sits in judgment on the world; when he sees that it is deserving of destruction he rises from the throne of judgment and sits on

> the throne of mercy. For the third three, he sits and feeds the whole world, from the horns of the wild ox to the eggs of lice. In the fourth [period] he plays with Leviathan, as it is said, 'This Leviathan, which you have formed to sport with' (Psalm 104: 26) . . . (An alternative explanation) What does he do in the fourth [period]? He sits and teaches Torah to the small children in school.
>
> (Babylonian Talmud (BT), *Avoda Zara* 3b)

The literary history of this passage is complex; it combines images of God which occur separately in other contexts. As it stands in its final form, it utilises images of God to emphasise four values which are central to rabbinic teaching. The first is that of learning; God himself, the giver of Torah, sets the example of loving engagement with it. The second is that of the balance of justice and mercy; vital as justice is, the world cannot survive without compassion. The third value is concern for all living things; if God spends his time sustaining the eggs of lice, how much more so should we take care of his creation. God's game with the Leviathan is his joyful anticipation of the coming of the Messiah, when justice, peace, enlightenment and happiness will prevail; but equally, the teaching of Torah to small children is a sign and guarantee of this paradise to come.

God is said to pray, and even to wear *tefillin* (BT *Berakhot* 7a, 6a). He even 'wrapped himself in a prayer-shawl like a precentor and demonstrated to Moses the order of prayer for the forgiveness of sin' (BT *Rosh Ha-Shanah* 17).[2] The projection on to God of the way of life commended for humans elicits innumerable pictures of God fulfilling his own *mitzvot* (commandments).

These homely images are counter-balanced by the use of special names and epithets coined by the rabbis to converse about God. Foremost among these is *shekhinah* (the dwelling, or presence), a noun formed from the common biblical root *shakhan* (dwell), used in such phrases as 'they shall make me a sanctuary, and I shall dwell in their midst' (Exod. 25: 8). Ephraim Urbach correctly observes, 'Shekhina does not mean the place where the Deity is to be found . . . but His manifest and hidden presence', and 'The concept of the Shekhina does not aim to solve the question of God's quiddity, but to give expression to His presence in the world and His nearness to man, without, at the same time, destroying the sense of distance' (Urbach 1987: 40, 65). Less certain is Urbach's contention that the *shekhinah* is to be *identified* with God. This may sometimes be true, but it is a mistake to look for consistency in rabbinic usage over the long period involved.

The two common biblical names of God, the 'personal' tetragrammaton, translated since the Septuagint by 'Lord', and the more general *Elohim*, are understood to refer to *middat ha-rahamim* (the Attribute of Mercy) and *middat ha-din* (the Attribute of Judgment) respectively (*Sifré Deuteronomy* 27).

Several additional expressions are used of God in the Talmud. *Ha-Maqom* ('the place' – 'the Omnipresent') is used by the early tannaim (second century), though it tended to be replaced later by *ha-Qadosh barukh hu* ('the Holy One, blessed be He'). *Rahmana* ('the Merciful'), presumably originally intended as an epithet for God, tends to be transferred to the Torah. *Gevurah* ('power' – omnipotence) indicates that God's word and power are unquestionable and unlimited; even his 'silence' is overpowering. *Ribbono shel Olam* ('Master of the Universe') occurs commonly in narratives as a term by which God is directly addressed; it appeals to his ability to respond effectively to claims on his justice (see Urbach 1987: Chs 4 and 5).

Unfortunately, the unreliability of our texts makes it difficult to date precisely the nuances and changes in usage. But putting together the six non-biblical terms mentioned, we can see that the 'pictures' of God they convey stress six aspects of experience:

Shekhinah	God's nearness to humans
Ha-Maqom	His enveloping presence
Ha-Qadosh barukh hu	Holiness, blessedness
Rahmana	Compassion, especially as expressed through his gift of Torah
Gevurah	Power, through his revealed will
Ribbono shel Olam	His responsive control of the world

Each of these aspects is confirmed in liturgical formulations and through a wealth of remarks and anecdotes throughout rabbinic literature. Collectively, they contribute towards a 'picture' of God which reflects and interprets Jewish experience of the ultimate.

Translators – the Aramaic targums

No one knows for certain when regular Torah reading became a feature of synagogue worship. Tradition ascribes its institution to Moses (BT *Bava Qama* 82a; Jerusalem Talmud (JT) *Megillah* 4: 1) – as we might say, 'lost in the mists of antiquity'. Philo (*De Somniis* 127), Josephus (*Against Apion* 2: 175) and the New Testament (Acts 15: 21) all refer to regular public reading of the Torah. Though the Mishnah assumes regular reading of both Pentateuch and *haftarah* ('Completion': reading of the Prophets), the earliest explicit references to fixed cycles of reading occurs in an anonymous, possibly fourth-century, passage in the Babylonian Talmud. There, the custom 'in the West' (the land of Israel), of reading the Pentateuch in a three-year cycle is contrasted with the Babylonian custom, now universal Jewish practice, of a one year cycle (BT *Megilla* 29b).

Regular Hebrew reading in an Aramaic-speaking society necessitated translation. This was no casual process, but involved professional *meturgemanim* (translators), who would translate verse by verse as the Torah was read. Several Aramaic *targumim* are extant,[3] and still find liturgical as well as scholarly use. Many Jews even today follow advice said to have been given by Joshua ben Levi to his sons in the third century to read the weekly Torah portion once in Hebrew and twice in translation (*targum*) (BT *Berakhot* 8b).

Every translator is an interpreter. Much rabbinic tradition is woven into the more discursive *targumim*, but even the more literal Onkelos found it necessary to deviate from the Hebrew text now and then to avoid misleading his audience. He feared that too literal a rendering of the Hebrew text might cause people to have a wrong 'picture' of God. Frequently, Onkelos 'tones down' biblical anthropomorphisms, often by substituting *shekhinah* (presence), *yeqar* (glory) or *memra* (word) for God. 'I shall dwell in their midst' (Exod. 25: 8) becomes 'I shall set my *shekhinah* amongst them'; 'They beheld the God of Israel and beneath his feet was . . .' (Exod. 24: 10) becomes 'They beheld the glory of the God of Israel and beneath his throne was . . .'; 'They heard the voice of the Lord God walking in the garden' (Gen. 3: 8) becomes 'They heard the sound of the *memra* of the Lord God walking in the garden'.

Moses Maimonides (1135–1204) seized on this as evidence that anthropomorphisms were always to be interpreted figuratively.

However, Moses Nahmanides (1194–1270) responded that not only was Onkelos manifestly inconsistent, if it really was his intention to avoid anthropomorphism, but that the term *shekhinah* was actually a synonym for God, not the designation of some separate 'created glory'.[4]

Judaism and the visual arts

There is widespread misapprehension that since the Ten Commandments forbade the manufacture and possession of idols, Judaism has discouraged the visual arts. The discovery, within this century, of early synagogues, such as those of Capernaum and Beth Alfa in Israel, or of Dura-Europos on the Euphrates with its elaborate third-century frescoes delineating biblical scenes, has demonstrated that Jews of the rabbinic period placed no ban on visual representation, even of the human form.[5]

Literary evidence supports the conclusion that the Jewish religious artists of Galilee and elsewhere were working within the parameters of what was eventually defined as *halakhah*, though not necessarily in accordance with the most restrictive interpretations. As we learn from the anecdote of Gamaliel in the bath-house of Aphrodite, attitudes varied; Gamaliel himself found the statue unobjectionable since it was clearly intended as decoration, not for worship (Mishnah, *Avoda Zara* 3: 4). The law developed through the Talmud and later tradition, and was defined by Joseph Karo (1488–1575) as follows:

> It is forbidden to make a representation of anything in the heavenly region, such as . . . angels, or a human form alone. . . This applies to a relief, but in sunken form, as in tapestry or wall painting, it is permitted. However, one may not make relief or sunken representations of sun, moon or stars unless this is for the purpose of instruction. . . Representations of animals, birds and fish, trees, plants and so on, may be made even in relief. Some say that representations of people and dragons are only forbidden if complete with all their limbs . . .
>
> (*Shulhan Arukh*, *Yore De'ah* 141: 4–7)

Owing to the unstable conditions of Jewish life, religious art has perforce been expressed most profusely in the decoration of artefacts such as the *kiddush* cup, the Passover dish, and the *Hannukah* candelabrum, as well as the illuminated manuscript. But the larger art forms, including stained glass windows and synagogue architecture, have also been practised when conditions allowed.

There is no direct representation of God. Kabbalistic Jews in countries where Christians cultivated icons went so far as to place cards with divine names before them as they prayed; these focus the mind on 'correct' aspects of God, but are not icons.

The early mystics – *Shi'ur Qomah*

The Mishnah (early third century) refers cryptically to *maaseh bereshit* (the 'work of creation') and *maaseh merkavah* (the 'work of the chariot'), esoteric studies of Genesis 1 and Ezekiel 1 respectively. The latter is developed in *Re'uyot Ezekiel* ('Visions of Ezekiel') and *Sefer ha-Razim* ('Book of Secrets'), and it is evident from several talmudic and midrashic sources that there were schools in the talmudic period in which these studies were cultivated. However, not homiletic speculation but active 'mystical ascent' characterises the full-blown mysticism which arose when these elements were combined with the radical understanding of the Song of Songs as a self-portrait of God.

Scholarly consensus today is that the oldest Jewish mystical texts were composed not later than the second century, though the extant texts were subjected to later modification. Among the treatises preserved are those collectively known as the *hekhalot* literature. *Hekhalot* means 'palaces', and refers to seven palaces through which adepts ascend till they come face to face with the godhead. We do not know by what means people actually 'journeyed' – there has been speculation, though no evidence, that it involved the use of drugs – but it is clear that a real experience, not a theoretical description, was the aim.

A short treatise called *Shi'ur Qomah* ('Measurement of Stature') actually ventures a description of *yotsrenu* ('our Creator' – God), as one might expect to behold him in the seventh palace. It lists God's limbs, their names and their measurements, drawing on the male imagery of the Song of Songs (especially 5: 10–16); the Jewish interpretation of the Song as celebrating the love of God (the male lover) and Israel (the female beloved) was known to Origen, and must go back at least to the second century. The Creator's limbs, according to this little book, are of the order of tens of millions of parasangs in length. Ten million parasangs are 180 billion handbreadths, and as each handbreadth is 'from one end of the world to the other' it may well be, as suggested by Joseph Dan,[6] that *Shi'ur Qomah* is actually trying to wean people away from an even more crudely anthropomorphic interpretation of the Song in mere human-size terms.

The anthropomorphism of *Shi'ur Qomah* greatly embarrassed the more rationalistic Jewish thinkers of the Middle Ages. Maimonides, in reply to a correspondent who enquired whether *Shi'ur Qomah* was a Karaite work or 'of the deep secrets of the sages', was scathing in his brief reply: 'In sum, it would be a great *mitzvah* to erase and destroy all trace of this work, for "You shall not make mention of the name of other gods . . ." (Exodus 23: 13); undoubtedly, whatever has measurements is "an other god".'[7] Others, misled by its pseudepigraphic attribution to the second-century rabbis Akiva and Ishmael, would feel constrained to 'explain it away' as ingeniously as possible.

Maimonides, the rationalist – denial of anthropomorphism

The Bible often speaks of God in human terms (anthropomorphism). We read, for instance, of God's 'mighty outstretched arm' intervening in history, or of his anger or pleasure, or of his taking an oath, or even changing his mind. But if God really has no physical form or dimensions, and is all-knowing and eternal, the creator who is himself beyond space and time, what sense can we make of such talk? The medieval Jewish philosopher, Moses Maimonides, devoted a large part of his 'Guide for the Perplexed' to solving this question. All the biblical passages, he held, were metaphors, intended to convey deep truth to simple people. For instance, when the prophet speaks of 'The eyes of the Lord, which run to and fro through the whole earth' (Zach. 4:10), he conveys in simple terms the idea that God's providence extends over everything on earth.[8]

If one cannot talk of God in human terms, are there any other ways of making positive statements about him? To the medieval philosophers, Jewish, Christian and Muslim, this was the problem of the 'attributes' of God. Are there attributes which may properly be ascribed to God? Can his 'essence' – that is, his real nature, rather than his dealings with us – be known? Though the Qur'ān is far more reticent than the Bible, far less given to anthropomorphism, it does apply several attributes to God, such as 'merciful', 'mighty', 'protector' and so on. Muslim philosophers often distinguished between essential and inessential attributes, accepting the essential ones as real attributes of God, not mere metaphor. Maimonides, however, is adamant that one cannot attribute any qualities whatever to God, and progress towards understanding him comes only from denial of the attributes. Even the description of God as 'the First' is a metaphor, for 'first' can only properly be applied to objects which exist in time, and God is beyond time. To describe him as 'First', or as 'the Last', simply signifies that he is not subject to any change whatsoever (Maimonides, *Guide*, I:57). This is how Maimonides expresses his thoroughgoing *via negativa*:[9]

> . . .Know that the negative attributes of God are the true attributes; they do not include any incorrect notions or any deficiency whatever in reference to God, while positive attributes imply polytheism, and are inadequate, as we have already shown. It is now necessary to explain how negative expressions can in a certain sense be employed as attributes, and how they are distinguished from positive attributes. Then I shall show that we cannot describe the Creator by any means except by negative attributes. . .
>
> After this introduction, I would observe that . . . God's existence is absolute, that it includes no composition, as will be proved, and that we comprehend only the fact that He exists, not His essence. Consequently it is a false assumption to hold that He has any positive attribute; for He does not possess existence in addition to His essence . . . still less has He accidents, which could be described by an attribute. Hence it is clear that He has no positive attribute whatever. The negative attributes, however, are those which are necessary to direct the mind to the truths which we must believe concerning God; for on the one hand, they do not imply any plurality, and, on the other, they convey to man the highest possible knowledge of God; e.g., it has been established by proof that some being must exist besides those things which can be perceived by the senses, or apprehended by the mind; when we say of this being, that it exists, we mean that its non-existence is impossible. We then perceive that such a being is not, for instance, like the four elements, which are inanimate, and we therefore say that it is living, expressing thereby that it is not dead. We call such a being incorporeal, because we notice that it is

unlike the heavens, which are living, but material. Seeing that it is also different from the intellect, which, though incorporeal and living, owes its existence to some cause, we say it is the first, expressing thereby that its existence is not due to any cause. We further notice, that the existence, that is the essence, of this being is not limited to its own existence; many existences emanate from it, and its influence is not like that of the fire in producing heat, or that of the sun in sending forth light, but consists in constantly giving them stability and order by well-established rule, as we shall show; we say, on that account, it has power, wisdom, and will, i.e., it is not feeble or ignorant, or hasty, and does not abandon its creatures; when we say that it is not feeble, we mean that its existence is capable of producing the existence of many other things; by saying that it is not ignorant, we mean 'it perceives' or 'it lives,' – for everything that perceives is living – by saying 'it is not hasty, and does not abandon its creatures,' we mean that all these creatures preserve a certain order and arrangement; they are not left to themselves; they are not produced aimlessly, but whatever condition they receive from that being is given with design and intention. We thus learn that there is no other being like unto God, and we say that He is One, i.e., there are not more Gods than one.

(Maimonides, *Guide*, I:59; Friedländer's translation pp. 81–3)

What of the simple believer who does conceive of God as possessing positive attributes? What such a person believes in, says Maimonides, is not God at all, and therefore that person is in effect an atheist.

I do not merely declare that he who affirms attributes of God has not sufficient knowledge of the Creator, admits some association with God, or conceives Him to be different from what He is; but I say that he unknowingly loses his belief in God.

(Maimonides, *Guide*, I:60; Friedländer p. 88)[10]

For all its apparent obscurity, the medieval debate on the attributes of God highlights the problems that still trouble us today when we try to make intelligible statements about God. If whatever we say about God is somehow wrong, can we really talk about God at all? And if we cannot talk about God, is the idea of God intelligible or communicable? Surely there must be some reference to our experience; to confine ourselves to abstract or negative terms detaches our understanding of God from the experience in which it is rooted.

Kabbalah

The influence of neo-Platonism on Jewish thought[11] brought to the fore the problem of how a perfect, unchanging God, whose nature could not be grasped in human terms, could have been responsible for the creation of the world, intervene in or even know its lowly affairs. If God is perfect and unchanging, one cannot ascribe to him intention, thought, word or action; these are processes in time, and necessarily involve change. Neo-Platonists solved this problem through the doctrine of emanation, according to which all that exists comes into being through successive emanations from the unchanging divine source. The One gives rise to the Many without itself changing.

Thirteenth-century Spanish Kabbalah drew heavily on the earlier *hekhalot* mysticism, but at the same time absorbed much of the philosophy of the intervening period. The classical exposition of this trend in Jewish mysticism is the *Zohar*, composed by Rabbi Moses de Leon towards the end of the thirteenth century but traditionally ascribed to the second-century teacher, Simon bar Yohai.[12] The *Zohar* interprets the emanations as the ten *sefirot* (sing. *sefirah*), the mediating channels or intelligences by which the material world is linked with the divine.

God himself is the *Ein Sof* ('without end' – infinite, absolute), about whom nothing can be said, and who cannot be grasped by any intellect. There can be no 'picture' of God. There can, however, be descriptions of the *sefirot*, and it is these which generate the rich imagery in mature kabbalistic writing.

The *sefirot* fall into three groups. The first triad corresponds to the 'world of thought' and consists of *keter* (the crown), followed by the masculine (active) potency of *hokhmah* (knowledge) and the feminine (passive) potency of *binah* (understanding). From the conjoining of masculine and feminine proceeded the second triad. The second triad corresponds to the 'world of soul' and consists of the masculine (active) potency of *hesed* (love, kindness) and the feminine (passive) potency of *din* (judgement), which between them generate *tiferet* (beauty). The third triad corresponds to the 'world of material things' and consists of the masculine (active) potency of *netsah* (victory, eternity) and the feminine (passive) potency of *hod* (glory), which between them generate *yesod* (the foundation). The tenth *sefirah* is *malkhut* (kingdom), the sum of the activity of the others.

Some of the *sefirot* have alternative names, and all function within a rich symbolic system. For instance, the first *sefirah*, *keter*, emanating from the infinite light of the *Ein Sof*, is also referred to as *attika* (the Ancient One), *nequdah rishona* (the first point), *nequda peshuta* (the simple point), *resh hivra* (the white head), *arikh anpin* (the slow to anger), *rum ma'alah* (the immeasurable height), or *ehyeh* (the 'I am'). The *sefirot* collectively comprise *Adam Qadmon* (the First Adam, or Primal Man), in whose image human beings are made. They are represented in the human body as follows:

Keter	head
hokhmah	brain
binah	heart
hesed	right arm
din	left arm
tiferet	chest
netsah	right leg
hod	left leg
yesod	genitals
malkhut	complete body

Representations of the *sefirot* in the form of a tree or even a male human body are sometimes produced. But are these representations of God? Are the *sefirot* in some way the essence of God, and is knowledge of them theosophy, actual knowledge of God? This question is addressed in the *Zohar* itself:

> Should anyone ask: Is it not written, 'You saw no image'? (Deuteronomy 4: 15), he may answer, 'The image I have seen is the one of which it is written, "He shall see the very form of the Lord", (Numbers 12: 8) and no other whatsoever, that he created and formed with letters.' That is why it says, 'To whom will you liken me, who is compared with me?' (Isaiah 40: 25) 'What likeness will you find for God or what form to resemble his?' (Isaiah 40: 18)
>
> Even this image does not exist in its place, but when it descends to rule over creatures, and extends over them, it appears . . . to each of them according to their (own) appearance, vision and shape . . .
>
> That is why he says, Though I appear to you in your own form, 'To whom will you liken me, who is compared with me?' (Isaiah 40: 25). For before the Holy One, blessed be he, created form in the world, he was alone, without form or appearance . . .

> But after he had created the image of the chariot of supernal man, he descended there, and was named by that image . . . that they might comprehend him through his attributes, how he would guide the world with mercy and justice, according to the deeds of men. For if his light would not extend over all creatures, how would they comprehend him, how would 'The whole earth is full of his glory' (Isaiah 6: 3) be fulfilled?
>
> Woe to anyone who compares him to any attribute, even of his own attributes, how much more so to any human attribute . . . He is described insofar as he rules over the attribute . . . but when he rises above it he has no measure, description or form.
>
> [This is] just like the sea, whose waters have no shape or form of their own, but take their form from the land over which they flow . . .
>
> (*Zohar* II, 42b)

The primary interpretation of this passage is expressed by David R. Blumenthal in his *Understanding Jewish Mysticism: A Source Reader* (Ktav, 1978):

> God was unknown before creation, and that aspect of Him cannot be known even by exploring the meaning of His name or its letters. After Creation, however, He chose to reveal Himself to man and He made known His various Names and/or attributes. Finally, to identify His names and/or attributes with Him, with His essence, would be wrong, for they are only labels, expressions of an unknowable essence behind the word.
>
> (Blumenthal 1978: 127)

So the picture is not of God himself, for that would be, literally, unthinkable. The picture is of his attributes, an insight into the consciousness or creativity of God, not into his essence. If we consider the sefirotic system as an expression of our deep experience of reality, we find that it affirms as God-determined absolutes ten aspects of human experience, and explores their relationships both among each other and with the created world. Such a system makes possible 'anthropopathy', the attribution to God of human feelings and emotions; the biblical words denoting God's joy, anger, power, grace, lovingkindness and so on are literally applied to God, not in his essence as the *Ein Sof*, but in his conscious self-revelation as he interacts with his created world.

Liturgy

Instances of personal prayer, such as those of Abraham and Hannah, are found in the earliest biblical stories. Even when the national worship was centred on the Temple, sacrifice did not replace prayer, but supplemented it; if Ezekiel and Leviticus focus on the sacrificial aspects of Temple worship, Psalms is the supreme expression of its prayer. Trito-Isaiah, welcoming all humanity to the new Jerusalem Temple, declared in the name of God, 'My house shall be called a house of prayer for all peoples' (Isa. 56: 7).

Yet the liturgical framework for prayer as it exists today was set only in the second century. What 'picture' of God did Gamaliel II and his collaborators convey through their prayer formulations?

The balance between scriptural reading and actual prayer indicated a God (a) whose will could be known through his revealed word and (b) who might be approached, addressed, even pleaded with by each humble individual without the need for mediation through priest or sacrifice. This picture of a God who does not require intermediaries – priests, sacrifices, rituals – is a revolutionary achievement of rabbinic Judaism. Yet priesthood was not rejected in principle. Given the appropriate circumstances, priest, sacrifice and ritual might all contribute to the bond with God; but at the same time it was unambiguously affirmed that each man and woman could approach God directly in the sincerity of their own heart.

The twice daily scriptural reading was the *Shema*. Its first paragraph, Deuteronomy 6: 4–9, has two themes, the loving acceptance of God's supremacy and of his commandments. The theme of the second paragraph (Deuteronomy 11: 13–21) is reward and punishment. The third paragraph (Numbers 15: 37–41) reinforced the experience of redemption, that God had brought Israel out of Egypt.

Shema was embedded in a group of blessings headed by a call to prayer, 'Bless the Lord who is to be blessed'. Two blessings preceded the *Shema*. The first praises God as creator of light and darkness, that is, as the one whose power is displayed daily through his orderly guidance of creation. The second declares his love of Israel, manifest through his revealing the Torah to them. Following *Shema*, the one morning or two evening blessings focus on God as redeemer and protector.

The main prayer at the three daily services is known by the rabbis simply as *tefillah* (prayer). It consists of nineteen (originally eighteen) short, thematic blessings. Each blessing has a 'seal', or ending, of the form 'Blessed are you, O lord, who . . .'. Most probably Gamaliel did no more than formulate themes and the structure of the whole, laying down precise wording for the endings but not for the themes.

The nineteen blessings commence with a set of three, standard for sabbaths, festivals and weekdays (endings are those of the standard Orthodox prayer books, sometimes abbreviated; themes are explained only where not obvious):

ENDING	THEME
Shield of Abraham	God of the patriarchs (Abraham, Isaac, Jacob); past and future redeemer
Restore the dead to life	Power of life and death, dispenser of life-giving dew and rain
Holy God	

The second group varies according to occasion. On Sabbaths and festivals it consists of short readings for the day. On weekdays it consists of thirteen (originally twelve) petitions, couched in collective terms, but open to the inclusion of individual personal intercessions. The concluding formulae of the thirteen are:

ENDING	THEME
Gracious giver of knowledge	
Who delights in repentance	
Who forgives sin	
Redeemer of Israel	Context – God who saves from the harsh conditions of life
Healer of the sick	
Who blesses years	Prayer for bountiful crops

Who gathers the dispersed of Israel	
Who loves justice	A reflection on injustice in the world
Who destroys slander and arrogance	Directed against treachery, injustice and heresy
Stay and trust of the righteous	A prayer for welfare of the faithful including proselytes
Who rebuilds Jerusalem	
Who makes the horn of salvation flourish	For the 'restoration of David', that is, the coming of Messiah
Who hears prayer	General prayer for the acceptance of the preceding petitions

The concluding group of three blessings is standard for sabbaths, festivals and weekdays:

ENDING	THEME
Who restores the *shekhinah* to Zion (Jerusalem)	Petition that the full service of prayer and sacrifice be restored and accepted with love
Thanksgiving	For God's 'daily miracles'
Peace	

The attitude in which the *tefillah* is said contributes to the picture of God it instils in the worshipper. One stands, in a serious frame of mind, feet together, hands folded over heart, eyes closed, in humble submission before the Almighty, and facing the Temple site. Steps are taken forward at the beginning, backward as one 'departs' from the divine presence at the end. At various points one bows humbly. There is a sense of smallness and unworthiness in the presence of the infinite; yet this awe-inspiring infinite being is addressed as a loving, caring parent, who through ages past has concerned himself deeply in the story of Israel of which the worshipper is part.

Prayers for each festival or special occasion incorporate appropriate imagery of God. The Passover prayers, for instance, abound with references to God 'who brought us out of Egypt'; the image of God as 'redeemer' emphasises his role in history and his concern for the poor and oppressed. The most powerful imagery is undoubtedly that reserved for the Ten Days of Penitence, spanning the period from the New Year to the Day of Atonement.

The *selihot* (prayers for forgiveness) services which precede the New Year are formulated around the *shlosh esreh middot*, the thirteen attributes of God based on Moses' prayer on behalf of Israel after the sin of the Golden Calf. These are the attributes – the 'picture of God' – derived from Exodus 34: 6–7:

TEXT OF EXODUS 34: 6–7	ATTRIBUTE[13]
Lord	The attribute of mercy, extended before sin has been committed
Lord	The attribute of mercy, extended after sin has been committed
God	in his pure attribute of mercy; alternatively, the one with power (to forgive)
merciful	to the guilty, assuaging their punishment
gracious	even to the undeserving
patient (long-suffering)	granting opportunity to the sinner to repent
abundant in goodness	preferring to show mercy in judgement
and truth	uncorruptible
keeping mercy to the thousandth generation	The attribute of mercy is far greater than that of justice (punishment is only to the third and fourth generations)

forgiving iniquity	sins committed deliberately but with malice
and transgression	sins committed in a rebellious spirit
and sin	accidental sin
by no means clearing the guilty, but visiting the sins of the fathers on the sons. . .	This is also understood as an instance of God's compassion, for though he will not forgive unrepented evil, he hesitates to punish, waiting for generations; if the 'sons' abandon their fathers' sins, there is no punishment.

In a small but significant change, the ending of the third blessing of the *tefillah* during the Ten Days of Penitence becomes 'Holy King', instead of 'Holy God'. The 'king' metaphor for God presupposes the role of king as head of the judiciary. Since this is a time for repentance, God is envisaged as a judge before whom all pass for judgement. Yet the king is very much a shepherd king, for the metaphor of sheep passing one by one before the shepherd also features in the liturgy of the day (derived from Mishnah *Rosh Ha-Shanah* 1: 2). And the image of king is blended with the more tender image of father in the ancient prayer *Avinu Malkenu* (Our father, our king!) featured twice daily through the penitential season.

As the Day of Atonement itself approaches, the twin images of father and king seem to move from the pole of judgement to that of forgiveness. The central blessing of the *tefillah* does indeed refer to a king, but a 'king who pardons and forgives our sins and the sins of his people the house of Israel, and each year makes our sins pass away. . .' Liturgical poetry on the Temple liturgy of Atonement helps dramatise the move.

To complete this brief sketch of the way God is pictured in Jewish prayer, here are a few verses of the *shir ha-kavod* (Song of Glory) which is sung responsively at the end of the Orthodox Sabbath morning service. The poet, probably Judah the Pious of Regensburg (*d.* 1217), struggles with the philosophical problem of how to talk of the ineffable. His solution is the classical one that, though he can say nothing of God as he really is, he can freely draw on biblical and rabbinic imagery which sought to describe God's deeds.

> I will chant sweet hymns and compose songs for my soul yearns for You . . .
> I declare Your glory, though I have not seen You; I portray You by imagery, though I have not known You.
> Through the acts of Your prophets, by the speech of Your servants,
> You gave a glimpse of the glory of Your majestic splendour.
> They described Your greatness and Your power from the display of Your mighty works.
> They likened You, but not as You really are; they likened You in accordance with Your deeds
> They represented You in countless visions; yet You are one in all the imagery.
> They saw You as aged and also as youthful; the hair of Your head now grey, now black.
> Aged in the day of judgement, youthful in the day of battle; as a warrior whose hands do battle for Him . . .
> With sparkling dew His head is covered. His locks with drops of the night . . .
> His glory rests on me; and mine on him; He is near to me when I call to Him.
> He is bright, he is ruddy; His clothes are red, as when He came from treading the winepress in Edom.
> He showed the *tefillin* knot to the meek Moses, when the Lord's likeness was before his eyes.
> He delights in His people, He glorifies the humble; He is enthroned by their praises, He glories in them.[14]

Feminism

What religious Jewish responses are there to the changing awareness of the role of the women's movement in society?

Hebrew, like English, separates its pronouns by gender. All nouns have gender, and most verb forms vary by gender. It is linguistically impossible to talk about God in Hebrew without committing oneself on gender. Even the dodges, ugly but manageable in English, of using 'inclusive' language, avoiding pronouns, or coining neologisms such as 'godself', cannot work. However much we may insist that grammatical gender is not to do with sex, the fact remains that the constant and consistent use of masculine language for God reinforces the concept of male superiority, and male dominance in society. This is not lessened by the theological certainty that it is nonsense to speak of God, who has no physical form, as male or female in 'godself'.

As Clifford Geertz pointed out in his essay on 'Religion as a Cultural System', religious symbols function both as models *of* the community's sense of reality and as models *for* human behaviour and social order. So the question is not just whether we think of God as male or female, but of how the ways we talk about God influence male and female roles in society.

Genesis 1: 27 runs, 'So God created humankind[15] in his own image; in the image of God he created him; male and female he created them'. This implies that in using our concept of God to model human behaviour we should not distinguish between male and female. Consistent with this, the rabbinic formulation of the 'imitation of God' incorporates virtues associated with female as well as male roles. 'After the Lord your God shall you walk' (Deut. 13: 5) is interpreted as *imitatio dei*:

> Said Rabbi Hama bar Hanina: How can a person walk after God? Is it not written 'For the Lord your God is a consuming fire' (Deuteronomy 4: 24)? But follow God's attributes. As He clothes the naked . . . as He visits the sick . . . comforts the bereaved . . . buries the dead . . . so should you.
>
> (BT *Sota* 14a)[16]

What is remarkable is the absence of distinctively male characteristics from those attributes of God we are called upon to emulate. It is God's care and compassion that we are exhorted to copy, not his vengeance and imposition of justice.

Are feminine images of deity, rather than just feminine attributes, to be found anywhere within the Jewish tradition? At least one verse speaks of our relationship with God as that of a slave-girl to her mistress:

> As the eyes of a slave follow his master's hand
> or the eyes of a slave-girl her mistress
>
> (Psalm 123: 2)

But this is hardly auspicious. Images of slavery and royalty are today as problematic as those of male dominance. Scripture, indeed, says:

> On the day the Lord spoke to you out of the fire in Horeb, you saw no figure of any kind; so take good care not to fall into the degrading practice of making figures carved in relief, in the form of a man or a woman, or of any animal on earth . . .
>
> (Deut. 4: 15–16)

The conscious search for God-imagery, even if not 'figures carved in relief', is an uncomfortable process for traditional Jews. Like Molière's *M. Jourdain*, astonished at the discovery that he had been talking grammar all his life, we have suddenly realised that we were using images all along. The task now is to find the right images.

We have spoken above of the common rabbinic use of the term *shekhinah* for God. This noun, which means something like 'indwelling', certainly has feminine gender, but so do all abstract nouns in Hebrew. Although the abstract noun does not occur in scripture, it is obviously derived from the verb *shakhan*, to dwell, as used in contexts such as 'They shall make me a sanctuary, and I shall dwell in their midst' (Exod. 25: 8). The difficult question, which we raised earlier in the name of Nahmanides, is whether it refers to God, or just to God's 'presence' in the world, that is, to some sort of emanation or radiant light from God.

> Said Rabbi Simon the son of Yohai: See how great is the love of the Holy One, blessed be He, for Israel, for wherever they have been exiled, the *Shekhinah* has accompanied them.
>
> (BT *Megilla* 29a)

Elsewhere, the *shekhinah* is said to have 'withdrawn' at the time of the destruction of the Temple, or even to be 'weeping in the inner houses' (BT *Hagiga* 5b).

It is highly unlikely that any of the rabbis who uttered these divergent statements about the *shekhinah* were thinking of it in gender terms. However, it is clear that they thought of the *shekhinah* as protecting and nurturing Israel. In this sense, it is legitimate for us today to draw upon this precedent for female imagery of God's relationship with people.

In the section on Kabbalah we referred to the masculine and feminine pairs of *sefirot*, for instance the masculine (active) potency of *hokhmah* (knowledge) and the feminine (passive) potency of *binah* (understanding) which engender the second triad. Such bisexual imagery affords a foothold within tradition for contemporary attempts to abandon exclusively male language, though in its original kabbalistic formulation it retains the concept of male dominance – male active, female passive.

If the availability of feminine imagery of God within Jewish tradition is limited, does it make sense to create new images? The attempt has been made by Jewish feminists. Rita M. Gross urges that, as a first stage, familiar forms of addressing God in prayer should be transposed to the feminine. For instance *ha-qedosha berukha hi* – 'the Holy One, blessed be She' – should be used in place of the current masculine form. Gross lists five basic goddess images that need translating into Jewish terms.

1. The 'coincidence of opposites' or 'ambiguity symbolism', close to the idea accepted in Jewish liturgy of God who creates both light and darkness.
2. Images of God the Mother, which must be joined with:
3. The goddess of culture in all its aspects, motherhood and culture being twin aspects of creativity.
4. The goddess as giver of wisdom and patron of scholarship and learning.
5. The assertion of sexuality as an aspect of divinity.

She sums up, 'Dimensions of deity that have been lost or severely attenuated during the long centuries when we spoke of God as if S/He were only a male are restored. They seem to have to do with acceptance and immanence, with nature and the cyclic round. Metaphors of enclosure, inner spaces, and curved lines seem to predominate. What a relief from the partial truth of intervention and transcendence; of history and linear time; of going forth, exposure and straight lines!'[17]

Views like those of Gross are strongly resisted, particularly in the Orthodox communities, where liturgical innovation of any kind is frowned upon and radical change is perceived as undermining authority. But the questions are being raised, experiments are taking place, and even the Orthodox are nervously toying with women's services and special forms of religious observance, as one sees in the growth of the 'Rosh Hodesh' (New Moon) movement.

Modern and Holocaust theologies

Jews have been involved in virtually all the theological movements of the modern world. Spinoza unleashed the most radical questioning of traditional ideas on God. Did his identification of God with the natural order (*deus sive natura*) make him an atheist or, as Novalis had it, 'a man intoxicated by God'? Though he himself was excommunicated by the Jewish community, his deist philosophy influenced Moses Mendelssohn. At the time Mendelssohn was advocating a 'God of Reason', the new Hasidic movement in Eastern Europe was popularising a modification of the kabbalistic theosophy described above. Jewish folk memory recalls a dispute between the Hasidic leader, Shneur Zalman, and Elijah, the Gaon of Vilna, as to the meaning of 'the whole earth is full of his glory' (Isa. 6: 3); this was a debate on the immanence or transcendence of God – was God in, or beyond, nature?

Evolution, existentialism, philosophy of language, postmodernism have all affected more recent Jewish thinking about God, yet perhaps no single event has presented as great a challenge as the Holocaust. The traditional 'picture' of God is that he is benevolent and all-powerful, a just and compassionate ruler of the world. If that is true, why did he not intervene to save innocent people, including a million and a half children, at the time of the Holocaust?

Of course, theologians, and indeed the Bible itself, have always worried about injustice in the world, about why the righteous often suffer and the wicked prosper. The whole book of Job is devoted to this problem. Contrary to Reform theologians such as Emil Fackenheim, the Holocaust did not raise a radically new problem on this score; it merely focused attention on a problem which has worried theists ever since Cain killed Abel.[18]

Richard Rubenstein pursued the vocation of Reform Rabbi without worrying unduly about the presence of evil in the world, until a chance meeting with Heinrich Grüber, Dean of the Berlin Evangelical Church, in 1966. He was deeply shocked by Grüber's contention that 'For some reason, it was part of God's plan that the Jews died. God demands our death daily. He is the Lord. He is the

Master; all is in His keeping and ordering.'[19] Part of the shock lay in the fact that these words proceeded from the mouth of a man who was clearly not motivated by anti-Semitism. Rubenstein has been accused of denying the existence of God, but he strenuously rebuts this:

> No man can really say that God is dead. How can we know that? Nevertheless, I am compelled to say that we live in the time of the 'death of God'. *This is more a statement about man and his culture than about God* . . . When I say we live in the time of the death of God, I mean that the thread uniting God and man, heaven and earth, has been broken. We stand in a cold, silent, unfeeling cosmos, unaided by any purposeful power beyond our own resources. After Auschwitz, what else can a Jew say about God?
>
> (Rubenstein 1966: 151–2)

And:

> I believe there is a conception of God . . . which remains meaningful after the death of the God-who-acts-in-history. It is a very old conception of God with deep roots in both Western and Oriental mysticism. According to this conception, God is spoken of as the *Holy Nothingness*. When God is thus designated, he is conceived of as the ground and source of all existence. To speak of God as the *Holy Nothingness* is not to suggest that he is a void. On the contrary, he is an indivisible *plenum* so rich that all existence derives from his very essence. God as the *Nothing* is not absence of being but superfluity of being.
>
> Why then do we use the term *Nothingness*? Use of the term rests in part upon a very ancient observation that all definition of finite entities involves negation. The infinite God, the ground of all finite beings, cannot be defined. The infinite God is therefore in no sense a thing bearing any resemblance to the finite beings of the empirical world. The infinite God is nothing. At times, mystics also spoke of God in similar terms as the *Urgrund*, the primary ground, the dark unnameable abyss out of which the empirical world has come.
>
> . . . whoever believes God is the source or ground of being usually believes that human personality is coterminous with the life of the human body. Death may be the entrance into eternal life, the perfect life of God; death may also end pain, craving, and suffering, but it involves the dissolution and disappearance of individual identity.
>
> Perhaps the best available metaphor for the conception of God as the Holy Nothingness is that God is the ocean and we are the waves. In

> some sense each wave has its moment in which it is distinguishable as a somewhat separate entity. Nevertheless, no wave is entirely distinct from the ocean which is its substantial ground.[20]

Like the attenuated, psychological prop God, introduced by the Reconstructionist Rabbi Harold Kushner in his popular 'When Bad Things Happen to Good People', Rubenstein's God has little in common with the transcendent and omnipotent God of biblical tradition.

Orthodox theologians retain the image of God who is loving and omnipotent, and who intervenes in history on behalf of his people, Israel; it is we who have fallen short of his demands and been unfaithful to his Torah. But many object that to uphold this view in the wake of the destruction of six million Jews, among them the spiritual leadership of Jewry, promotes the image of a God whose demands are totally unreasonable and whose decisions as to when and how to intervene are arbitrary.

The image of God as hidden, or distant, was linked by the prophets of the exile to Israel's disobedience. Yet, as Samuel Balentine has shown, even in scripture God's hiding is not necessarily a judgement, but 'a subject for lament and protest as innocent suppliants charge that they have done nothing to warrant divine abandonment'.[21] The same ambiguity on the silence of God characterises Holocaust theology.

In our view, it is possible to retain diverse, even contrary images of God, as we have seen in both scripture and rabbinic tradition. The critical task is to relate these images to experience, not to define some entity from whose nature all the underlying experiences can be logically inferred. In terms of the *midrash* cited earlier, God appears sometimes as a warrior, sometimes as gentle elder. To assert 'this is the same God' is to affirm the underlying unity of all experience, not the inferential integration of our descriptions of that experience. All our 'pictures' are pictures of the one God; to accord privilege to any one of them at the expense of the others is to commit idolatry.

NOTES

1. Rabbi Yohanan (third century) in Babylonian Talmud, *Megilla* 31a.
2. The text of this prayer, the 'thirteen attributes' of Exodus 34, is given below in the section on liturgy.

3. For an introduction see John Bowker (1969) *The Targums and Rabbinic Literature*, Cambridge, Cambridge University Press. Much research has been completed since that date, and several Targumim have been translated into English. T&T Clark of Edinburgh are publishing a series of the Aramaic Bible. Volume 6, the *Targum Onkelos to Genesis*, by Bernard Grossfeld, appeared in 1988 and has an excellent introduction.
4. Ramban (Moses Nahamides) on Genesis 46: 1. We referred above to Urbach's account of the use of the term *shekhinah* in rabbinic literature.
5. Popular works on Jewish art include Cecil Roth (1971) *Jewish Art*, London, Vallentine, Mitchell; Gabrielle Sed-Rajna (1985) *Ancient Jewish Art*, New Jersey, Chartwell Books; and catalogues of the main Jewish museum collections, especially those of the Israel National Museum in Jerusalem.
6. Joseph Dan (1989) 'The religious experience of the Merkavah' in Arthur Green (ed.) *Jewish Spirituality: From the Bible Through the Middle Ages*. London, SCM Press, p.296.
7. *Maimonides: Responsa*, ed. A.H. Freimann, Jerusalem 5694/1934, p. 343.
8. Maimonides, *Guide*, I: 44. *The Guide of the Perplexed by Moses Maimonides* (trans Shlomo Pines with an Introduction by Leo Strauss), 2 vols, Chicago, University of Chicago Press, 1963.
9. The *via negativa* (negative way), the doctrine that one cannot affirm anything of the transcendent God, only deny attributes, may be traced back to the Christian Pseudo-Dionysius in the fifth century, and has had many Christian and Muslim, as well as Jewish, adherents.
10. I have substituted 'unknowingly' for Friedländer's pre-Freudian 'unconsciously'.
11. On medieval Jewish philosophy, including neo-Platonism, see Colette Sirat (1985) *A History of Jewish Philosophy in the Middle Ages*, Cambridge, Cambridge University Press and Editions de la Maison des Sciences de L'homme.
12. For a detailed analysis of the literary history of the Zohar see Gershom G. Scholem (1941) *Major Trends in Jewish Mysticism*, Jerusalem, Schocken, Chapter 5, and Isaiah Tishby's introduction to his Hebrew translation of *Zohar* texts (*Mishnat ha-Zohar*, Jerusalem, 1961), translated into English by David Goldstein as *The Wisdom of the Zohar* (3 vols), the Littman Library, Oxford, Oxford University Press, 1989.
13. These interpretations are largely culled from Babylonian Talmud *Rosh Ha-Shana* 17a and *Yoma* 36b, *Mekhilta* on Exodus 34, *Targum Onkelos*, and Obadiah Sforno's commentary.

14. *Authorised Daily Prayer Book*, Centenary Edition, ed. Lord Jakobovits, London, 1990, p. 420–2.
15. The New English Bible text, which I have used, actually has 'man' here. I have emended this to 'humans', as this is a more accurate interpretation of the Hebrew term *Adam*. The New English Bible was published before the rise of feminism.
16. See Maimonides *Mishneh Torah: Hilkhot Deot* 1: 6 for a reconstruction of this passage.
17. Rita M. Gross (1983) 'Steps towards feminine images of deity in Jewish theology', in Susannah Heschel (ed.) *On Being a Jewish Feminist*, New York, Schocken Books, p. 234–47.
18. For a fuller exposition of this argument see Norman Solomon (1991) *Judaism and World Religion*, Basingstoke, Macmillan, and New York, St Martin's Press, chapter 7.
19. Richard L. Rubenstein (1966) *After Auschwitz*, Indianapolis, Bobbs-Merrill, p. 54.
20. Richard L. Rubenstein (1970) *Morality and Eros*, New York, McGraw-Hill, pp. 185–6.
21. Samuel E. Balentine (1983) *The Hidden God*, Oxford and New York, Oxford University Press, p. v.

FURTHER READING

Heschel, S. (ed.) (1982) *On Being a Jewish Feminist*, New York, Schocken Books.

Lachower, F. and Tishby, I. (eds) (trans D. Goldstein) (1989) *The Wisdom of the Zohar* (3 vols), Oxford, Oxford University Press for Littman Library of Jewish Civilisation.

Maimonides, Moses (trans S. Pines, with an introductory essay by Leo Strauss) (1963) *Guide of the Perplexed* (2 vols), Chicago and London, University of Chicago Press; also *The Guide for the Perplexed* trans M. Friedländer (1904) 2nd edn, London, Routledge and Kegan Paul.

Roth, C. (rev. edn B. Narkiss) (1971) *Jewish Art: An Illustrated History*, London, Vallentine Mitchell.

Rubenstein, R. (1966) *After Auschwitz*, Indianapolis, Bobbs-Merrill.

Scholem, G.G. (1941) *Major Trends in Jewish Mysticism*, Jerusalem, Schocken Books.

Sed-Rajna, G. (n.d.) *Ancient Jewish Art: East and West*, Secaucus, NJ, Chartwell Books Inc.

Urbach, E.E. (trans I. Abrahams) (1987) *The Sages*, Cambridge, MA and London, Harvard University Press.

6. Sikhism

Beryl Dhanjal

The Sikh Gurūs amassed 1,430 pages of poetry on the subject of *Akāl Purakh* (God) without exhausting the possibilities, and, not infrequently, they expressed the impossibility of providing an adequate description. Guru Nanak often explained that mere language was inadequate to express the wonder, the immense awe, or even the ecstasy engendered by such awe, *visamād*. We are incoherent and suffer such limitations in expression that we are unable to offer any adequate description. Guru Nanak said:

> The more we say, the more there remains to be said.
>
> If I knew, would I not say?
>
> Does anyone know how to write this account?
>
> How shall I address Thee? How shall I praise Thee? How shall I describe Thee? How shall I know Thee?
>
> In describing him, there would never be an end.
>
> Millions of men give millions of descriptions of him, but they fail to describe him. If anyone shall try he shall afterwards repent.
>
> If he can be described in writing then describe him; but such description is impossible. O Nanak, call him great; only he himself knows how great he is.

> Were one tongue to become a hundred thousand, and a
> hundred thousand to become twentyfold more,
> I would utter the name of the One Lord of the world
> hundreds and thousands of times with all my tongues.

In this way I should ascend the stairs of the Lord and
become one with him.
On hearing the matters of heaven, even the worms become
jealous.

(The above quotations are a few culled from *Japjī Sāhib* alone, so they represent but a small sample from Guru Nanak's works.)

In addition to relating something of what Guru Nanak said of God, it is also necessary both to consider what others have said since his day, and to look at popular images. Some images are brand new and growing.

Orientalism and western models

Yet, thus far, what have people had to base their views on? The writings which have been influential have often been works by a western-educated élite and by European men. Sikhism has been written about by J.D. Cunningham, M.A. Macauliffe, and others, and they have seen Sikhism in terms of that model of religion which they carry unconsciously in their own heads: the Christian model. Even if people are non-believers, their very language still dictates the model and the concerns and institutions which they see as religion.

Yet, the curious thing is that when Sikhs themselves write of Sikhism, they too often write in the same terms. Is there then a Sikh tradition to which we must adhere in a faithful manner to avoid falling into orientalism, and to be true to the teaching of the Gurūs? Thus far, even Sikh writers have followed the well-trodden path. If they have resented orientalism and the efforts of westerners to write Sikh theology, they have not suggested any other model which might be more helpful in giving a wider understanding. Writers say that God is one, omnipotent, infinite, eternal, absolute, immense, omnipresent, spirit and light etc., which is not untrue, but nor is it distinctive.

Much writing concentrates more on history than theology. A recent booklet from the Sikh Missionary Society contains thirty-four pages of 'history' and two and a half on actual belief. This is not an uncommon situation.

W.H. MCLEOD

It has often been said that anyone who tries to produce a systematic theology for Sikhism will attract criticism. The Sikh Gurūs were not theologians and some think that their work should not be analysed as theological material. It is therefore ironic that Hew McLeod's book, *Gurū Nānak and the Sikh Religion* (1968) was criticised for its treatment of the *janam sakhīs*, but less was said about his chapters on the teachings of Guru Nanak, in which he suggested a systematic theology based upon the Gurū's teachings. The theological work has been quoted almost verbatim, many times, without acknowledgement and usually by his critics. It was an important book, and since it was written it has been difficult to think in terms other than those which McLeod proposed.

McLeod writes of the nature of God and the divine self-expression. The nature of God includes his unity, that he is simply *Ik*, the One. God is both *nirguṇa* (without qualities) and *saguṇa* (with qualities). As to his *nirguṇa* aspect, we can say nothing for we can form no impression. But of his *saguṇa* aspect we can say something, for these are the aspects by which we can know and picture him. God is creator, destroyer and sustainer. God is formless, ineffable, immanent, eternal, sovereign. He is great, and he takes the initiative towards humans. The divine self-expression may be seen through the *śabad*, God's word heard in the heart, the *Nām*, Name, the *Gurū*, the divine preceptor, the *hukam*, the divine order and *sach*, truth.

This is a fair summary of Nanak's teaching. Is there any more to be said? For Guru Nanak, there was always more. McLeod also constantly rethinks. *Gurū Nānak and the Sikh Religion* would not be the same book if he were to write it now.

But for many Sikhs, theology cannot and should not be attempted for non-Christian religions. Anyone who tries is liable to be accused of a form of orientalism, of trying to bend Sikh thought to fit it into western categories, producing a sort of systematised western form which therefore is no longer true to the original teachings of the Gurūs.

Some say that Sikh Gurūs were interested in direct experience of God; they were not interested in writing systematic accounts of theology, and Guru Nanak was not a theologian. Here is an argument erected against McLeod. But would this argument ever have been propounded had it not been for McLeod? He wrote about the Gurū's approach, saying that it was not systematic, but that even so, it was not inconsistent. On the contrary, one of the claims that can be made, and was indeed made by McLeod, is that the Gurū was entirely consistent. On this point, there has never been any argument. If the views of the Gurū are clear and consistent, then surely arranging them in order to demonstrate how clearly this is so, can hardly be a harmful exercise.

In attempting to describe the Gurū's thoughts, one might try to choose some characteristic words, and some scholars use that approach. The pitfall, though, is that in doing so, although one is selecting from Nanak's vocabulary, one is choosing what one wishes to emphasise, which might not reflect the Gurū's priorities: he might not give the same emphasis. Perhaps a sensible approach would be to look at word frequency with a computer. One might choose and methodically follow one poem, but that would give only a taste. Selecting from many possible terms means that one might give undue attention to some parts and too little to others. But there is much to learn from the very choice of words. McLeod has chosen the terms in which he sees the basic concepts of Sikhism. He refers in all of his later publications to *Akāl Purakh*, the 'One Beyond Time'. This is indeed a characteristic phrase from the Gurū.

Akāl Purakh is now the term McLeod substitutes for the English word 'God', and it is also an expression often used by some other (though not all) scholars. McLeod (1989: 49) has come to believe that in writing about Sikhism, in order to approach a Sikh understanding, one should discard English vocabulary which is associated with very specific concepts and use Panjābi concepts instead.

Mūl Mantra

Guru Arjan chose a special piece by Guru Nanak as the very first words of the Gurū Granth Sāhib. The *Mūl Mantra* is the basic credal statement, the root of all belief. This is the Gurū's terse summation of the one he worships. It does seem a good starting point for our study because it comes first of all and because it is quoted at the beginning of every subsequent piece. Macauliffe has a story that the Gurū was asked why the words *Sat Nām*, True Name, were always written as an introduction to his hymns. He replied:

> The Name is the God of all Gods. Some propitiate Durga, some Shiv, some Ganesh, and some other Gods; but the Gurū's Sikhs worship the True Name and thus remove all obstacles to salvation. Accordingly, the prefatory words, the True Name, are written in all compositions.
>
> (Macauliffe 1909, vol. 1: 138)

By being used before all other verses, the *Mūl Mantra* is given the status of an invocation, a *mangalacharan*. McLeod says that the title, *Mūl Mantra*, was given by Bhai Gurdas. Guru Nanak said that *Harinām*, the Name of God, was the *Mūl Mantra* (McLeod 1968: 163). It is, most importantly, a description of God.

Guru Nanak chose to begin with the simple number 1.

1 Ouṃkar	The one creator of the *oum̐*, the mystic syllable
Satinām	whose Name is True
Karatā Purakh	the Creator
Nirbhau	fearless
Niravair	free from hostility
Akāl murat	whose form is timeless, immortal
Ajonī	unborn
Saibhaṃ	self-existent
Gurparaśadi	by the grace of the Gurū
Japu	murmuring, inward recitation
Ādi	beginning
Sach	truth, reality
Jugad	in the beginning of time
Sach	truth
hai bhi	[He] is also
Sach	truth
Nanak	Oh, Nanak !
hosī bhī	[He] will be
Sach.	truth.

Any Sikh scholar or commentator can write paragraph after paragraph on any one word, so laden with meaning is each word. Yet Guru Nanak feels his words are inadequate. In the *Japjī* he follows the words he uses directly by saying:

> By thinking, I cannot think of him, even if I think a hundred thousand times. In silence, I cannot keep silent, even if I remain meditating.

> Hundreds and thousands of cunning devices and not even one will get you there. How can one become true? How is the veil of falsehood to be broken? By walking in the way of his order.

Among the twenty-two words, *sach* (true, truth, reality) appears four times. Thus it would appear to be one of Guru Nanak's priorities. In addition, many more of the words really describe this truth – that God was true when time began, has been true throughout the ages, is true today and will be true in the future. Nanak also managed to squeeze a human being's proper response towards God into this tiny space: *japu* – meaning repeat, meditate on the name, murmur it in constant prayer.

ONE

The first symbol in the Gurū Granth Sāhib is the numeral one, *Ik*. God is pictured first as a numeral: the 1 *ouṃ* creator. The *ouṃ* is the mystic syllable, considered by some as one of the holiest names of all for God, the eternal reality, transcendent, absolute, without qualities. *Ik ouṃkar* emphasises the sole reality of God, the self-existence as against all that is other.

Ik ouṃkar always calls to mind the negative expression, *Niraṅkar*, without form, formless. Although he created all forms, he is formless. There are several other terms which express the same thing. *Niraṅkar* is one of the most important terms. Although *Akāl Purakh* is formless, his presence is visible to the enlightened believer because he is immanent in his creation. Guru Nanak says:

> You have thousands of eyes and yet no eye, thousands of forms, yet no form, thousands of feet and no foot, and no fragrance. But you have thousands of fragrances. I am dazed by such a wonder.
>
> (Gurū Granth Sāhib: 663)

Guru Nanak is known as *Nānak Niraṅkarī*, Nanak who is at one with the Formless One.

SACH

Truth comes at the beginning of the list. There is one and he is truth, reality: 'Truth is his name' – *Sat Nām*. This is often emphasised: *Sāchā Sāhib Sachu Nāi* – 'True is the Lord, True is his Name' (*Japjī, pauṛi* 4). 'He is the only one who is true' (Gurū Granth Sāhib: 412). By comparison, everything else is transient, and untrue.

> He was true in the beginning, throughout the ages, is true now and will be true in the future also . . . He is the only one . . . Wherever you look, the True One is there.
>
> (*Japjī, pauṛi* 24)

There are many instances when the Gurūs said that the place where the True One is to be found is within the heart. Of all the expressions used for God, *sach* and compounds using the word, like *Sat Nām* (True Name), make it perhaps the single most important word.

NĀM

Sach is frequently linked to *Nām* – whose Name is true, reality. Of all the descriptions, God is surely the True Name, and the Name is creation. 'What you have created is your name, it is that by which we can know you' (*Japjī, pauṛi* 19).

KARATĀ PURAKHU

God unfurled creation with a single command (*Japjī, pauṛi* 3). He alone is the object of praise who created the universe (Gurū Granth Sāhib: 765). He makes and unmakes, builds and demolishes, creates and destroys (Gurū Granth Sāhib: 413). He is the sustainer. He is the gardener who tends the trees and cares for the garden (Gurū Granth Sāhib: 765). His authority is total. He is the one Sovereign Lord. There are a very large number of verses emphasising God's absolute power.

NIRBHAU NIRVAIRU

These qualities are seen by Sikhs as qualities which can relate to *Akāl Purakh* alone. There is no one else who has no fear and no hostility. To say that he has no hostility re-emphasises that *Akāl Purakh* is all love. Although *Akāl Purakh* has no fear, humans should fear *Akāl Purakh*. Fear, the Gurū said, is hard to bear. 'But without fear no one crosses [the ocean of existence], but if one dwells in fear, then to it is added love.'

AKĀL MURAT

Akāl is to Sikhs as Allāh is to Muslims. Like *nirbhau* and *nirvairu*, *a-kāl* is negative. *Kāl* is time, so the negative, *akāl*, means without time, timeless, eternal. Apart from using common names for deities, like Harī and Rām, the Gurūs used many words to describe God and many of them are used in the negative, defining reality in terms of what it is not, which is traditional in Indian thought.

AJONĪ SAIBHAṂ

Ajonī means that God has never come to earth as an *avatāra*, or been born. He is self-existent.

> God has no mother, no father, no son and no relatives. He has no wife, no sexual desire. He has no family. He is completely detached, and he is infinite; but it is his light that shines in his creation; and his light that is in everyone and everything.
>
> (Gurū Granth Sāhib: 579)

GURPARAŚADI

'By the favour of the Gurū.' Sikhs believe that knowledge comes by the grace of the Gurū. If humans demonstrate their devotion, then God may look kindly on them and show his love.

Other qualities

Apart from the qualities mentioned in the *Mūl Mantra* there are many others used in the Gurū Granth Sāhib.

Since God is formless, unborn, uncreated, indescribable, can he be pictured at all? Is listing negative adjectives the best we can do? God in his fullness is beyond understanding. In his ultimate sense, he is unknowable and unpicturable. But having admitted as much, there remains the possibility that he is not totally unknowable, because partial understanding is possible. Wherever you look, he is there. And even closer: 'The Lord pervades every heart' (Gurū Granth Sāhib: 579), and 'Behold the Lord within yourself!' (Gurū Granth Sāhib: 598).

But God is not merely a passive object for humans to try to picture. He takes the initiative himself. He shows himself and we see what he shows. Ultimately, he decides who is to be united with himself. 'The True King unites the believer with himself' (Gurū Granth Sāhib: 18). 'Nanak, all we receive is by the grace of the Beneficient One' (*Japjī, pauṛi* 24). But he is generous; he gives and gives. 'In every age, he goes on giving. The recipients grow tired' (*Japjī, pauṛi* 3).

Divine self-expression

McLeod (1968: 189) also uses 'divine self-expression'. This he summed up in six key words: *śabad* (word), *nām* (name), *Gurū* (divine preceptor), *hukam* (divine order), *sach* (truth) and *nadar* (grace). The first five words are 'expressions of God'; 'all are used to expound the nature, content and method of divine communication to humans, of the divine truth which, when appropriated, brings salvation; all share a fundamental identity' (McLeod 1968: 190).

God expresses himself in the *śabad* (word) which he, as Satgurū, communicates to the individual heart. If that heart has been blessed with grace, then the individual will be able to perceive *Akāl Purakh* around and within himself or herself, and will understand the means of attaining him, and see the path to be followed.

Inadequacy of the account

There is no end to his gifts, his creation; there is no end to his sight, his hearing. The limit of the secrets of his heart cannot be known. There is no limit to the physical worlds he has created. His own limits can't be known . . . The more one says, the more there is to be said. Only he knows how great he is.

Apart from the difficulties in picturing *Akāl Purakh*, it is difficult to capture the words and ideas of a master like Guru Nanak, and to convey them adequately. Elusive thoughts flood the mind; word pictures, concepts piled upon concepts, surprising, amazing, such a feast of ideas, of sheer magical poetry; one is faced with the impossibility of choice. The tenth Gurū, Govind Singh, lists about 950 epithets for God in a single poem, *Akāl Ustat*.

The immensity of the conception makes it difficult to look at theological definitions and choose one which will make sense: monotheism, monism, pantheism – arguably all of them, simultaneously.

Nirguṇa and *saguṇa*

God is of course *nirguṇa*, beyond imagination, understanding and description. But by revealing himself in the creation, he has presented us with a chance to appreciate all of his praise-worthy qualities, and has given us a chance to see and know him. There is nothing humans can do as regards the *nirguṇa* aspect of God. They can acknowledge it is there but, as far as their own efforts are concerned, it is the second – *saguṇa* – aspect that they must address. However, in using the term *saguṇa*, the Sikh Gurūs were not thinking of the more usual meaning of the term used to describe an *avatāra*.

Devotion to steel

Normally, weapons are kept in gurdwaras. Often, in front of the *manjī* (throne) on which the Gurū Granth Sāhib is installed, there may be some silvery metal circles, and some arrows. Sometimes there are swords and daggers. The circles are *chakras* (quoits), an

Indian weapon designed for throwing. The traditional *chakra*s were sharp around the edges and are reputed to be capable of decapitating people. The Sikh symbol, *niśan sāhib*, which is seen on the pennants outside gurdwaras and printed on Sikh literature, shows two curved swords surrounding a *chakra*, intersected by a double-edged sword. Devotion to weapons might strike people as curious. It conflicts with the generally pacifist perception of religion in modern times in the West.

There are many well-known poems by Guru Govind Singh in which he expresses his devotion to God. The favourite must be his *Jāp* (quoted in the volume *Sacred Writings* in this series), and there are many other inspiring passages:

> . . . for God is but one; he who denies this is deluded and fooled. Worship the One who is Master of all; worship him alone. See him present in all creation a single form, an all pervading light.
>
> There is no difference between a temple and a mosque, nor between the prayers of a Hindu and a Muslim. Though differences seem to mark them, all men are in reality the same.
>
> Gods and demons, celestial beings, men called Muslims and others called Hindus – their differences are trivial, of no consequence and the result of locality and dress. . .
>
> All are the same, none is separate, a single form, a single creation.
>
> As the sparks fly upward in their thousands from a fire, each separate and distinct then reuniting with its source;
>
> Or as fine ground dust from a pile flies up and fills the air, and then subsides to earth again;
>
> As waves rise endlessly in the vastness of the ocean, their water still at one with the water around them;
>
> So does all life emerge, and having manifested themselves, they likewise return.
>
> (*Dasam Granth*, *Akāl Ustat*: 15–17)

But Govind Singh also saw other sides to God. There is a doctrine known as *pīrī mīrī*, which is traditionally said to have developed from Guru Hargovind's wearing of two swords, symbolising worldly and spiritual power. *Pīr* is the word used today for holy men in Pakistan. *Pīrī* is the spiritual authority and *mīrī* is a temporal authority, ruling like a prince. Gurūs, and the ultimate, came arrayed as princes. The God Govind Singh pictured was *Sarab Loh* (all steel), *Akāl* (immortal), *Mahānloh* (great steel), *Sarb Kāl* (all death), *Mahan Kāl* (great death) and *Asipani* (sword in hand). He was the symbol and source of bravery.

In fact, Guru Govind Singh produced very long lists of epithets for God, and some were very unusual. Reveller, Great Enjoyer, Destroyer of all, Annihilator of all, Establisher of all, Unfathomable, Movement of the winds, *Jogī* of *Jogī*s, *Tantra* of *Tantra*s, *Mantra* of *Mantra*s, Doer of fearsome deeds, Creator of maladies, Enjoyer of all, Lover of lovers, Life of all life. Guru Govind and Guru Nanak chose very different words. Guru Govind Singh's selection of expressions certainly captures the idea of power, might and majesty.

In one work in the *Dasam Granth*, the *Śastar Nām Mālā*, all of the possible names of the weapons are given and they are personified. It is simply a catalogue of weapons. Kahan Singh of Nabha, in *Mahān Koś*, says that the piece is not easily understood, which is true, for it is very obscure, and perhaps only comprehensible to those with special knowledge of these matters. The weapons (and Kahan Singh lists five kinds) are divided into daggers, swords, *chakra*s, spears, guns, which may account for the five weapons (one of each?) which were required by early *Rahitnāmā*s. The weapons are personified and are, for Guru Govind, the medium for the worship of God. God in the form of a sword is invoked:

> I bow with love and devotion to the Holy Sword.
> Assist me that I may complete this work.
> Thou art the Subduer of countries, the Destroyer of the armies of the wicked, in the battlefield thou greatly adornest the brave.
> Thine arm is infrangible. Thy brightness refulgent, thy radiance and splendour dazzle like the sun.
> Thou bestowest happiness on the good, thou terrifiest the evil, thou scatterest sinners, I seek thy protection.
> Hail! Hail to the Creator of the world, the Saviour of creation, my Cherisher, hail to thee, O Sword!
> I bow to the Scimitar, the two-edged Sword, the Falchion, and the Dagger.
> Thou, O God, hast ever one form; thou art ever unchangeable.
> I bow to the holder of the Mace
> Who diffused light through the fourteen worlds.

I bow to the Arrow and the Musket,
I bow to the Sword, spotless, fearless, and unbreakable;
I bow to the powerful Mace and Lance
To which nothing is equal.
I bow to him who holdeth the discus,
Who is not made of the elements, and who is terrible.
I bow to him with the strong teeth;
I bow to him who is supremely powerful,
I bow to the Arrow and the Cannon
Which destroy the enemy.
I bow to the Sword and the Rapier
Which destroy the evil.
I bow to all weapons called Shastar (which may be held)
I bow to all weapons called Astar (which may be hurled or discharged).

(*Bachitar Nāṭak* 87; translated in Macauliffe 1909, vol. 5: 286)

It is perhaps from this preoccupation with God as a sword that comes the allegation about goddess worship among the early *Panth*. Caṅdī, the goddess, was seen as an incarnation of *Bhagautī* (the sword), and therefore, as a symbol of power. Sikhs insist that the word *Bhagautī* means sword. It is used daily as the opening words of the *Ardās: Prithme Bhagautī simarke*, translated by Macauliffe (1909, vol. 5: 331) as 'Having first remembered the sword', but translated in modern times as 'Having first remembered God'. (*Ardās*: line 1)

Many early accounts refer to Guru Govind Singh and the goddess. *Gurbilās* literature, such as *Gurbilās Dasvīn Pataśāhī*, gives the *Khālsā* a mystic birth from God, the Sword and Devi (Caṅdī), the goddess. Other accounts talk of *hom*s and sacrifices, human sacrifices even, to make the goddess appear. It is said that the Gurū had employed some Brahmans to perform the ritual and materialise the goddess. When the Brahmans ran away in terror, the Gurū threw all their materials into the *hom* pit. There was a flash of flame, and, seeing it from afar, people thought that the goddess had appeared. The Gurū drew his sword and set out for Anandpur. When the people asked if the goddess had appeared to him, he raised his sword aloft. Macauliffe said that he did so to show that his sword could achieve as much as a goddess, but people misunderstood, and some people believed that she had given him the sword.

Certainly, the goddess was an eighteenth-century interest of the

Panth. Bhai Vir Singh once undertook research, comparing and contrasting as many as ten different accounts of the events. Until modern times, these tales were an accepted part of *Khālsā* lore. Whatever the arguments about the goddess, *Bhagautī* is taken as 'sword' or God now. If the early *Khālsā* were assuming *kṣatriya* status, picturing God in the shape of the sword would not be out of place.

It is true that in India the implements, tools of one's trade, the things necessary to help a person make a living, are reverenced once a year. Cunningham (1849: 316) says that throughout India:

> the implements of any calling are in a manner worshipped, or in Western moderation of phrase, they are blessed or consecrated. This is especially noticeable among merchants who usually perform religious ceremonies before a heap of gold; among hereditary clerks or writers who similarly idolise their inkhorn; and among soldiers and military leaders, who on the festival of Das-hara consecrate their banners and piled up weapons. Govind withdrew his followers from that undivided attention which their father had given to the plough, the loom and the pen, and he urged them to regard the sword as their principal stay in this world.

Cunningham saw it as a 'veneration for that which gives us power, or safety, or our daily bread'. People in India do reverence the tools of their trade. It is not so curious that Sikhs should reverence weapons. When Guru Govind created the *Khālsā* he introduced a new initiation ceremony. The initiation became *khaṇḍe kī pāhul*, the initiation of the double-edged sword.

Some writers have interpreted this as power and glory for the *Khālsā*, for those who were initiated and were given the name or title *Siṅgh*, which was a *kṣatriya* title. In the *Mahān Kośּ*, Kahan Singh describes *Siṅgh* as a person who has taken '*khaṇḍe dā amritdharī Gurū Nānakpanthi Khālsā*', *khaṇḍe dā amrit* meaning the 'nectar of the sword'.

Although there is much uncertainty about what did happen at Anandpur in 1699, most accounts mention the requirement to bear arms. Grewal and Bal (1967: 119) have suggested that the *Khālsā* were becoming *kṣatriya*, without reference to Brahmans. In fact, the only *varṇa* retained was *kṣatriya*, and for such men, God was pictured as a sword. In *Prācīn Panth Prakās*, Rattan Singh Bhangu observed: 'All weakness would be beaten out of them, and each, having taken the baptism of the sword would be firmly attached to the sword'.

Gurbilās Dasvīn Pataśāhī bears this out. *Kṣatriya* had become rare and in the *Kālyug*, the rule fell to lower orders. The new *kṣatriya*s were the Sikhs. The religion of the sword was created for the purpose. The *Khālsā* were to bear their five weapons. The *kaṛāh praśād* that was given to them in gurdwaras was also touched with the sword, and their *amrit* was stirred with one. Until recently, the *kaṛah praśād* was cut with a sword at the point in the *Ardās* when the assembly mentioned the words *degh tegh fatah*, 'may victory attend our charity and the sword'. (However, recently some Sikhs have been saying that people should no longer follow this observance, because a new directive has been issued to the effect that during the *Ardās*, nothing should be done to cause a distraction, and people should concentrate on the words and deal with the *praśād* after the service has ended.)

Words in common use: *Sat Nām* and *Vāhigurū*

Sach is not only one of the words used most often, it is also one that has stood the test of time, for it appears at the very beginning of the Gurū Granth Sāhib. It is also a word which is commonly used today. It often appears in combination with *Nām* as *Sat Nām*.

The other word of popular devotion is *Vāhigurū*. *Vāh*! is an expression of wonder. It may sound too colloquial but it literally means a heartfelt, awestruck, 'Wow!'. *Vāhigurū* was not a word used by Guru Nanak in his *bānī*. It appeared later.

In the *janam sakhī*s people did repeat the words '*Gurū Gurū*'. In the B 40 manuscript, it says *Lage Gurū Gurū japaṇī* (They began repeating *Gurū! Gurū!*). McLeod (1989: 16) says that this seems to be how *Nām simaraṇ* was understood, and that this is a considerable divergence from the technique Nanak himself had sought to teach, which was a more arduous discipline. McLeod (1980: 222) mentions the basic formulae that are familiar to any reader of *janam sakhī*s, and one of these is '*vāh gurū akhī*', uttering praises to the Gurū. By this stage, this was not a greeting but a powerful formula.

Another interesting point made by McLeod (1980: 251) is that in *janam sakhī* usage, Nanak is generally referred to as Baba Nanak not as Gurū. Gurū is used when there is stress upon his status as supreme teacher, and as Gurū to others. But Nanak's own Gurū was not human and perhaps in recognition of this, the word Gurū was used very infrequently and carefully during the early period. Maybe when '*Gurū! Gurū!*' and '*Vāhigurū!*' were first used, they were aware of Nanak's usage of the word, and felt that it referred to God. Later the expressions referred to Gurūs. *Niraṅkar*, the Formless One, is also a popular *janam sakhī* term. Nanak Niraṅkarī is used as soon as Nanak is born. So he was born in union with the Formless One. Sometimes the *janam sakhī*s do refer to Baba Nanak actually seeing the Formless One with his own eyes.

In the *janam sakhī*s, Guru Nanak is shown as saying '*Vāh Gurū*', in the course of an incident when the Gurū arrived in Delhi and saw a dead elephant. He was informed that it belonged to the ruler, Ibrahim Lodhi. But ultimately, all things belong to God. Baba Nanak is shown as telling the keepers that the animal was alive and that they should rub its forehead and say '*Vāhigurū!*'. The elephant stood up to the astonishment of all!

According to Macauliffe (1909, vol. 2: 107), Guru Ram Das said:

> O Emperor, in the Sat, the Treta, the Dwapar and the Kal ages God was worshipped under the names of Wasdev, Hari, Gobind, and Ram respectively. The Guru hath made of the initials of these four names the word Wahiguru which is praise of God and the Guru.

There is also a hymn in Macauliffe (1909, vol. 2: 207), in which Guru Amar Das described the pleasure obtained in praising God under the name of '*Wāh! Wāh!*' In a note, Macauliffe mentioned that '*Wāh!*' meant 'Bravo!'.

> The True One causeth Himself to be applauded through the Guru's instruction.
> Wah! Wah! is his praise and eulogy, some pious men know this.
> Wah! Wah! are true words by which man meeteth the True One.
> Nanak, by uttering Wah! Wah! God is obtained;
> His praise is obtained by good acts.
>
> The tongue is adorned by uttering the words Wah! Wah!
> By these perfect words God is found
> Greatly blest are those from whose mouths Wah! Wah! proceedeth.
> They who utter Wah! Wah! shall be illustrious, and the people shall come and worship them.

> Wah! Wah! is obtained by good acts, Nanak; He who uttereth it shall obtain honour at the gate of the True One.
>
> (Macauliffe, 1909, Vol. 2.2: 207)

The poem has nine verses, showing perhaps the relish the Gurū found in this joyful, colloquial expression.

Vāhigurū is often used in the *Dasam Granth*. Whereas *1 ouṃ kar sat gurparaśadi* preceded everything in the Gurū Granth Sāhib, in the *Dasam Granth* everything is preceeded by *1 ouṃkar Sri Vāhigurū Jī kī Fatah*.

VĀHIGURŪ JĪ KĀ KHĀLSĀ SRĪ VĀHIGURŪ JĪ KĪ FATAH

Many writers say that the *Khālsā* were enjoined to salute each other with *Vāh Gurū Jī Kā Khālsā; Srī Vāh Gurū Jī Kī Fatah*. Latif (1891: 264) thinks that there were regulations aimed at giving Sikhs a 'distinct national character', such as wearing blue clothing but not red. But,

> The object of other institutions, such as the principle of devotion to steel, and the exclamation of 'Wah Guru', is obvious, for the steel made them vowed soldiers, while the repetition of the phrase 'Wah Guru', revived every moment religious fervour in their mind, and constantly awakened them to a sense of their duty and obligations to the community of which they had become members.

Cunningham (1849: 315) says that:

> The proper exclamation of community of faith of the Sikhs as a sect is simply 'Wah Guru!' that is 'O Guru!' or 'Hail Guru!' The lengthened exclamations, 'Wah Guru ki Fath!' and 'Wah Guru Ka Khalsa!' (Hail! virtue or power of the Guru!, or Hail! Guru and Victory! and, Hail the state or church of the Guru!) are not authoritative, although the former has become customary.

The notion of an exclamation of community of faith is not unimportant. It should be borne in mind that all groups in India, Hindus and Muslims, had their own exclamations, colours, signs, practices, greetings, external identity markers etc., e.g., *Kānphat Jogīs* wore earrings and said '*Adeś!*' as a greeting.

Fatah (victory), Cunningham says, has joined the other notions, *degh* (cooking pot) and *tegh* (sword), and these words rose from the 'notions' of the Gurū even if he didn't ordain them. The words were used on Sikh coinage by leaders from Guru Govind Singh's friend, Banda to Ranjit Singh (who ruled 1799–1839). The inscription means 'hospitality, the sword and unending victory granted by Nanak and Guru Govind Singh'.

Cunningham (1849: 316) says that the *Gur Ratnawali* gives the

> fanciful and trivial origin of the salutation, *Vahiguru*: Wasdev, the exclamation of the first age, or Satyug, Har Har, the exclamation of the second age; Gobind Gobind, the exclamation of the third age; Ram Ram, the exclamation of the fourth age, or Kalyug; whence Wah Guru in the fifth age or under the new dispensation.

So it appears that from being an expression in praise of the Gurū, the word *Vāhigurū* moved to become a noun designating God. There were no more human Gurūs when the personal succession ended, but Gurū was embodied in the *saṅgat*, the assembly, the Gurū-Panth and in the Gurū Granth Sāhib – the Gurū-Granth.

The eternal Gurū and God merge and this development is reflected in the changes in the use of the term *Vāhigurū*, which is now required by *Sikh Rahit Maryādā*. It says that a Sikh should greet others with the salutation, '*Vāhigurū Jī Kā Khālsā, Vāhigurū Jī kī Fatah*'. Despite this, most Sikhs usually greet each other with '*Sat Srī Akāl*' (True Timeless One).

Vāhigurū is repeated frequently in the *Ardās*, the Sikh prayer. Those saying it are required to say *Vāhigurū* at intervals while the prayer is being read.

Akāl Purakh and *Vāhigurū* are both expressions in popular use. The words *Sat Nām* and *Vāhigurū* are inscribed in large letters across the front of many gurdwaras. They are also words very frequently uttered by people in the ordinary course of daily life. When people are faced with sadness they often intone: *Sat Nām, Sat Nām, Sat Nām Jī, Vāhigurū, Vāhigurū, Vāhigurū Jī, Sat Nām, Sat Nām, Sat Nām Jī, Vāhigurū Jī* . . . etc., over and over again. It gives them comfort. People often exclaim '*Vāhigurū!*', meaning a variety of things, according to circumstances. They often say 'As *Vāhigurū* wills', or '*Vāhigurū* knows best'.

Icons and art

For the most part, modern gurdwaras are places totally devoid of icons of any kind and, indeed, many have little art. Historic ones may be richly decorated with marble, gold, frescoes etc., but modern gurdwaras are quite bare.

There are no pictures at all in many gurdwaras, and many devout people believe that the true picture of the Gurū is in the *bānī*, so there is no need for anything else. However, there is another school of thought; some Sikhs have pictures of Gurūs, various martyrs and historic events in the gurdwara. One gurdwara in Southall has commissioned a collection of paintings about the Gurūs and Sikh history for the purpose of educating young people and visitors. However, these pictures are hung in the *laṅgar* (communal eating area) and not in the hall where the Gurū Granth Sāhib is enthroned.

The Gurū Granth Sāhib is placed on a throne, and that denotes its position as Gurū, teacher. Words therefore are transmitted directly. Modern gurdwaras are large halls intended for assemblies. They are arranged like the court of a king, and the position of the Gurū Granth Sāhib, in front of the people, and raised above them, shows its position as God's word.

The *saṅgat*, the assembly, the company of holy people, is also a way of seeing the Gurū. The *Khālsā*, being in the form of the Gurū, also has God within it. In practical ways, serving the congregation is therefore service to God. So the assembly is a very definite way of picturing *Akāl Purakh*.

Disfunctional symbols

New ideas replace old ones. Once it was important to touch the *kaṛāh praśād* with a sword, when the sword was mentioned in the *Ardās*. Now, people have forgotten why it was done. Ideas about the sword are perhaps no longer understood as they once were. The concerns, even of the *Singh Sabha* scholars, differ from today's accepted orthodoxies. Their interests and concerns differed from the generations who preceded them.

Probably few people who read it can resist sometimes getting lost in the pages of the *Mahān Kośʹ*, Kahan Singh of Nabha's great encyclopaedia, usually because what one wanted to check is not included at all, and one becomes engrossed in all manner of strange and unexpected items. Weapons cover pages; many concepts of God are barely noted. Bhai Sahib's biography has a beautiful photograph of his own weapons, including several walking sticks, an umbrella and a sitar as well as swords, daggers, guns etc. These things assumed an importance a few years ago which perhaps they lack today.

There is also, it has to be admitted, a gulf between academic studies of Sikhism and popular practice. The concerns of scholars and those of ordinary people are rather different. The two sides might gaze across in mutual incomprehension. Ordinary people might relish and love Sikh spirituality, but have few ideas as to how to express it.

Monotheism and syncretism

How Sikhs see God probably depends on their background. Many Sikhs say that they think that Sikhism is monotheistic, and they refer to the Oneness of God. They find it difficult to see how the Trinity works. But language is often used without defining terms or without much awareness of what they actually mean.

The belief that Sikhism is monotheistic dates from days gone by when Sikhism was seen as a hybrid between Hinduism and Islam. Monotheism was thought to have been an Islamic contribution to a sort of syncretic belief, other notions having been culled from Hinduism. Various parts of both 'parents' were also firmly rejected, according to this model. It is an outdated model.

Some writers have adopted one model for Sikhism and Islam. They saw both as holding fast to God as an omnipotent reality. Both hold to a strict code of conduct. Perhaps the society of the *saṅgat* is not too unlike the Muslim *millat* (congregation, community of believers). The parallels between Gurūs and Ṣūfī *Pīrs* in Panjab are close; the idea of a common kitchen and staying in a common hostel are also not unknown. But the idea that Sikhism exists because of the action of Islam on Hinduism and the growth of syncretistic movements in medieval India is a notion commonly believed.

Christopher Shackle (1978) has done valuable research into the language of the Sikh Gurūs, and has shown that the claim that

Sikhism is a religion of syncretism, a blending of Islam and Hinduism, is false. He says that there is not a direct influence from Islam as is claimed in many secondary sources. Although Guru Nanak uses Muslim names for God, he does so for poetic purposes. The Gurū was aware of Islam, but was not borrowing from it. Shackle said that many loan words are words concerned with ruling and royal authority, which is not surprising in view of the circumstances of the life and times of the Gurū, and his early career and family links with local government and the bureaucracy.

Experience

What is important about Nanak's God is not merely picturing him, but experiencing him. The men who wrote the Gurū Granth Sāhib were more interested in experience than theory. God is experienced through his creation. It is real but, unlike him, it will pass away and change. God is formless, but seen through his revelation. Humankind is required to turn towards God, to direct loving passionate devotion towards him, and to fear him. Lodge truth within your heart, and act in accordance with truth. God is accessible through his Name.

New pictures of God

Over the past decade in Britain there has been a spiritual development in Sikhism unlike any other in the past. It is not a revivalist movement, but something quite new. Young people who have grown up here have become interested in the religions of their forefathers who came from South Asia. The reasons for the growth of spiritual religion in these communities are several. A major point is the level of education of the young people. They have been born and raised in Britain, have attended schools here and undertaken further education here. So their background is in many ways British. Despite much emotional talk by older people of heritage languages and mother tongues, the most useful language for many of the young is English. Learning to read the sacred language of the Sikhs will attract a minority, but it will be only a minority.

The traditional gurdwaras are probably going to need to come to terms with the fact that picturing, knowing, and experiencing God may provide for a greater need than fighting old Panjabi political battles. Teachers in schools in Britain, if they have dealt with religion, have already taught it in their own terms. Even if schools do not teach religious studies well, the whole language and culture revolve around a certain kind of religious centre. Our picture of God underlies our world and our understanding, even if we are not 'religious'. Young Panjabis growing up here have had no other models. Therefore, like it or not, a peculiar kind of spiritual hybrid is growing among these communities.

The new impetus from the Indian side comes from various *Sants*. They are charismatic and exciting. Some *Sants* can attract followings of young men who enjoy driving *Bābā Jī* from home to home in the middle of the night, and they enjoy the charismatic personalities of the teachers. This kind of religion is alive, direct, worth getting out of bed before dawn to experience. But much of what it is going to be about, and how God will be pictured, is going to depend on the personalities and teachings of the *Bābās*. There is not going to be one outcome, but several. There are other young people who are adrift, knowing little about Sikhism, but being 'fundamentalist' about what they neither know nor understand.

New cults are rising, and established ones are growing. These communities are settled, peaceful and rich compared with those in India. Their elders never bought books, but the young will buy books, eventually; they will also write books. What they choose to write and choose to emphasise is going to be what matters to them. It is highly unlikely that the matters which have concerned people in Panjab in the past are going to appeal to young people in countries like Canada and Britain in the future. So the way of picturing God will change.

Some think that God made human beings in his own image. Perhaps, too, humans return the compliment and make God in their own image. New images are being created all the time. Probably what will emerge will be a more 'spiritual' approach, with emphasis on the original teachings of Guru Nanak, a cross-fertilisation from the *Sant* tradition of Northern India with the spiritual concerns of the West.

FURTHER READING

Cunningham, J.D. (1849) *A history of the Sikhs*, Oxford, Oxford University Press (repr. 1981, New Delhi, S. Chand).

Grewal, J.S. and Bal, S.S. (1967) *Guru Gobind Singh: A Biographical Study*, Chandigarh, Panjab University.

Latif, S.M. (1891) *History of the Punjab: From the Remotest Antiquity to Present Time*, Calcutta, Calcutta Central Press Company (repr. 1984, Lahore, Progressive Books).

Macauliffe, M.A. (1909) *The Sikh Religion*, Oxford, Oxford University Press (repr. 1983, New Delhi, S. Chand).

McLeod, W.H. (1968) *Gurū Nānak and the Sikh Religion*, Oxford, Clarendon Press.

McLeod, W.H. (1980) *Early Sikh Tradition: A Study of the Janam Sakhīs*, Oxford, Clarendon Press.

McLeod, W.H. (1984) *Textual Sources for the Study of Sikhism*, Manchester, Manchester University Press.

McLeod, W.H. (1989) *The Sikhs: History, Religion and Society*, New York, Columbia University Press.

Shackle, C. (1978) 'Approaches to Persian loans in the Adi Granth', in *Bulletin of the School of Oriental and African Studies*, vol. XLI, pp. 73–96.

7. Chinese Religions

Xinzhong Yao

Whether or not there is 'God' in Chinese religions was not clear to the earlier sinologists. Some of them, led by De Groot, strongly believed that Chinese religion essentially was a kind of animism, and there existed no God, only animist spirits or multiple gods. Others, however, represented by James Legge, insisted that a form of monotheism ante-dated animism, with a belief in one God as the supreme Being (De Korne 1926: 13). Today, though there are still some scholars who insist that Chinese religion is essentially some kind of polytheism or animism, few would deny that there was a belief in God in Chinese religion, especially in its early history.

According to the records of historical works, the religious activities of the ancient Chinese can be traced back to the time of the Yellow Emperor (2698–2598 BCE), who was believed to have set up the first temple and conducted the first sacrificial rituals. During the next two centuries, to the time of Yao and Shun (2357–2206 BCE), the polytheistic beliefs and activities merged into the belief in one God who was called '*Shang Ti*' (*shang* here means 'above', 'high' and 'first', *ti* means 'Lord', 'Sovereign'; see the 'Canon of Shun' of the *Book of History*, in Waltham 1971: 12). Though there is no hard evidence to prove this legend, at least, as a leading historian and archaeologist in modern China, Kuo Mo-jo, says,

> By the time of the Yin [i.e., the Shang Dynasty 1765–1123 BCE] the idea of a supreme God was already in existence. In the beginning He was called *Ti*, and later on *Shang Ti*. During the transitional period from the Shang to the Chou (1122–221 BCE), He was then called *T'ien* (Heaven). From the oracle text, we can know that the Yin people believed in a supreme Being as a personal God who could issue orders and had the

> sense of good and evil. . . . This is perfectly similar to the God of ancient Israel.
>
> (Quoted in Chiu 1984: 56)

These early concepts and descriptions of the supreme power were accepted by the late state religion and thus played a decisive role in the religious thinking and activities of the Chinese community.

Shang Ti – a supreme Lord

The idea of God in Chinese religion was first expressed by the concept of *Shang Ti* or *Ti* in the Shang Dynasty, probably even earlier. When Howard Smith talks about the religious life in the Shang Dynasty, he observes,

> The most distinctive ideas of a peculiarly Chinese world-view were already in evidence: a cult of ancestors, which resulted in a highly organised sacrificial and mortuary ritual, the belief in a supreme being who presides over a hierarchical structure in the spiritual world which was intimately related to man's life and destiny . . . and the belief that the main purpose of religion was to maintain a harmonious relationship between heaven, earth and man.
>
> (Smith 1968: 11)

Our knowledge about *Shang Ti* comes from two basic sources. One is the inscriptions on the oracle bones which were used in the divination of the Shang kings and remained underground, undiscovered for more than three thousand years, the other is the records in various historical books, especially in the *Book of History* and the *Book of Poetry*,[1] which are generally believed to be works of the early Chou Dynasty.

In the inscriptions of the oracle bones, *Ti* appeared in several different forms, from which the leading palaeographers have drawn their respective conclusions. One of them is that the form of *Ti* 帝 is a symbol of a flower. The flower implies the zenith of growth and shows the plant's greatest beauty and glory. From this understanding originated the Shang people's concept of the supreme God – 'the origin of life, the potency of fertility, the power of eternity, regeneration, and the majestic glory of the universe' (Chiu 1984: 55–6). Another explanation of *Ti* is that the form is a symbol of a spirit-tablet, and it is 'the first ancestor-spirit' of the royal house who 'was regarded as the supreme *Ti*' (Smith 1968: 5).

Though there are still arguments among historians, archaeologists and palaeographers concerning the meaning and origin of the character *Ti*, we can certainly say that the forms of this character in the oracle inscriptions show that *Shang Ti* is a supreme Lord and has absolute authority and power. In the *Book of Poetry*, *Shang Ti* is mentioned as the source of goodness, infinite being and final judge, and his help is described as '*Shang Ti*'s blessing'. In the *Book of History*, *Shang Ti* or *Ti* is recorded as having been consulted, sacrificed to, besought and worshipped by the kings. He is conceived of as dwelling above, and the gods of his pantheon are both nature deities and deified royal ancestors, who all work for him as his agents in charge of controlling nature, and the destiny and welfare of the royal family and the nation.

The power and authority of *Shang Ti* are shown first by his omnipotence in the natural world. Weather and climate, natural calamities and disasters, changes of seasons and the harmony of the universe are all under his control. For example, *Ti* can send or stop the wind, clouds, thunder and rain. The wind is called the agent of *Ti*, or messenger of *Ti*, and clouds are regarded as the ministers at the right and left hand of *Ti*. We can read in the oracle inscriptions that *Ti* ordered thunder to strike in the months of spring, and that all natural phenomena were governed on his behalf. However, the Lordship of *Shang Ti* does not imply that he is the creator of the world. This is where the Chinese *Shang Ti* differs from the Judaic God: *Shang Ti* as the ruler and commander is not the same God as the creator. When Kuo correctly sees a 'perfect similarity' between them, he perhaps has failed to see this essential difference.

The authority of *Shang Ti* is expressed especially by his domination in the human world; all human affairs such as good fortune and bad fortune, happiness and sorrow, harvest and famine, victory and defeat in war, building and destruction of cities, promotion and demotion of officials, also depend upon the will of *Shang Ti*. He is held in awe and veneration, and his will is consulted through various divinations and other religious activities. For example, before any action such as attack or defence was prepared, the Shang kings would have divinations performed to inquire whether or not the action would meet with the approval of *Ti*. If the result of the divination was 'yes' or any other kind of auspicious answer, it meant that the action had been approved, and would be supported by *Shang Ti*; otherwise, they had to drop their plan or wait until they obtained approval from this absolute God. When King Pan-geng decided (*c.* 1402 BCE) to move the capital to Yin, he sought permission from *Shang Ti* and took this permission as one signal of *Shang Ti*'s 'being about to renew the virtuous service of my high ancestor, and secure the good order of our kingdom' (the *Book of History*, 'The Pan-geng', in Legge 1879: 111).

The authority of *Shang Ti* can also be identified by the fact that only a king is entitled to worship him through the mediatorship of the ancestral kings. The former kings, at death, would go up to heaven and sit beside *Shang Ti* as his agents. They certainly had a direct concern with their descendants on earth and could greatly influence *Shang Ti*'s attitude towards the king below. For this reason, ancestral worship became an essential part of the worship of *Shang Ti*, which was of the highest significance for the continuation of the monarchy. If the kings did not worship their ancestors or did not perform appropriate sacrifices to them, the spirits of the ancestors would advise *Shang Ti* to withdraw the support which he had given to the dynasty. Therefore, the Shang kings took great care in their ancestor worship and developed an elaborate system of sacrifice and rituals in conjunction with the great sacrifice to *Shang Ti*.

Supported by his ancestors and favoured by *Shang Ti*, the Shang king occupied a central position in the human world. It was the king who was the direct mediator between the Shang people and their God, and the king therefore had great responsibility, both to the people and to *Shang Ti*. The fortune of kings became essential to the fortune of the state because only those kings who were protected by *Ti* could bring good fortune to the people.

Shang Ti gave his favour to the royal House because 'the former king was always zealous in the reverent cultivation of his virtue, so that he was the fellow of *Shang Ti*' (the *Book of History*, 'The Tai-jia', in Legge 1879: 99).[2] However, whether or not this dynasty would continue depended also upon every king's performance and virtue. That is to say that the favour of *Shang Ti* was not fixed and unchangeable. '[The Ways] of *Shang Ti* are not invariable – on the good-doer, he sends down all blessings and on the evil-doer, he sends down all miseries' (the *Book of History*, 'The Instruction of Yi', in Legge 1879: 95). Therefore, the Shang kings had to be cautious in administration: fearful and trembling as if they were in danger of falling into a deep abyss . . . and examining everything to see whether or not it was in harmony with the will of *Shang Ti*.

Normally, a king could enjoy *Shang Ti*'s favour because of his ancestors' heritage. However, he could also lose this favour due to his bad performance or evil behaviour, and that meant that the old dynasty would be replaced by a new one, just as in the replacement of the Hsia Dynasty by the Shang Dynasty and the Shang by the Chou. Thus, the transformation from one dynasty to another was conceived as nothing less than a transformation of *Shang Ti*'s favour and support. When the founder of the Shang Tang rose against the Hsia, in order to justify his action he offered sacrifices to *Shang Ti* and announced: 'The Way of Heaven is to bless the good, and make the bad miserable. It sent down calamities on the [House of] Hsia, and made manifest its guilt. Therefore, I, the little child, did not dare to forgive [the criminal]' (the *Book of History*, 'The Announcement of Tang', in Legge 1879: 90). When the Chou began to rise against the Shang dynasty, King Wu of the Chou first accused the Shang king of 'not serving *Shang Ti*', so that he must override the Shang to 'aid *Shang Ti* and secure the tranquillity of the four quarters' (the *Book of History*, 'The Great Declaration', in Legge 1879: 126). Poems describe in detail the idea of the Chou people about *Shang Ti*, and how the Chou developed under the care and help of *Shang Ti* from a state into a dynasty. The first paragraph of one poem reads:

> Great is *Shang Ti*,
> Beholding this lower world in majesty.
> He surveyed the four quarters [of the Kingdom],
> Seeking for some one to give establishment to the people.
> Those two earlier dynasties
> Had failed to satisfy him with their government;
> So, throughout the various states,
> He sought and considered
> For one on whom he might confer the rule.
> He turned his kind regards on the west
> And there gave a settlement [to the first ruler of the Chou].

(The *Book of Poetry*, in Legge 1879: 389; also see Waley 1937: 255)

In this way, the Chou developed from a small tribe into a great power, and at last, though the Shang had hundreds of thousands of descendants, it gave way to and was subject to the Chou as soon as *Shang Ti* gave his order (the *Book of Poetry*, 'The King Wen', in Legge 1879: 379).

T'ien – an absolute power

The God of the Shang people, *Shang Ti*, outlived their dynasty, and *Shang Ti* was worshipped by the next dynasty, the Chou, as its supreme God. However, the importance of *Shang Ti* gradually diminished and his role was overshadowed by the Chou's own God, *T'ien* (Heaven, Lord of Heaven), who was worshipped either together with *Shang Ti* (since the Chou was originally a state of the Shang Dynasty), or alone, becoming an absolute ruler in later Chinese history. In the religious sense, this transformation cannot be said to be a change from one God to the other. *Shang Ti* and *T'ien* are essentially the same; they are not two separate gods but two names or titles for the same Lord of the universe.[3] This is proved not only by their identification in the religious life of the Chou dynasty (because the Chou, previously a state of the Shang, developed into a dynasty), but also by their combination in the religious worship of all Chinese imperial history: Majestic *T'ien*, or August *T'ien*, is often worshipped in conjunction with *Shang Ti*.

T'ien has been used in two basic senses: as a personal God and as impersonal power or nature.[4] This resulted in an argument among the first Christian missionaries in China about whether or not *T'ien* should be regarded as a synonym for the Christian God. In the seventeenth century, when a Chinese emperor wanted to settle the dispute between the Jesuits and the Franciscans and Dominicans by adopting the word *T'ien* for God, the impersonality of this term evoked strong objection and protest from the latter, and the decision of the emperor was then overridden by the pope's decree that a personal '*T'ien Zhu*' or Lord of Heaven would be an appropriate name for God.

Though the two basic senses of *T'ien* are mixed in historical texts and religious terminology, and no easy distinction can be drawn in most of the religious situations, we may well say that, in the earlier part of the Chou dynasty, *T'ien* was regarded as a Supreme Being, possessing anthropomorphic qualities. In the Chou bronze texts, *T'ien* was depicted as a pictograph of a line or a circle above a human, which means 'The One above human beings' or 'the Great Man'. From this fact, some scholars conclude that *T'ien* was an innovation, representing the Chou ancestral kings. However, others believe that *T'ien*, as a term representing the highest God, had appeared in the Shang inscriptions, and it was equivalent in meaning and usage to *Ti*, the Supreme Lord of the universe (Eno 1990: 183). For the Chou people, *T'ien* had full authority and power to endow or withdraw his mandate of governing the human world. By extending this idea of the Mandate of Heaven and its succession as the legitimacy of government, a new title, 'the Son of Heaven', was adopted for the Chou kings, and later became a general title for all of the Chinese emperors.

In the records of the Chou dynasty, *T'ien* was described not only as a creator of the universe and human beings – '*T'ien* gives birth to the multitudes of the people' (the *Book of Poetry*, in Waley 1937: 252), but also as the supreme power and ruler, and was credited with many other anthropomorphic features. He was awe-inspiring, of dread majesty, and to be feared; he conferred on humans their moral sense, and granted the right to rule to those he favoured. His will was glorious, might be known, and must be complied with.

One of the most significant features of *T'ien* is his morality and universality. The Chou dynasty won the world from the Shang, so the Chou kings paid special attention to how to legitimise their rebellion. In this respect, they gradually developed a new religious awareness that the supreme God must be both righteous and universal. The supreme God could not be merely a patron deity of a ruling tribe or class. God treated the people equally and granted his blessing only to the moral ones. The Chou Kings claimed that *T'ien* was *the* God of morality. He would endow his mandate, *T'ien Ming*, to a righteous king to govern a given state, and he would take away the mandate from an unworthy king. From this concept, the Chou people strongly believed that the prosperity or decline of the state, and the welfare of the people, depended totally upon the will of *T'ien*. The ruin of the former dynasties, the Hsia and the Shang, was the direct will of *T'ien*. Because the last kings of these dynasties were so debauched and cruel, the people complained to *T'ien*. '*T'ien* had compassion on the people of the four quarters' (the *Book of History*, 'The Announcement of the Duke of Shao', in Legge 1879: 184), and withdrew his favouring decree from these kings, and this led to their ruin. Poems in the *Book of Poetry* vividly describe this process. When a king made mistakes, *T'ien* would send down calamities to warn him. If this was not effective, he would angrily send down more serious disasters such as death and disorder in the world: the troubles would multiply like flames, till they were beyond help or remedy. When *T'ien* completely despaired of the king, he would enlighten the people and give his favour to the sage who would carry out the Mandate of *T'ien* to set up a new dynasty (the *Book of Poetry*, in Legge 1879: 408–10, 418–19).

In contrast to *Shang Ti*, who liked to destroy a state himself, the will of *T'ien* was carried out indirectly. For example, the last king of the Shang was said to have indulged in drinking and to have dug pools which were filled with wine so that he and his concubines could swim in it. Though this was one of the indirect causes which led to the ruin of the Shang, King Wu of the Chou dynasty connected it with the will of *T'ien*:

> When *T'ien* was sending down his favouring decree, and laying the foundations of [the eminence of] people, [spirits] were used only at the great sacrifices. When *T'ien* sends down his terrors and the people are thereby greatly disordered and lose their virtue, this may be traced invariably to their indulgence in spirits; yea, the ruin of the states, small or great, has been caused invariably by their guilt in the use of spirits.
>
> (The *Book of History*, 'The Announcement about Drunkenness', in Legge 1879: 174)

The Chou people, like the Shang people, also insisted that only the king could sacrifice to their God, but they put more emphasis on the belief that a king, or the son of *T'ien*, could not obtain *T'ien*'s support unless his moral nature was pure. *T'ien* could not be served by a tyrant or a debauchee; the sacrifices of such a ruler would be of no avail, the divine harmony would be upset, and catastrophe would manifest the wrath of *T'ien*. As time went by, the mandate of *T'ien* was gradually identified with the will of the people: '*T'ien* loves the people, and the sovereign should reverently carry out [this mind] of *T'ien*' (the *Book of History*, 'The Great Declaration', in Legge 1879: 127). It is this teaching of the state worship of *T'ien* that became the basic principle of Chinese religion and politics.

Yu Huang – a heavenly sovereign

The leading power in the political field would also be a dominating power in religious life. Worship of *T'ien*, performed by the royal house, strongly influenced the ordinary people's religious beliefs and practices. For as long as three thousand years, *T'ien* was the centre of the state religion in China. Worship of *T'ien* was seen as such an essential connection between human authority and the spiritual power, and the blessings from *T'ien* were seen as such an essential factor for the prosperity of the whole nation, that people's attitude to him would naturally be sincere. This can be seen not only from the religious text books but also from the popular language which expresses the religious commitment of the common people. For example, 'the wrath of *T'ien* and the resentment of men' is a common saying for the evil effects of bad politics; while 'the plan of a matter is up to humans, but its success depends upon *T'ien*' reveals a total dependence of human beings upon God.

However, we have to concede that the worship of *T'ien* was a privilege of the royal house and it was seldom a religious affair for ordinary people. Whenever the latter happened, only two explanations were possible: either a new dynasty was appearing or a rebellion was rising. These rebellions and new dynasties would claim that they were carrying out the mandate of *T'ien* and that they were supported and favoured by *T'ien*. As soon as they settled down, they would, as quickly as their predecessors, perform sacrifices to *T'ien* to restrengthen this divine tie. The exclusion of the people from this worship, on the one hand, preserves *T'ien*'s revered and majestic image; on the other hand, however, it results in the people's alienation from him and encourages them to turn to other spiritual powers. This may be one of the reasons why most Chinese popular religious beliefs and practices have been connected with polytheism or animism, rather than with the monotheism associated with *T'ien*.

Thus, a clear division between the state religion and popular religious life was formed. This division led to a new type of God-worship in popular religion which was a syncretic product of the state religion, Taoism and Buddhism. While *T'ien* still exerted his influence on the people and the community, the God *Yu Huang* (the Jade Emperor) or *Yu Huang Shang Ti* (the Jade Emperor Lord on High), gradually occupied the mind of the ordinary Chinese people.

Though there must have been other supreme gods anteceding God *Yu Huang*, the name of *Yu Huang* first appeared in the literature of the Tang dynasty (618–907 CE). His worship in its present form was recorded in the Sung Dynasty when it was said that certain gods appeared in dreams of an emperor, and sent him letters from *Yu Huang* from Heaven. As a result of these dreams, the emperor decreed that temples and statues be set up to him, and conferred upon him the title of 'Most High, Creator of Heaven, Bearer of the Sceptre, Regulator of the Calendar, Incarnation of the Tao, the Jade Emperor, Grand Emperor of Heaven' (Maspero 1981: 90). From that time, God *Yu Huang* captured the mind of the common people and worship of him became the most important part of popular religious life. He was conceived of as Sovereign over the world of gods, of human beings and of all the spiritual beings.

Yu Huang is a syncretic God of Chinese religions. From the worship of the state religion, he got his original authority and power. In fact, for the common people, *Yu Huang* is not very different from *Shang Ti* and *T'ien*, or they have never bothered to differentiate these titles: *Yu Huang* is *Shang Ti*, *T'ien* is also equated with *T'ien Ti* – the Emperor of Heaven, and *Yu Huang* is even popularly called *Lao T'ien Yeh* – the old Lord of Heaven. *T'ien*, *Ti* and *Yu Huang* not only share most of their personal features, but also exert similar influence on human affairs.

The Taoist heritage is apparent, and indeed *Yu Huang* is often called the God of Taoism. He is not only a sovereign of the world and a conductor of the law of nature, but also an incarnation of *Tao*, and sometimes he is said to be the current supreme God of the Taoist religion, one of the Three Pure Ones who are the Triad of the Past, the Present and the Future, and who appeared or will appear in sequence. He also gained status from Buddhism. Some of the Buddhists insisted that *Yu Huang* came from one of the Buddhist deities – Indra, who was also sometimes called *Yu Ti*, though Taoists claimed that *Yu Huang* was the equal of Buddha as Saviour of the World. Buddhist ideas of heaven provided for him a place in heaven, and *buddha*s are often used to help in establishing his authority. However, the most striking feature of *Yu Huang* is his resemblance to the emperor. In the popular religion, he is the counterpart in Heaven of the emperor on earth, and has his palace, his ministry and even his wife and concubines. Wearing the dragon-embroidered robe and pearly headgear, *Yu Huang* is seated on his throne, surrounded by his ministers, and deals with all the affairs of the three worlds of the gods, the humans and the ghosts. These features make many scholars express a serious doubt about his position as God, and insist that he is nothing more than a head of the spiritual world or an executor of the natural law.

NOTES

1. The *Book of Poetry*, which is traditionally believed to have been edited by Confucius, has altogether 305 poems and has been commonly regarded by ancient and modern scholars as one of the most trustworthy documents concerning the religious life of the later Shang and the Western Chou dynasties. The *Book of History*, which was believed to be another classic edited by Confucius, covers the history of early China to the early time of the Spring and Autumn (*c.* 628 BCE).
2. Legge, in his translation of *The Shu King* (*Book of History*), adopted several terms, such as 'God', the 'Sovereign in the Heavens', 'Spiritual Sovereign', to translate *Shang Ti* or *Ti*, and 'God' or 'Heaven' to translate *T'ien*, while Waley in the *Book of Songs* uses 'God on High' for *Shang Ti* and 'Heaven' for *T'ien*. Waltham, in his modernised edition of Legge's translation, unifies these terms by adopting 'God' for *Shang Ti* and 'Heaven' for *T'ien*. In this chapter, whenever citing these terms from the translations, we restore their Chinese names: *Shang Ti* and *T'ien*.
3. It seems that in the translations of Chinese classics, not much emphasis has been put on this aspect. The most obvious example is that *T'ien* is represented by 'It', and *Shang Ti* by 'He', as shown in a poem of Waley's translation of the *Shi Ching*, 'Mighty is God on High, Ruler of His people below; Swift and terrible is God on High, His charge has many statutes; Heaven gives birth to the multitude of the people, But its charge cannot be counted upon . . .' (Waley 1937: 252).
4. While in this book, the term of *T'ien* is used mainly in the first sense, in the volume, *Attitudes to Nature* in this series, *T'ien* (Heaven) is used mainly in the second sense.

FURTHER READING

de Bary, Wm. Theodore (1960) *Sources of Chinese Tradition*, New York, Columbia University Press.

Chiu, Milton M. (1984) *The Tao of Chinese Religion*, Lanham, University of America Press.

De Korne, John C. (1926) *Chinese Altars to the Unknown God*, Grand Rapids, Michigan, Smitter.

Eno, Robert (1990) *The Confucian Creation of Heaven – Philosophy and the Defense of Ritual Mastery*, Albany, State University of New York Press.

Legge, James (1879) *The Shu King, The Shi King* (repr. 1970 in *The Sacred Books of China* Part I, in F. Max Müller (ed.) *The Sacred Books of the East*, vol. III, Delhi, Motilal Banarsidass.

Maspero, Henri (1981) *Taoism and Chinese Religion* (trans Frank A. Kierman), Amherst, University of Massachusetts Press.

Smith, D. Howard (1968) *The Chinese Religions*, London, Weidenfeld & Nicolson.

Thompson, Laurence G. (1987) 'T'ien', in M. Eliade (ed.) *Encyclopedia of Religion*, vol. 14, pp. 508–10, New York, Macmillan.

Waley, Arthur (1937) *The Book of Songs*, London, Allen & Unwin.

Waltham, Clae (1971) *Shu Ching – Book of History*, London, Allen & Unwin.

8. Japanese Religions

Wendy Dossett

God, in the western sense, does not generally figure in Japanese religion. Around two per cent of the Japanese population are Christians, and they have imported, in varying degrees, the God of the western Christian tradition. But the focus of wider Japanese religious experience is less on an omnipotent God than on more animistic spirits, such as *kami*, the indigenous deities of the nation, and on the various heroes of the Buddhist tradition of Japan.

Western scholarship conceives of the traditions of Shinto and Buddhism as distinct and autonomous. However, they exist symbiotically in Japan. The interdependence of the two traditions is reflected in the tendency to participate in both traditions, in an overlap of ways of speaking about *kami*, *buddha*s and ancestors, and in iconography.

Although most Japanese would claim not to be religious, the richness and ubiquity of iconography, religious art, and the mass of customs which can be traced to religious origins, present something of a counter claim. Almost every house has either a *butsudan* or a *kamidana*, or even both, in which to enshrine family ancestors, and before which to recite *sūtra*s or prayers. Thousands of young people train in the arts of *ikebana* (flower-arranging) and *cha-no-yu* (the tea ceremony). Many children practice *kendo* (the way of the sword) and other martial arts. All these customs and practices can be traced to, or have been influenced by, Zen Buddhism. The characteristic style of Japanese painting also owes much to Buddhism. Traditional Shinto held the emperor to be a god. This belief, many would argue, is slow to leave the religious consciousness of the Japanese, and the emperor remains a living icon. *Sumo* wrestling is a tremendously popular Shinto ritual. These few examples go some way towards illustrating the contention that 'religious pictures' of different kinds are very much part of Japanese culture.

So, while 'Picturing God' may not be a useful expression under which to examine the religious life of the Japanese, the culture is replete with religious 'pictures', of the Buddha, enlightenment, the *kami*, nature, and of reality 'as it is'. In this chapter we shall examine these aspects of Japanese religions in terms of their symbols which appear in religious art and iconography.

A distinctive facet of Japanese religion is the immanence or closeness of the human realm, and that of the *kami*, *buddha*s and ancestral spirits. The 'numinous' is not so far away, it is here, implicit in this world. This has a significant effect on the way these realms and religious ideals are depicted and talked about. All symbols in Japanese religions indicate something beyond themselves, something that cannot be encapsulated in words and pictures. But at the same time these signs and symbols are often *in themselves* that which they are signifying. A symbol 'participates' in what it indicates to a degree that might seem exotic to readers from comparatively aniconic religious or cultural backgrounds. Images are invested with the very power they represent. Rituals are efficacious in themselves. They are not only provisional or metaphorical ways of indicating the relationship between the human and the other worlds; these two worlds are so close that simply by participating in humanity, one is participating in both.

One might argue, for example, that the widespread belief in fortunetelling, lucky charms (*o-mamori*), and the efficacy of prayer for mundane benefits, is a way of showing or picturing the experienced closeness of the two worlds. At many Shinto shrines, for example, there are booths in which one can simply choose a number from one to ten, and receive on a small slip of paper a blessing, a recommendation for action, a warning or words of wisdom. Such an exchange would be rendered meaningless were it not that the *kami* of the shrine are believed to be intimately concerned with human activity and will ensure that the choice of number is not arbitrary. The 'other' is very much implicit in the human world order. The distinction between *kami* and humanity is not as clear as one might expect. The gods are all around.

The term *kami* functions in the Japanese language as an honorific. Usually it denotes spiritual power and authority. The usual English translation of *kami* is 'deity' or 'god', but it could be argued that the term, rather than denoting a class of ontological beings, has an adjectival function which sacralises what are seen as the (morally ambivalent) powers of the universe. Alternatively, Ian Reader (1991: 27) describes *kami* as representing

> a life force, a source and manifestation of energy found in the world and as such [they] are benefactors of the benefits of that force, upholders of life and its goodness. However, just as nature itself, they are unpredictable and, just as humans, are prone to pique, jealousy, rage and other disruptive human habits...

Kami are pictured as so tangible that they actually reside in shrines, and are 'physically' transferred to portable shrines (*mikoshi*) and taken into the streets during festivals (*matsuri*). Their presence is embodied in a 'divine symbol' of some kind, often a mirror symbolising the 'stainless mind of the *kami*' (Ono 1962: 23), or a sword, stone or jewel. Some shrine precincts have carved images of dogs, foxes and other animals or humans. These are often dressed and decorated, highlighting the very human way that the *kami* powers are thought of. Images or statues of actual *kami* are quite rare, as early clan Shinto was aniconic. However, due to the later influence of Buddhist iconography, and the theoretical fusion of the two traditions (*Honji-suijaku*),[1] some Shinto deities which were particularly thought of in terms of the Buddhist cosmology, were depicted iconographically. The *kami* Hachiman, for example, is often depicted as a Buddhist priest.

As well as sanctifying and personifying natural and spiritual forces, the term *kami* can also be applied to human beings. The great cultural heroes of Japan and the War Dead are venerated as *kami*. Before the dismantling of State Shinto in 1946, the emperor was a *kami*. Religious leaders, mainly of Shinto-related new religious movements, are often referred to as *kami*. Living *kami* (*ikigami*) need not be depicted in provisional or symbolic ways, since they can be related to in person.

The *kami* idea also embraces natural phenomena. The sun, the elements, and natural features, such as mountains, are *kami*. Mountains such as Mount Fuji and Mount Ontake have always been destinations for pilgrims. *Kami* are thought of both as occupying the mountains and, at the same time, as actually being identified with the mountains. The mountains themselves are *kami*, not just symbols or symbolic residences. Thus a pilgrimage is not just a symbolic act, it is a real visit to the *kami* world. Buddhism also has its sacred mountains, one of the most famous being Mount Koya, residence of Kukai, or Kobo Daishi (774–835), the founder of Shingon. The sanctity of Buddhist mountains is part of the same tradition of Japanese mountain worship.

The forces of *kami* are thus implicit in the human realm, and are related to in very human and immediate ways. Buddhist notions too, despite the tendency in the West to think of them as other-worldly, if not world-denying, can be discerned very much in the here and now.

The type of Buddhism which predominates in Japan is Mahāyāna. This is characterised by devotional practices, and the belief that *nirvāṇa* is a real possibility in this life. While there are many schools of Buddhism which espouse seemingly contradictory doctrines about the ability of humanity to achieve enlightenment, and while the social function of Buddhism is (paradoxically, considering its worldly orientation) to provide death rituals, Japanese Buddhism generally stresses that the conditions necessary to achieve the religious goal are available in this life.

However, true to the central Mahāyāna concept of *upāya*, or skilful means,[2] Japanese Buddhism maintains that all Buddhist languages and pictures are provisional. Thus in Jodoshinshu, one of the largest denominations of Japanese Buddhism, the idea that Amida Buddha, the great *bodhisattva* who works ceaselessly to bring sentient beings to enlightenment, resides in a Western Paradise or Pure Land, is simply a provisional way of picturing the functioning of enlightenment, which is helpful to sentient beings (because it can be imagined or visualised). This is not to say that believers consciously or continuously demythologise their cosmology, but rather that, when pushed to do so in certain situations, they would relinquish their belief in Amida and the Pure Land as real existing entities, without detracting from the meaning of the picture.

Language and iconography, therefore, have an ambivalent function in the Pure Land Schools (of which Jodoshinshu, literally the 'True Pure Land School', is the largest). Amida images in temples are addressed in person, most people talk of Amida and the Pure Land as if they were 'real'. The writings of Shinran, the founder of Jodoshinshu, stress less the provisionality of the Amida–Pure Land concept, and more the individual selfless surrender to the all-powerful compassion (*daihi*) of the Buddha. Pure Land devotional literature provides many examples of literal belief (and therefore, according to the tradition, efficacious belief).

Zen, of course, stresses much more the provisionality of all language, and is in spirit iconoclastic. The great corpus of Buddhist literature is viewed as totally provisional, and thus, in many respects, redundant. Zen advocates the search for enlightenment beyond the boundaries of dualistic language. Language, concepts, images and practices, while perhaps having some use, are more likely to be distractions from the task of 'seeing reality as it really is'. However, even Zen must provisionally utilise 'means' to attain and describe its 'ends'. One of the most noted 'means' in Zen is the *koan*, an apparent riddle designed not to be solved, but to illustrate the provisionality and therefore the absurdity of linguistic concepts, and to propel the disciple out of the habitual mode of discriminative thinking and into real insight.

Since 'insight' in Zen is seeing reality non-discriminatively, reality is left very much in its place. In Zen, reality should be experienced rather than talked about. The Zen 'arts' can be seen in this context. Rigorous training in martial arts, *ikebana*, or *cha-no-yu*, results in the ability to be absolutely spontaneous in expression. While these arts are not iconographic in the usual sense, they represent Zen ideals and human participation in them. The perfect reflection of 'reality in its isness' (Suzuki 1959: 16) is the ultimate goal of any Zen art.

Zen painting, influenced by Taoist ideas about the sanctity of nature, provides perhaps the clearest example of this reflection of reality. Helmut Brinker (1987: 11–12) cites a Zen master:

> Before a man studies Zen, to him mountains are mountains and waters are waters; after he gets an insight into Zen ... mountains to him are not mountains and waters are not waters; but after this when he really attains the abode of rest, mountains are once more mountains and waters are waters.

Zen paintings, of nature, of animals, of monks going about their tasks, sitting, or laughing, and so on, are therefore pictures of reality, or of enlightenment (*satori*). The tradition of the grotesque in Zen art further illustrates the notion that our tendency to discriminate is misguided. Zen paintings rarely have iconographic status, as icons require dualistic relationships (art–artist, art–viewer, sign–signified, etc.) to function; but they are, provisionally at least, pictures of ultimate truth.

In contrast to Zen minimalism, the great Japanese 'pantheon' of *buddhas* and *bodhisattvas* is saturated with layer upon layer of symbolic meaning. The iconography is tremendously rich and varied, reflecting the richness of the tradition. Numerous *buddhas* and *bodhisattvas* are acknowledged, both in temple-centred sects, and in the general religious consciousness of the Japanese. Each figure has a different character, and represents a different aspect of Buddhist thought. The relationships between the figures are highly complex, and are seen differently, both through history and depending on different orthodox standpoints.

One of the most popular figures in the pantheon is Kannon (Skt. Avalokiteśvara), the *bodhisattva* of compassion. Statues and pictures of Kannon (who is often depicted as female in Japan) often have several heads, indicating the *bodhisattva*'s great insight, or many arms, showing superhuman capacity to aid all suffering sentient beings. The Sanjusangendo temple in Kyoto enshrines an overwhelming 1001 bronze images of Kannon, impressing any visitor with Kannon's immense capacity to become manifest wherever there is suffering.

Jizo Bosatsu (Skt. Kṣitigarbha) also enjoys a popular following as comforter of the grieving and guardian of children and women in childbirth. He is usually pictured as a simple human monk, though Albert C. Moore (1977: 191) argues that some small images of him suggest a phallic cult.

Popular *buddhas* include: Yakushi (Skt. Bhaiṣajyarāja), the 'medicine Buddha', whose cult in Japan is one of the oldest; Miroku (Skt. Maitreya), the future Buddha, often depicted as an ascetic; and Shaka (Skt. Śakyamuni), the historical Buddha, who plays a central cultic role in many Japanese Buddhisms. Often pictured in attendance on the *buddhas* and *bodhisattvas* are the Guardian Kings of Buddhism.

Fudo Myo-o is a popular figure and champion of the righteous. He is normally depicted as fearsome, furious and powerful, and he carries a lasso and a sword to bind and destroy evil-doers. Statues and pictures, unlike those of most other *buddhas* and *bodhisattvas*, who are surrounded by the light of enlightenment, show him amidst the flames which burn illusion. He is believed to be a manifestation of the Great Sun Buddha, Mahāvairocana (Jap. Dainichi Nyorai) of

Shingon Buddhism. Dainichi is seen as the source of the universe, and is associated in Japan with Amaterasu-o-mikami, the sun goddess of the Shinto pantheon (Matsunaga 1969: 193).

Shingon is esoteric in nature, and holds that the truths of the universe can be apprehended only by initiates through complex symbolic and ritual forms. Two such forms are the *mudra* and the *maṇḍala*. *Mudra*s are the bodily actions of the Buddha, usually hand signals, performed in order to awaken the *buddha*-nature of the practitioner, and *maṇḍala*s are geometric designs which symbolise existence, to be drawn, contemplated or visualised. According to Moore (1977: 187) the religious purpose of a *maṇḍala* is to 'aid the worshipper to find his way to the Buddha-centre of the universe and thus be reintegrated'. For Nichiren Buddhists the *maṇḍala* designed by Nichiren (1222–82), showing the name of the *Lotus Sūtra* and the *buddha*s, *bodhisattva*s and *kami* which protect it, is the 'supreme object of devotion' (*gohonzon*).

As well as the symbolic forms of *mudra* and *maṇḍala*, words have a special religious function within Japanese Buddhism. Nowhere is the strong relationship between a symbol and that which it symbolises more striking than in the invocations performed by Nichiren and Pure Land Buddhists. *Namu Myohorenge-kyo*, which means 'I pay homage to the name of the *Lotus Sūtra*', is repeated by Nichiren Buddhists in the belief that simply the name of the *sūtra* carries within it the essence of Buddhism. For believers in Pure Land Buddhism, uttering the *nembutsu*, '*Namu Amida Butsu*', is the sole practice, and for Shinran's Jodoshinshu, the utterance comes not from the effort of the practitioner, but from the grace of Amida Buddha.

The importance and centrality of sanctified words can be seen not only in the formulae of certain Buddhist denominations, but also in Japanese religion and culture in general. Calligraphy, the celebrated Japanese art form, imbues written Japanese with ritual and symbolic significance. Temples and shrines of any Japanese religion will give a central place to works of calligraphic art, as will many Japanese households. The written names of ancestors occupy focal points in *butsudan*s and *kamidana*s, and the names of *buddha*s, *bodhisattva*s, religious leaders and heroes, along with their famous statements, may also be enshrined. Religious poetry in written form is given ritual status, the content and the form being identical in terms of meaning. The names of *kami* function in the same way. The written name of a *kami* (on a folded piece of paper called *ofuda*) represents the power of the *kami* itself.

For the Japanese, different religions are relevant to, and useful for, different rites of passage, at different times of life, and to express the different world-views that an individual holds in different situations. Generally, it is rare that one religion is seen as superior to another in terms of absolute truth, and, with one or two exceptions, religions are not seen as static universal truths for all humanity.

This general orientation allows for the multiplication of symbols and provisional languages that are so present in Japanese culture. It facilitates the borrowing and adaption of rich and elaborate cosmologies, which has occurred so often through history, and it also allows for the general tendency not to perceive different symbols and what they indicate as in conflict or contradiction with each other.

NOTES

1. *Honji-suijaku* literally means 'true nature – trace manifestation' – and is the term applied to the assimilation of Shinto deities (trace manifestations) into the Buddhist world-view. For a detailed discussion of this theory and its impact on iconography and Japanese culture see Alicia Matsunaga's *The Buddhist Philosophy of Assimilation*, Rutland Vermont, Tuttle, 1969.
2. Michael Pye, in his *Skilful Means: A Concept in Mahayana Buddhism*, London, Duckworth, 1978, examines in detail the provisionality of Buddhist language.

FURTHER READING

Brinker, H. (trans George Campbell) (1987) *Zen in the Art of Painting*, London, Arkana.

Getty, A. (1928) *The Gods of Northern Buddhism: Their History and Iconography*, Oxford, Clarendon.

Matsunaga, A. (1969) *The Buddhist Philosophy of Assimilation*, Rutland Vermont, Tuttle.

Moore, A.C. (1977) *Iconography of Religions* (Chapter 6), London, SCM Press.

Ono, S. (1962) *Shinto: The Kami Way*, Rutland Vermont, Tuttle.

Pye, M. (1978) *Skilful Means: A Concept in Mahayana Buddhism*, London, Duckworth.

Reader, I. (1991) *Religion in Contemporary Japan*, London, Macmillan.

Suzuki, D.T. (1959) *Zen and Japanese Culture*, London, Routledge and Kegan Paul.

Index